ENGLISH CULTURE AND THE DECLINE OF THE INDUSTRIAL SPIRIT, 1850–1980

Second Edition

England was the world's first great industrial nation. Yet the English have never been comfortable with industrialism. Drawing upon a wide array of sources, Martin Wiener explores the English ambivalence to modern industrial society. His work reveals a pervasive middle- and upper-class frame of mind hostile to industrialism and economic growth. From the middle of the nineteenth century to the present, this frame of mind shaped a broad spectrum of cultural expression, including literature, journalism, and architecture, as well as social, historical, and economic thought.

Now in a new edition, Wiener reflects on the original debate surrounding the work and examines the historiography of the last twenty years. Written in a graceful and accessible style, with reference to a broad range of people and ideas, this book will be of interest to all readers who wish to understand the development – and predicament – of modern England.

Martin J. Wiener is the Mary Jones Professor of History at Rice University. His previous books include *Between Two Worlds: The Political Thought of Graham Wallas* (1971), *Reconstructing the Criminal* (Cambridge, 1990), and *Men of Blood: Violence, Manliness, and Criminal Justice in Victorian England* (Cambridge, 2003).

ENGLISH CULTURE AND THE DECLINE OF THE INDUSTRIAL SPIRIT, 1850–1980

Second Edition

MARTIN J. WIENER

Rice University

CAMBRIDGE
UNIVERSITY PRESS

PUBLISHED BY THE PRESS SYNDICATE OF THE UNIVERSITY OF CAMBRIDGE
The Pitt Building, Trumpington Street, Cambridge, United Kingdom

CAMBRIDGE UNIVERSITY PRESS
The Edinburgh Building, Cambridge CB2 2RU, UK
40 West 20th Street, New York, NY 10011-4211, USA
477 Williamstown Road, Port Melbourne, VIC 3207, Australia
Ruiz de Alarcón 13, 28014 Madrid, Spain
Dock House, The Waterfront, Cape Town 8001, South Africa

http://www.cambridge.org

First edition published 1981
First paperback edition published 1982
Second edition first published 2004

Printed in the United States of America

Typeface ITC New Baskerville 10/12 pt.   *System* LATEX 2$_\varepsilon$ [TB]

A catalog record for this book is available from the British Library.

Library of Congress Cataloging in Publication Data
Wiener, Martin J.
   English culture and the decline of the industrial spirit, 1850–1980 /
Martin J. Wiener. –
2nd ed.
        p. cm.
   Includes bibliographical references and index.
   ISBN 0-521-84376-6 – ISBN 0-521-60479-6 (pbk.)
        1. England – Civilization – 19th century.   2. Industrialization – England –
History – 19th century.   3. Industrialization – England – History – 20th
century.   4. Industries – England – History – 19th century.   5. Industries –
England – History – 20th century.   6. England – Civilization – 20th century.
7. Industries – Social aspects – England.   I. Title.
DA533.W59   2004
942.08–dc22   2004052117

ISBN 0 521 84376 6 hardback
ISBN 0 521 60479 6 paperback

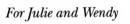

For Julie and Wendy

The life of nations no less than that of men is lived largely in the imagination.

– Enoch Powell (1946)

Contents

Preface to the first edition

"Capitalism," Fritz Stern has remarked, "is too serious a subject to be left to the economic historian alone."[1] Such is also the case with industrialism. In the course of writing a quite different book on British social thought in the late nineteenth and early twentieth centuries, I became aware of a distinctive complex of social ideas, sentiments, and values in the "articulate" classes, embodying an ambiguous attitude toward modern industrial society. In the world's first industrial nation, industrialism did not seem quite at home. In the country that had started mankind on the "great ascent," economic growth was frequently viewed with suspicion and disdain. Having pioneered urbanization, the English ignored or disparaged cities.

The more I explored these incongruities, the more important they seemed to become. Instead of peripheral curiosities, they turned out to lie near the heart of modern British history. Taken together, they bore witness to a cultural *cordon sanitaire* encircling the forces of economic development – technology, industry, commerce. One could begin to see this mental quarantine take shape in the social changes (and nonchanges) of the Victorian era, watch it give from then on a particular softly rustic and nostalgic cast to middle- and upper-class culture, and finally observe it intertwine with the modern fading of national economic dynamism. To follow the unfolding of this complex of attitudes was to highlight, in a novel way, the importance of the conservative (with a lowercase "c") frame of mind in modern Britain. What first appeared to me as incongruities, in short, came to provide a key to the reinterpretation of the past century and a quarter of British domestic history.

The complex of attitudes I examine here (as I note in Chapter 1) has not been uniformly demonstrated throughout British society, nor is my attention generally focused on "public opinion" in the statistical sense, as when each individual in the population is taken to be of equal significance. This book explores sentiments, attitudes, and values among the English elite, though that elite is very broadly defined, in the conviction that here lies the most important key to unlocking the puzzles of modern British history.

Cultural values and attitudes often reveal themselves in imaginative literature. It is important, however, to make clear that when we examine such literature our purposes are not those of English studies. Cultural history is different from literary history, and an enterprise entirely separate from literary criticism. We shall be examining (among many other nonliterary sources) the public reception and public image of writers and their work – not, as a rule, the subtleties of their art, which are lost on many of their readers. We are dealing here with precisely those aspects of their work that literary critics tend to pay least attention to – what they most share with the widest audience.

All the attitudes and sentiments I examine, and the social developments I link them to, have been previously noted, but only separately. Historians of literature, art and architecture, society, politics, and economics[2] have all observed aspects of this complex. No one has yet brought all these aspects together to view them as parts of a coherent cultural pattern. My approach, therefore, is synthetic. I draw upon a wide variety of evidence, and also the results of scholarship in many specialist fields. The subject definitions of the specialist fields of historical inquiry are essentially arbitrary divisions of convenience. It is important on occasion to transcend them, to make connections and uncover affinities that might otherwise pass unnoticed. I agree with Raymond Williams, who has argued that "it is with the discovery of patterns of a characteristic kind that any useful cultural analysis begins, and it is with the relationship between these patterns, which sometimes reveals unexpected identities and correspondences in hitherto separately considered activities, sometimes again reveals discontinuities of an unexpected kind, that general cultural analysis is concerned."[3] I hope to reveal some such patterns and to illuminate some of their relationships and consequences.

Williams's interest in the connections between literature (in a broad sense) and society has been unusual among British scholars, who have inclined to avoid such "vague" areas, making sharp distinctions between ideas and sentiments – the realm of imagination – on the one hand, and "real life" on the other.[4] This is unfortunate. One of my hopes for this work is that it will contribute to breaking down this artificial barrier and to widening historiographical sensitivities. Ideas are indeed "real" and have consequences.

In the writing of this book I have incurred many debts. A Younger Humanists Fellowship from the National Endowment for the Humanities enabled me to spend a year in London drawing upon the treasure trove of the British Library, and the Dean of Advanced Studies and Research at Rice University helped with research expenses. Julie R. Jeffrey assisted in the early research, John Fowler proofread the final version, and Linda Quaidy, Holly Leitz, and Josephine Monaghan typed several drafts. Indeed, Ms. Quaidy and Ms. Leitz bore up cheerfully under a succession of "final" versions. Edmund Stillman, of the Hudson Institute Europe, offered support and an occasion to present some of these ideas for the first time. Members of Eric Hobsbawm's seminar at the Institute of Historical Research listened patiently to an early version of Chapter 4 and made useful suggestions. Meetings of the Pacific Coast, Rocky Mountain, and Midwest Conferences on British Studies gave me opportunities to spin out other threads of this fabric. The following individuals read all or part of the manuscript and offered valuable advice: Luther P. Carpenter, Thomas Haskell, T. W. Heyck, Francis Loewenheim, Michael B. Miller, Carol Stearns, and Robert K. Webb. Most of all, Meredith Skura's rigorous, imaginative, and supportive criticism drew out my best efforts.

Martin J. Wiener
October 1980

Introduction to the new edition

This book germinated during a time in which, as never for centuries, British "educated opinion" had lost its confidence about the nation, its state, and its direction. The simultaneous end of empire, re-emergence of Scottish and Welsh nationalism, and loss of economic superiority to its European neighbors placed those who governed and those who formed opinion in Britain in a novel situation of uncertainty. Articles and books appeared with titles like "Whither Britain?" and even a special issue of the influential monthly, *Encounter*, entitled *Suicide of a Nation?*. Harold Wilson made the theme of the 1964 election campaign that ended thirteen years of Conservative rule the revival of national dynamism, the "forging of a new Britain in the white heat of the technological revolution," although his government thereafter floundered in the unfriendly eddies of a swiftly flowing contemporary world. Six years later, Labour was turned out in a campaign in which fresh promises of national rebirth were this time chiefly employed by its opponents, led by Edward Heath. Heath's Conservative government also failed to deliver on these promises, collapsing in the midst of a world oil crisis, worsened for Britain by a miners' strike. A decade of political promises had sorely disappointed; national "revival" turned out to be a more complex and elusive goal than a mere change of political parties. By 1974, in a climate of unparalleled gloom about public affairs, a serious rethinking of modern British history was overdue.

Up to this point, the new concerns about Britain's present state and direction had had little effect on professional history-writing, which even as a more politically radical new generation was beginning to make its mark remained within well-worn "Whig" paths of a "master narrative" of progress. The chief innovation at the time was the establishment, led by Eric Hobsbawm and E. P. Thompson, of "history from the bottom up," shifting attention downward to the working classes as the central figures of the story of advance and the casting of trade unionists and working-class political activists, rather than middle-class radicals and enlightened Whigs and even humanitarian imperialists as the "heroes." The "forward march

xiii

of Labour" rather than the advance of free and democratic yet orderly social and political life became the new central theme in the writing of the history of the previous two centuries. However, the energetic debates among historians in the 1960s and early 70s had yet to really take notice of the kind of drastic questioning of the nation's current situation then prevalent in the discussion of public affairs.

While the Heath government, and the country, went through the turmoil of that *annus horribilis*, 1973–74, I was in Britain on sabbatical leave, studying twentieth-century thinking in Britain about national "modernization." The current troubles and this century of thinking seemed to need each other as context. I had been trained primarily in intellectual history, and I found the terms in which economists argued about questions of economic growth and retardation too narrow. I firmly believed that, as J. M. Keynes once remarked, contemporary "practical" men of affairs owed more than they ever acknowledged to the ideas of men no longer living. Yet I had become, along with many other intellectual historians of my generation, dissatisfied with a narrow and elitist focus on a small number of exceptional minds. My angle of vision was broadening, to embrace the far less sophisticated and rigorous ideas, and sentiments, held by large numbers of persons, which formed more a framework for thinking than a specific set of ideas – what Germans call the "Zeitgeist," or the "mental climate" of a period and place. I had come to believe that, as the controversial politician Enoch Powell had once put it, "the life of nations no less than that of men is lived largely in the imagination."

Was there a gradually formed "imagination" that lay behind the British public troubles of the 1970s? While writing an earlier book on the late-Victorian and Edwardian thinker and socialist activist Graham Wallas, I had become aware of a change in the character of the nineteenth-century "bourgeoisie" as it was triumphing (as the conventional histories had it) over the old aristocratic order: it was taking on many of the trappings – material and mental – of that order. No sooner had they "triumphed" than business, industry, and urban life seemed to be again indicted for their many failings. At the same time, a newly intense concern with national identity emerged, a concern in which the past and its imagined virtues played a central role. What did all this mean, and did it have something important to say about Britain's contemporary problems?

At this juncture I encountered the writings of the young generation of Marxists around the *New Left Review*. Beginning in the 1960s, writers like Tom Nairn and Perry Anderson had been asking why the expected transformation to Socialism had failed to come off. In seeking an answer to this political question, they offered a model of British history that resonated with my perceptions. Because of the unique timing of its industrial revolution, Britain, they argued, had never really had a full "bourgeois revolution" – the powerful existing ruling class had been able to accommodate and absorb the new bourgeoisie. The result was a peculiar state, less "modern" than it pretended to be. If Nairn and Anderson's model were taken in a broader, more than merely political sense, it could provide an explanation for both present-day socioeconomic "stalemate" and the flourishing over the past century of a surprisingly anti-modern middle-class culture.

My emerging picture of an "industrial spirit" that was tamed and contained over the previous century of British cultural history, along with some of the political and economic consequences of such containment, was set out in two talks delivered in the spring of 1974: one to a scholarly seminar directed by the Marxist historian E. J. Hobsbawm, the other to an audience of business and political leaders at a conference at Ashridge Management College organized by the Hudson Institute Europe. In these talks, particularly the latter, I sought to bring the worlds of historical scholarship and public policy discourse into fruitful contact, suggesting recent implications of historical developments and historical roots of present dilemmas and perhaps planting some seeds of thought to germinate later.

Thereafter, I returned to teaching in America, and to a number of academic and personal obligations that slowed progress on the writing of the book, which was not published until the beginning of 1981. By the time it appeared, another Labour government had bogged down in social stalemate, and its Conservative replacement was itself entering a crisis period. Margaret Thatcher's government was coming under increasing pressure to reverse its radical new policies of tighter money and freer markets. It was an opportune moment for reappraising the basic lines of modern British history, and the book received a good deal of notice from journalists and politicians as well as the more expected complement of professional historians. As Richard English and Michael Kenny observed, it was "the first major 'declinist' text to be taken up by both an academic and a wider audience."[1] It was cited by both members of the government, as an account of a century-old wrong direction that it was seeking to rectify, and by some of its critics, as a basis for their indictment of the government's "betrayal of British industry" (the title of a 1982 television special based on the book). Each side naturally took from the book that which best suited its immediate agenda, but both were responding to a genuine effort on my part to write a history that made current dilemmas more comprehensible.

English Culture and the Decline of the Industrial Spirit proposed that in the late nineteenth and early twentieth centuries a cultural reaction against

---

[1] Richard English and Michael Kenny, eds., *Rethinking British Decline* (2000), p. 25.

the disruptive force of the industrial revolution "inoculated" the rapidly growing middle and upper-middle classes with values and attitudes resistant to economic innovation and growth. National identity became associated not, as it appeared by the mid-nineteenth century that it might be, with industrialism, technology, capitalism, and city life, but with values rooted in slow-changing "country" ways of life. This reaction was nurtured by institutions like the public schools and Oxbridge and by the opportunities available to adopt quasi-aristocratic lifestyles. As a result, the rise of "industrial values" was contained, and the status of industrial and technological careers remained decidedly inferior to that of careers in government or the professions. The broad outcome was an economy less dynamic and a polity less supportive of economic development than would otherwise have been the case.

Beyond (but not unconnected to) the immediate interest in its implications for current policy issues, the book also stimulated a great deal of scholarly discussion and investigation. Indeed, one of its contributions has unquestionably been to accelerate the development of business history, technological history, and the study of the social and cultural influences on economic behavior in British history. For twenty years critics have focused on the specific question of economic behavior and the supposed influences of educational institutions and aristocratic lifestyles on it. Could national economic growth have been significantly faster? Did public schools and old universities in fact retard such growth? Were industrialists and potential industrialists "gentrified" in their attitudes and way of life, and insofar as they were, did that clearly retard economic development?

Here there was certainly much open to criticism. The product of an intellectual historian, the book, it can be argued, credited ideas with more power than they merited, and in plowing new ground, it had often to work with an insufficient evidentiary base. Questions like the future careers of public school graduates or the country estate–buying propensities of industrialists had yet to be thoroughly studied, and in such matters the book of necessity painted a broad brush, elucidating themes and selecting examples rather than quantifying large amounts of evidence. As F. M. L. Thompson, the book's most recent critic, observed in 2001, "culture is a fickle guide, so flexible, anxious to please, and so easily moulded to suit any one of a range of preconceptions, that it is unwise for historians to trust it beyond the limits of independent corroboration from other types of more objective witnesses."[2] Among other things, Thompson, like some previous critics, questioned whether there had ever been such

---

[2] *Gentrification and the Enterprise Culture: Britain 1780–1980* (2001), p. 160. Besides Thompson's, the leading critical works are Bruce Collins and Keith Robbins, ed., *British Culture and Economic Decline* (1990), W. B. Rubinstein, *Capitalism, Culture and Decline in Britain,*

a thing as an "enterprise culture" (a term that does not appear in the book; it was coined by some of the book's Conservative admirers) or whether the process of "gentrification" (the adoption by businessmen and industrialists of "gentry" or "aristocratic" styles of life) had had, in fact, measurable deleterious consequences on economic growth. As a result of the industrious scholarship of the book's critics and other historians, much more is now known about these issues than was the case in the late 1970s, when this book was composed. No doubt, it would be quite a different work if it were undertaken today. Yet it still conveys some important things, both about the climate of thought in 1970s and 80s Britain and about the long sweep of British history. For a century and more, technologists and businessmen have expressed their sense of being denied the social status accorded to those in the professions or government. Many such persons, after reading the book, wrote the author during the 1980s repeating such sentiments. These have been too widely shared and too persistent over generations to not be telling of something important, however merely "cultural."

Furthermore, not only did most critics go rather overboard in their reaction to a work that was soon closely associated with the hated Thatcher government, they also tended to misread the book's argument as more drastic than it actually was – not as a partial but as a full explanation for British economic retardation; and even in its chosen specific territory of culture, as a portrait not of the containment or "domestication" of industrial values but of their defeat. In addition, nearly all critics focused on one half of the book's portrait – the economic behavior of the business class – and ignored the other half – the influence of counterindustrial values and attitudes on political discourse and policies (in which the long-lasting effects of empire played a crucial role, one that the book did not credit as much as it should have).[3] The book concluded by turning to politics and suggesting that Thatcher's greatest challenge might not be the money supply or the trade unions, both in the forefront of attention in the first years of her government, but the dominant frame of mind of the nation's political and economic leaders. So, arguably, it proved, and insofar as Blair's "New Britain" differs from the Britain of Wilson and Callaghan, it owes a debt to the "cultural" agenda as well as to the more concrete legislative and fiscal policies of the "Thatcherite" era in between.

1750–1990 (1991), and Peter Clarke and Clive Trebilcock, eds., *Understanding Decline* (1997).

3 This, indeed, was a point never made by critics, but indeed it should have been explored at some length. In the twentieth century, the possession of the world's most extensive empire helped support a large bureaucratic-professional class and its pseudo-gentry "custodial culture" oriented more toward preservation of the status quo than toward innovation.

Thus, even after absorbing the many valid objections of its critics, this book remains a milestone in the historiography of modern Britain, having made several different kinds of contributions. First, of course, because of the interest it stirred, far more is now known about the history of the British economy and, in particular, the "culture of economic behavior" in nineteenth- and twentieth-century Britain, and, indeed, about the "politics of modernization." But the work proved both symptomatic and influential well beyond the "relative economic decline" debate. The study of economics as cultural activity has rapidly developed, both within and outside the field of history. Outside, professional economics has become much more receptive to cultural, institutional, and behavioral angles of approach. Inside, business history has in Britain virtually exploded as a field of study, while in particular the study of what might be called the "birth of the industrial spirit" in the eighteenth century is beginning to transform our understanding of the industrial revolution, arguably the most important development in history since the invention of agriculture.[4] Indeed, one may now speak of a new emerging scholarly consensus on the origins of the Industrial Revolution that gives a greater role than ever before to a set of exceptionally close relations in eighteenth-century Britain between many scientists, craftsmen, and businessmen – what has been labeled a widely diffused "engineering culture."[5]

Beyond this, this book was one of the first works to highlight the peculiar hybridity of the British elite and how much longer and slower the "decline" of the aristocracy had been than had previously been assumed. It was also one of the first to draw attention to the growing preoccupation with national identity in twentieth-century Britain. The "literature of national identity" first discussed here has since become the subject of a large number of studies. "From about twenty years ago," Robert Colls observed in 2002, "historians and critics started asking the national question again."[6] No cessation seems in prospect.

English Culture and the Decline of the Industrial Spirit remains after more than two decades a vivid portrait of one face of modern British history, a stimulant to thought about the relations between culture and society in Britain, and, more generally, a founding text of the study of British national identities and a notable example of a work of history that played a part in the politics and public life of its own time.

[4] See Margaret C. Jacob, *Scientific Culture and the Making of the Industrial West* (1997), and Joel Mokyr, *The Gifts of Athena: Historical Origins of the Knowledge Economy* (2002).

[5] Jack Goldstone, "Efflorescences and Economic Growth in World History: Rethinking the 'Rise of the West' and the Industrial Revolution," *Journal of World History* 13 (2002), 374. For the full development of this argument, see Goldstone's forthcoming book, *The Happy Chance: The Industrial Revolution in the Perspective of World History*.

[6] Robert Colls, *Identity of England* (2002), p. 4.

PART I

The setting

1

The Janus face of modern English culture

Bladesover is, I am convinced, the clue to almost all that is distinctively British and perplexing to the foreign inquirer in England . . . Grasp firmly that England was all Bladesover two hundred years ago; that it has had Reform Acts indeed, and such-like changes of formula, but no essential revolution since then; that all that is modern and different has come in as a thing intruded or as a gloss upon this predominant formula, either impertinently or apologetically . . . Everybody who is not actually in the shadow of a Bladesover is as it were perpetually seeking after lost orientations. We have never broken with our tradition, never even symbolically hewed it to pieces, as the French did in quivering fact in the Terror. But all the organizing ideas have slackened, the old habitual bonds have relaxed or altogether come undone.
—H. G. Wells, *Tono-Bungay* (1908)

Cultural values and economic lag
The leading problem of modern British history is the explanation of economic decline. It has not always been thus. Until the later nineteen-sixties the generally accepted frame for the history of Britain over the previous century was that of a series of success stories: the bloodless establishment of democracy, the evolution of the welfare state, triumph in two world wars, and the enlightened relinquishment of empire. Such a happy frame, however, became increasingly hard to maintain as, having steered clear of the rocks of political turmoil or military defeat, the British found themselves becalmed in an economic Sargasso sea. As successive governments, Labour and Tory, saw their varying panaceas for lifting the economy to the level of growth of Britain's neighbors and competitors yield only frustrating failure (despite even the unforeseen windfalls of North Sea gas and oil), the realization began to sink in that the problem had a long history. "The English disease," Correlli Barnett argued in 1975, "is not the novelty of the past 10 or even 20 years . . . but a phenomenon dating back more than a century."[1] The intractability of the problem made it ever clearer that it was rooted deep in the nation's social structure and mental climate. The more closely Britain's twentieth-century eco-

nomic decline is examined, the more social and psychological elements are to be found intertwined with economic factors. The German director of the London School of Economics, Ralf Dahrendorf, concluded after studying Britain for some years that "economic performance and cultural values are linked," and that "an effective economic strategy for Britain will probably have to begin in the cultural sphere."[2]

All manner of historical explanations for British economic decline have been put forward, ranging from the exclusively economic to those involving political, social, and psychological components, and spanning the ideological spectrum from Marxist to Keynesian to free-market standpoints. It is without doubt a complex problem, and lacks any simple or generally accepted solution. Although it is true that, as E. J. Hobsbawm has sternly enjoined, "economic explanations of economic phenomena are to be preferred if they are available,"[3] such explanations as have been put forward, by their inadequacies, have only made clearer the problem's character. Strictly economic explanations either have been based on questionable assumptions or have left large space for "residual" factors, which would appear to be social and psychological.[4]

In a world perspective, it seems difficult – and unhelpful – to separate sharply culture and economics. Development economists have repeatedly come up against the limitations of purely economic analysis. Most leading development theorists have agreed that economic motivations alone – however necessary – are not sufficient to redirect a society's path.[5] Culture, society, and ideology have been portrayed as central to the development process. This awareness has spawned a large body of literature, emanating particularly from social psychologists and development specialists, that elaborates models of social–psychological change undergone by members of modernizing societies. These studies all brought out the importance of such factors, difficult to quantify, as character, world outlook, values, and attitudes in the economic transformation of societies.[6] This approach has not been limited either to social psychologists or to American scholars. The Swedish Nobel Laureate Gunnar Myrdal, in his massive *Asian Drama*, showed in detail the social and cultural upheaval involved in – and apparently necessary to – development.[7] The example of India virtually overwhelms anyone following a narrow approach to economic development. India's experience since independence has been frustrating for economic planners at home and advisers from the West. Repeatedly, schemes of fiscal and financial policy, foreign aid, and programs of industrial and agricultural investment foundered on the intangible resistances built into perhaps the world's most conservative culture.[8]

Another Asian society, Japan, by its contrasting success, has also underlined the fact that economic behavior does not take place in a cultural vacuum. We have come to see that Japan's startlingly rapid development owes at least as much to peculiar characteristics of Japanese society and culture – the "tribal" character of work relationships and the inner discipline that makes possible remarkable adaptability, for example – as to the country's specifically economic techniques. No one can fully understand the Japanese economic miracle without grasping the working principles of Japanese culture.[9]

How did specifically English cultural elements influence economic life? Despite all the publicity given trade union "obstructionism," this question is in the final analysis primarily about "bourgeois," or elite, rather than popular English culture (although there exists no precise line of division between them). Elites have disproportionate influence upon both the effective climate of opinion and the conduct of affairs. The values of the directing strata, particularly in a stable, cohesive society like modern Britain, tend to permeate society as a whole and to take on the color of national values, and of a general *mentalité*. In economic matters, as has been observed, bosses tend to get the workers they deserve; the attitudes and behavior of workers are deeply influenced, even if only in reaction, by the attitudes and behavior of employers.[10] How, then, has English middle- and upper-class culture affected the nation's economic development?

Progress and its discontents
For a long time, the English have not felt comfortable with "progress." As one social analyst has perceived, "progress" is a word that in England has come to possess a curiously ambiguous emotive power. "It connotes tendencies that we accept, even formally approve, yet of which we are privately suspicious."[11] It is a historic irony that the nation that gave birth to the industrial revolution, and exported it throughout the world, should have become embarrassed at the measure of its success. The English nation even became ill at ease enough with its prodigal progeny to deny its legitimacy by adopting a conception of Englishness that virtually excluded industrialism.

This suspicion of material and technological development and this symbolic exclusion of industrialism were intimately related in Britain. They appeared in the course of the industrial revolution, but, instead of fading away as the new society established itself, they persisted and indeed were extended and strengthened. In the later years of Victoria's reign they came to form a complex, entrenched cultural syndrome, pervading "educated opinion." The idealization of material growth and technical innovation that had been emerging received a check, and was more and more pushed back by the contrary ideals of stability, tranquility, closeness to the past, and "nonmaterialism." An "English way of life" was defined and widely accepted; it stressed nonindustrial noninnovative and nonmaterial qualities, best encapsulated in rustic imagery – "England is the country," in Stanley Baldwin's phrase (by his time already a cliché). This countryside of the mind was everything industrial society was not – ancient, slow-moving, stable, cozy, and "spiritual." The English genius, it declared, was (despite appearances) not economic or technical, but social and spiritual; it did not lie in inventing, producing, or selling, but in preserving, harmonizing, and moralizing. The English character was not naturally progressive, but conservative; its greatest task – and achievement – lay in taming and "civilizing" the dangerous engines of progress it had unwittingly unleashed.

Over the years, this outlook contended with an industrial reality that sometimes was proclaimed as a source of pride. The resulting conflicts of social values – progress versus nostalgia, material growth versus moral stability – were expressed in the two widespread and contrasting cultural symbols of Workshop and Garden (or Shire). Was England to be the Workshop of the World or a Green and Pleasant Land? This question, with its presumed incompatibility of industrial and rural values, lay at the back of a great many English minds.

Rural myths did not have to be opposed to industrialism. In later-nineteenth- and early-twentieth-century America, nostalgia abounded for what was often seen as a simpler and happier time; rural life was often idealized and much was made of its moral importance to the nation. These sentiments, however, rarely came together into a critique of progress itself or of economic development, as in England, except in the hands of a few intellectuals, whose distinctive strain of almost anarchic individualism reflected their awareness of being outside the cultural mainstream. Even rural panegyrists, and those nostalgic for an earlier America, rarely disdained manufacturing or commerce. The ideal of the American yeoman-farmer was of an agrarian technologist and capitalist, a businessman producing for a market, ever ready to invent or adopt technical or commercial improvements. Men like Jefferson welcomed the development of commerce and manufactures as an essential part of civilization, while idealizing the "rural republic." Industry would and should come, planted in the rural landscape, the one as American as the other.[12] Even nostalgia had a modernizing character in America, as made clear by Henry Ford and his historical reconstruction of Greenfield Village in the nineteen-twenties. This project was a sentimental evocation of the simpler America of Ford's early years, and at the same time a celebration of technological progress.[13] Americans may have idealized their "garden," but it was, in contrast to the English vision we shall explore, an economically dynamic, technically progressive garden.

In England, the symbols of Machine and Garden, Workshop and Shire, were in more direct opposition. These symbols embodied a tension that had become implanted deep within middle- and upper-class culture over at least the previous century. Much of the peculiar character of English domestic history over this period was the result of a nation, or at least an elite, at war with itself.

This inner tension in modern English culture is something of a puzzle. Why did hostility to industrial advance persist and even strengthen in the world's first industrial society? Why did such hostility so often take the form of rural myth making? Some answers lie in the peculiar pattern of nineteenth-century British social history.

The revolution that never was

Nineteenth-century Britain was a pioneer of modernization. Yet, the path it took to modernity was one all its own. Britain's transition was marked by admirably peaceful gradualism, but also, thereby, by a certain incompleteness. From this incompleteness stemmed long-lasting cultural consequences.

Modernization has never been a simple and easy process. Wherever and whenever it has occurred, severe psychological and ideological strains and stresses have resulted, though they have not always taken the dramatic form they found in Germany, or received so much attention.[14] In Britain these tensions have been particularly easy to overlook, as the transition to modernity was relatively smooth and involved no political upheaval. However, that very mildness, I shall suggest, fostered a self-limiting element in Britain's development. The industrial revolution in other countries came at least partly from without and thus challenged and disrupted traditional social patterns. In Britain, on the other hand, industrialization was indigenous, and thus more easily accommodated to existing social structures, which did not need to change radically.

The often-hailed Victorian achievement, seen in this light, was Janus-faced. If society was transformed, with a minimum of violence, the extent of the transformation was more limited than it first appeared to be. New economic forces did not tear the social fabric. Old values and patterns of behavior lived on within the new, whose character was thus profoundly modified.[15] The end result of the nineteenth-century transformation of Britain was indeed a peaceful accommodation, but one that entrenched premodern elements within the new society, and gave legitimacy to antimodern sentiments. The cultural and practical consequences would become clear only in the twentieth century.

The ambiguity of the Victorian achievement has been perceived by some observers, both on the Right and on the Left. Conservative politician Sir Keith Joseph has located the source of Britain's contemporary economic problems in the fact that it "never had a capitalist ruling class or a stable *haute bourgeoisie*." As a result, he has argued, "capitalist or bourgeois values have never shaped thought and institutions as they have in some countries."[16] This interpretation has expressed an important truth, but in a partial and misleading form: It blurs capitalism and bourgeoisie. The key to the peculiar pattern of modern British history is that the two have been distinct. The nation had the world's first (except perhaps for Holland) essentially capitalist ruling class: the eighteenth-century landed aristocracy and gentry. What Britain never had was a straightforwardly bourgeois or industrial elite. This crucial distinction has been usefully elaborated by two Marxist historians, Perry Anderson and Tom Nairn. Anderson and Nairn emphasized the importance of the fact that the industrial revolution began in Britain while the ruling landed aristocracy was becoming still richer, more self-confident, and an even more tightly knit oligarchy. This aristocracy, however, was no longer feudal but was essentially capitalist. "There was thus," Anderson argued, "from the start no fundamental antagonistic contradiction between the old aristocracy and the new bourgeoisie."[17] Consequently, no bourgeois revolution ensued; in its place was accommodation. Yet these two classes, if both capitalist, were not capitalist in the same way. The capitalism of the aristocracy, although varying in individual cases, was basically rentier, not entrepreneurial or productive. Thus the accommodation between aristocracy and bourgeoisie meant an adaptation by the new middle classes to a comparatively aloof and passive economic role. The rentier aristocracy succeeded to a large extent in maintaining a cultural hegemony, and consequently (as we shall see) in reshaping the industrial bourgeoisie in its own image. The Victorian retreat of the aristocracy was more political than psychological. The landed elite gave way only slowly to the industrialists, so that, as Peregrine Worsthorne put it not long ago, "the transference of power, protracted over a century, resembled a merger rather than a conquest; a marriage (in many cases literally) rather than a rape." The result was, in Worsthorne's phrase, the "civilizing [of] the bourgeoisie."[18]

Aristocratic hegemony persisted also – indeed, more obviously – in Britain's emerging rival, Germany.[19] Because the political histories of the two nations contrasted so dramatically, for a long time Britain was wrongly seen as taking a path of development opposite to that of Germany – a path of complete bourgeois triumph as against Germany's holding onto "feudalism." Britain was supposed to be the archtypal "nation of shopkeepers" – a Napoleonic gibe that was false when first uttered, and still false, if less obviously so, when repeated by German writers before and during the first World War. In truth, Britain and Germany both underwent powerful industrial revolutions in the midst of strong and resilient aristocratic societies.

That this encounter of industry and aristocracy led to different economic (not to mention political) outcomes in the two countries can be explained by many factors, chief among them the chronology of economic change, the degree of aristocratic openness, and, perhaps most crucial, the character of each aristocracy. Because the industrial revolution in Germany took place later and more suddenly than it did in Britain, the German industrial bourgeoisie had less time to become accepted by and absorbed into the older elite. Second, the Prussian aristocracy, in particular, was less ready than the English aristocracy to accept wealthy businessmen into its ranks, regardless of how much they hastened to remake themselves on the *Junker* model.[20] For both these reasons, the new industrialists and entrepreneurs of Imperial Germany were more likely than their longer-established English counterparts to retain their preoccupation with production.

Beyond this, however, the two aristocracies were different enough to influence their respective middle classes in quite distinct ways. The Prussian aristocracy was still an aggressive, authoritarian military caste; English lords and gentry had, with prosperity, long since shed that character. Moreover, the *Junkers*, for all their caste pride, were not wealthy on the English scale, and had to continue to struggle ruthlessly to protect and develop their economic and political position. In spite of their romantic pretensions, the *Junkers* became, as Fritz Stern observed, ever more "agrarian industrialists."[21] It was perhaps this combination of militarism and economic pressure that made Bismarck's government appreciate the geopolitical value of economic development, and that underlay the historic arrangement of 1878-9, in which industry traded political support for the economic support of tariff protection (and, ultimately, *Weltpolitik*).[22] Particularly after 1879, the industrial bourgeoisie in Germany was moving toward an aristocratic model less hospitable than the English to "free enterprise" or political liberalism, but more suitable to maintaining a fierce drive toward economic growth (closely associated with national power).[23] In Germany, thus, capitalism and liberalism were devalued far more than industrialism, whereas in England it was industrialism and not capitalism or liberalism whose development was inhibited. In this way, the conjunction of modernization with an entrenched aristocracy led in Germany to obstructed political development, and in Britain to inhibited economic development.

The British form of accommodation yielded both gain and cost. The gain was political and social stability, and a "humanization" of the rawness of early industrialism. The cost was, as Nairn put it, "the containment of capitalism within a patrician hegemony which never, either then or since, actively favoured the aggressive development of industrialism or the general conversion of society to the latter's values and interests."[24] Lasting social and psychological limits were thus placed on the industrial revolution in Britain. As Correlli Barnett concluded in his history of modern British military leadership, "the social and intellectual values of industrial society never ousted those of the aristocracy."[25] Out of this successful aristocratic–gentry holding action a distinctly English "culture of containment" developed. The social conflict was never clearly resolved, but internalized within the compromise that emerged: a new dominant bourgeois culture bearing the imprint of the old aristocracy. The tensions within this compromise culture were reflected in anxieties and discontents surrounding the idea of material progress, and in the emotions laden onto the cultural symbol of England as a garden. Beyond this, these tensions shaped not only bourgeois culture, but also, through culture, behavior. A variety of modern British practices that has served to humanize urban industrial society – new towns and green belts, the love of gardening, even a wariness of most modern architecture – owes a debt to this social compromise. Less attractive patterns of behavior also show their mark – chief among these is persistent economic retardation.

The consolidation of a "gentrified" bourgeois culture, particularly the rooting of pseudoaristocratic attitudes and values in upper-middle-class educated opinion, shaped an unfavorable context for economic endeavor. Economic historians, economists, civil servants, and even political leaders held sentiments and ideals that served to restrain rather than stimulate economic growth. Often even those seeking growth showed at the same time the influence of their cultural environment, which worked to "muffle" or "domesticate" such growth. Industrialists themselves were crucially affected in developing their view of the world and their role in it. They too gravitated toward what they saw as aristocratic values and styles of life, to the detriment, more often than not, of their economic effectiveness. The outcome was the spectacle (not necessarily all for the bad) of an industrial society diffidently led by men with "mind-forg'd manacles" restraining their concepts and their actions. How this came about is our story.

2

Victorian society: accommodation and absorption

England . . . owes her great influence not to military successes, but to her commanding position in the arena of industry and commerce. If she forgets this, she is lost.
—*Annual Register* (1867)

Sixty-four years that favored property, and had made the upper middle class; buttressed, chiselled, polished it; till it was almost undistinguishable in manners, morals, speech, appearance, habit, and soul from the nobility.
—John Galsworthy, *The Forsyte Saga* (1922)

"Nine English traditions out of ten," an old don in a C. P. Snow novel says, "date from the latter half of the nineteenth century."[1] This period saw the recasting of British life. Modern British political, commercial, and social institutions are predominantly the creation of Victorian reform and accommodation. Similarly, twentieth-century social values bear the imprint of Victorian arguments. Much of the criticism of mid-Victorian Britain by men like Mill, Arnold, Ruskin, and Dickens, for example, was amplified by social trends under way, and helped shape the outlook of succeeding generations of educated opinion. A distinctive English world view was being formed in the crucible of the mid-Victorian ferment of social ideas. It proved highly suitable to the new upper stratum taking shape at the same time, a stratum produced by the coming together of businessmen, the rapidly expanding professional and bureaucratic classes, and the older gentry and aristocracy. The central institution of the consolidation, the public school, came into its own in this period. From the eighteen-forties, old schools were revived, new schools were founded, and a common ethos began to crystallize. It was an ethos that readily absorbed one side of mid-Victorian social thought, institutionalized it, and propagated it. By Victoria's death, her nation possessed a remarkably homogeneous and cohesive elite, sharing to a high degree a common education and a common outlook and set of values. This shared outlook represented an adaptation by the traditional landed ruling class (as was widely noted at the time), but it also marked a crucial rebuff for the social revolution begun by industrialization.

A re-formed elite

The early years of Victoria's reign were widely thought at the time to be bringing about the triumph of the middle classes. It was frequently claimed that the parliamentary reform in 1832 and the repeal of the Corn Laws in 1846 were pulling out the props from the political and economic supremacy of the landed aristocracy. Marx and Engels went so far as to assert in 1850 that "the only remaining aristocracy is the bourgeoisie."[2] Was, in fact, the death knell tolling for the English aristocracy as a ruling class? In the long view, no doubt. Yet not before the aristocracy had succeeded in both prolonging its reign and educating its successors in its world view.[3] Power was peacefully yielded in return for time and for the acceptance of many aristocratic values by the new members of the elite. Hostility on both sides began to wane. After 1846 the interests of landlords were no longer clearly opposed to those of industry or capital. The greater landlords drew an increasing proportion of their incomes from railways, canals, mines, and urban property, and the growing scale of business organization was producing a new class of big businessmen, wealthier than their predecessors yet less directly involved in management and enterprise. For men of these groups, the old class antagonisms meant less and less, and a process of mutual accommodation was soon under way. In 1850 the *Economist* had criticized capitalists who advertised in the newspapers their desire to purchase land in order to acquire status. By 1870 it had changed its tune, observing that:

> Social consideration is a great and legitimate object of desire, and so great is the effect of this visibility of wealth upon social consideration that it would pay a millionaire in England to sink half his fortune in buying 10,000 acres of land to return a shilling percent, and live upon the remainder, rather than to live upon the whole without land. He would be a greater person in the eyes of more people.[4]

English history's normal pattern of ready absorption of new into old wealth, broken in the late eighteenth century by the explosive growth of geographically and religously isolated industrial wealth, resumed with a vengeance. In such Establishment spheres of activity as "society," the military (particularly the Volunteers), the Church of England, and the public schools and universities, the process of accommodation and absorption accelerated in the second half of the century. As Harold Perkin has noted, "the seeds of many of the aristocratic directorships of late Victorian England – in 1896 167 noblemen, a quarter of the peerage, were directors of companies – were no doubt sown on the playing fields of mid-Victorian public schools."[5]

The children of businessmen were admitted to full membership in the upper class, at the price of discarding the distinctive, production-oriented culture shaped during the century of relative isolation. "The main point about landowners – in England at least – is that they did not acquire their land in order to develop it, but in order to enjoy it," observed H. J. Habbakuk.[6] The adoption of a culture of enjoyment by new landowners and aspiring landowners meant the dissipation of a set of values that had projected their fathers as a class to the economic heights, and the nation to world predominance. In its place, they took up a new ideal – that of the gentleman.[7] This new ideal was in its essentials the older aristocratic ideal purged of its grosser elements by the nineteenth-century religious revival. Indeed, Bertrand Russell – himself a hereditary peer – was to suggest that "the concept of the gentleman was invented by the aristocracy to keep the middle classes in order."[8]

And so, in a sense, it did. Through these mechanisms of social absorption, the zeal for work, inventiveness, material production, and money making gave way within the capitalist class to the more aristocratic interests of cultivated style, the pursuits of leisure, and political service. Similarly, the modern industrial town was abandoned, whenever the means existed, in favor of a rural, preferably historic, home. The sons of the enormously successful mill owner John Marshall, for instance, let the business slide and became country gentlemen in the Lake District.[9] Fledgling gentry, F. M. L. Thompson observed, "could be more aristocratic than the aristocrats in their anxiety to conform to the rules of country life."[10] The London merchant banker Baron von Schroeder (to take one instance of many) bought a country house in Cheshire about 1868, became a magistrate in 1876, and was high sheriff and returning officer at the time of the first county council elections in January 1889. He was a well-known follower of the Cheshire hounds. In Cheshire, as elsewhere, it was increasingly difficult to distinguish between the habits of a banker, like "Fitz" Brocklehurst, a Liberal and a Unitarian, who insisted on spending three months in every year shooting in Scotland, and those of the aristocracy. Several generations would complete the transformation. J. M. Lee, examining the Cheshire elite, instructively compared the careers of James Watts, born in 1804, and his grandson, James Watts, born in 1878: The former was a Manchester businessman, possessed of only the most rudimentary education. A Congregationalist and an active participant in Liberal politics, he became mayor of Manchester during the eighteen-fifties. From the huge profits of a warehouse trade in fancy goods, he built an impressive country house, Abney Hall. His grandson was sent to Winchester and New College, Oxford, rowed for his college at Henley, and followed all the fashions of his generation, "even to the extent of taking an American wife!"[11]

The peculiar flexibility of the English aristocracy snatched a class victory from the brink of defeat, and helped alter the course of national development. At the moment of its triumph, the entrepreneurial class turned its energies to reshaping itself in the image of the class it was supplanting. That self-conscious spokesman of a bourgeois revolution, Richard Cobden (1804-65), watched with dismay his troops deserting the cause:

> We have [he complained to a friend in 1863] the spirit of feudalism rife and rampant in the midst of the antagonistic development of the age of Watt, Arkwright and Stephenson! Nay, feudalism is every day more and more in the ascendant in political and social life. So great is its power and prestige that it draws to it the support and homage of even those who are the natural leaders of the newer and better civilisation. Manufacturers and merchants as a rule seem only to desire riches that they may be enabled to prostrate themselves at the feet of feudalism. How is this to end?[12]

As capitalists became landed gentlemen, JPs, and men of breeding, the radical ideal of active capital was submerged in the conservative ideal of passive property, and the urge to enterprise faded beneath the preference for stability.

The gentrification of the Victorian middle classes proceeded as well through a second social trend of the period: the rise of the modern professions. Professional men – lawyers, doctors, public officials, journalists, professors, and men of letters – came into their own during the reign of Victoria. They grew numerous and distinct enough to be considered a class, or more strictly speaking, a subclass, with an influence on English opinion and culture far out of proportion to its size. By the second half of the nineteenth century there was a professional upper middle class in Britain alongside the capitalist class.

Throughout the century, old professions like law and medicine restructured themselves to emphasize expertise, expanded in numbers, and achieved enhanced status. Even the clergy followed a similar pattern. At the same time, new professions proliferated. The establishment of the Royal College of Surgeons in 1800, the British Medical Association in 1856, and the Law Society in 1825 placed the

traditional secular professions on a new footing of secure respectability.[13] One after another, new professions, greatly influenced by the
model of the older ones, began to detach themselves from the world
of business and organize themselves – civil engineers in 1818, architects in 1834, pharmacists in 1841, actuaries in 1848, and so on, all
revealing an aspiration to use their claims of expertise and integrity to
rise above the rule of the marketplace. Between 1841 and 1881, the
nation's population rose by 60 percent, whereas the seventeen main
professional occupations increased their numbers by 150 percent,
thereby coming to constitute a substantial portion of the middle
class.[14]

The growth of the professions bolstered the emerging cultural
containment of industrial capitalism. Professional men as a class were
characterized by their comparative aloofness from the struggle for
income. The scale of professional prestige was largely determined by
distance from flagrant "money grubbing." T. H. S. Escott (1844-
1924), author of the most informative contemporary survey of late-
Victorian Britain, explained that GPs and solicitors had lower occupational status than barristers and clergymen partly because the
former had to undergo the "vulgar" commercial process of receiving
money directly from their clients.[15] Professional aloofness was of
course partly a myth. Individuals often competed for clients, and the
maintenance of high professional standards also served to limit entry
and thus bolster incomes. Nevertheless, as Harold Perkin argued,
"once established, the professional man could generally rely on a
steady income not subject to the same mutual competition as rent,
profits and wages. To a certain extent, then, he was above the economic battle."[16] Furthermore, professionals valued services and intangible goods such as those they provided higher than the material
goods whose production was the concern of much of the nonprofes-
sional middle class and working class. This bias toward services,
together with the independence of their status from the vagaries of
the market, served to detach professional men from the mental and
emotional world of the industrial capitalist.

Of course, professionalization also carried other values more at-
tuned to an industrial world view: the career open to talent and
effort, specialization, and efficiency. But these values were not as
encouraged in English society as they were, for example, in America.[17]
Professionalization did not have a single, universal meaning: Its
actual forms derived from the interaction between its multiple tendencies and its social environment. The English environment magni-
fied the older gentry face of professionalization at the expense of its
newer bourgeois one.[18] The very modes by which an English profes-

sion typically defined itself set its members off from the world of capitalism. As one historian observed:

> The process of incorporation, acquisition of an expensive and pala-
> tial headquarters in central London, establishment of an apprentice-
> ship system, limitations on entries, and scheduling of fees, are all
> manifestly designed to "gentrify" the profession and make it accept-
> able to society. This aspect of professionalization is profoundly anti-
> capitalist, and hence at odds with much of the rest of nineteenth-
> century British society.[19]

The existence of a powerful aristocracy in Britain reinforced the anticapitalist tendencies within professionalization. Here, conse-quently, more than elsewhere, the development of the professions was separating many of the most able men from the world of com-merce and industry. A perceptive contemporary pointed this out: Matthew Arnold, poet and school inspector, observed in 1868 that professional men, admitted to an education with aristocrats, tended to model themselves on the aristocracy. Consequently, Arnold claimed, "in no country . . . do the professions so naturally and generally share the cast of ideas of the aristocracy as in England." In England the professions, including the emerging civil service, were "separate, to a degree unknown on the Continent, from the commercial and indus-trial class with which in social standing they are naturally on a level." The result was the spectacle of

> a middle class cut in two and in a way unexampled anywhere else; of a
> professional class brought up on the first plane, with fine and gov-
> erning qualities, but without the idea of science; while that immense
> business class, which is becoming so important a power in all coun-
> tries, on which the future so much depends . . . is in England brought
> up on the second plane, but cut off from the aristocracy and profes-
> sions, and without governing qualities.[20]

The shaping of a gentleman
Ironically, the educational system that Arnold's father did so much to shape played a leading role in fixing this separation, and the attitude and values that went with it, upon English society. The public school was of particular importance, for this "peculiar institution" unique to England had become by the end of Victoria's reign the shared forma-tive experience of most members of the English elite. For all their vaunted independence, the public schools, through new institutions like Headmasters' Conference, converged on a common model. Despite the absence of state direction, they came to constitute a system,[21] one that separated the next generation of the upper class from the bases of Britain's world position – technology and business.

The decade of the eighteen-sixties had seemed to be destined to be a time of sweeping reform in secondary education. A spreading awareness of the need to modernize the unsupervised hodgepodge of existing schools led to the creation of two royal commissions. The Clarendon [Public Schools] Commission, appointed in 1861, was to examine the nine most prestigious endowed schools, and the Taunton [Schools Inquiry] Commission, created three years later, was to look at all the other endowed schools. Their reports did indeed lead to acts of Parliament, but the thrust for fundamental reform was deflected. The main effect of the prolonged attention was to establish the nine ancient public schools, more or less as they were, as *the* model of secondary education for all who aspired to rise in English society. After examining in detail the faults of the public schools, the Clarendon Commission turned to their greater merit:

> These schools have been the chief nurseries of our statesmen; in them, and in schools modelled after them, men of all the various classes that make up English society, destined for every profession and career, have been brought up on a footing of social equality, and have contracted the most enduring friendships, and some of the ruling habits of their lives; and they have had perhaps the largest share in moulding the character of an English Gentleman.[22]

There was change – new schools appeared, new subjects were introduced, improvements in physical facilities and innovations in school procedures were made – but only the minimum necessary to preserve and extend the social dominance of the public school pattern. This aim was attained: In the later nineteenth century the sons of the middle classes flocked in increasing numbers into schools modeling themselves upon the "Clarendon nine." What was usually desired was expressed in a fictional parent's enthusiasm for the reinvigorated Shrewsbury: "Just the very place: new buildings, old traditions. What could possibly be better?"[23]

The most obvious example of the public schools' detachment from the modern world was the virtual absence of science of any sort from their curricula. In the teaching of science the public schools lagged far behind schools of lesser social standing. It was first taught in private and Dissenting academies in the eighteenth century, and by Victoria's accession it was a normal part of the curriculum in most such schools, and in many grammar schools.[24] Yet it did not penetrate the schools of the upper class for some years thereafter, and then only over determined obstruction.

At Rugby, the pioneer of public school science instruction, the first science teachers were barely tolerated. J. M. Wilson, an astronomer, was allowed after 1859 to offer four hours a week of "natural philosophy" as long as it did not interfere with the fourteen hours he put in on algebra, geometry, and trigonometry. For this science instruction no room could be found on the premises at Rugby, and "the experiments were performed out of sight, in the cloakroom of the Town Hall a hundred yards away down the road from the school, with the apparatus locked up in two cases so that the townspeople could use the space for other purposes at night."[25] This was the situation the Public Schools Commission found at the most scientifically minded of the leading schools! Even after the commission urged the development of science instruction, the pace of change was slow. Graham Wallas (1858-1932), at Shrewsbury between 1871 and 1877, later recalled that "we had no laboratory of any kind, and I never heard in my time of any Shrewsbury boy receiving a science lesson."[26]

This neglect of science rested on an educational ideology. Its positive face was exaltation of the Greek and Roman classics as the basis of any liberal education. Its negative side was a fear of science as antireligious, which sharply waned as the century drew on, and an association of science with vulgar industry, artisans, and commercial utility, which did not diminish so readily. Headmasters, more or less equating the classics (together with Christianity, of course) with civilization and ideal mental training, were eloquent in defense of a purely classical curriculum, and they were backed up by most educated persons of note. No less a figure than Gladstone added his views: "What I feel is, that the relation of pure science, natural science, modern languages, modern history and the rest to the old classical training, ought to be founded on a principle . . . I deny their right to a parallel or equal position; their true position is ancillary, and as ancillary it ought to be limited and restrained without scruples."[27]

Most significant for the future, science was linked in the public mind with industry, and this damaged its respectability in upper-class eyes. Industry meant an uncomfortable closeness to working with one's hands, not to mention an all-too-direct earning of money. The question of science teaching was enmeshed in the class system: Despite the tradition of Hooke, Boyle, and their contemporaries of the great days of the Royal Society, it was not until the twentieth century that experimental science was fully accepted again in England as a fit occupation for a gentleman. The fact that the classics were a mark of social class worked to prevent the application of parental pressure for "modern" instruction. As the Taunton Commission concluded in 1868:

> They [the great majority of professional men and poor gentry] would, no doubt, in most instances be glad to secure something more than classics and mathematics. But they value these highly for their own sake, and perhaps even more for the value at present assigned to them in English society. They have nothing to look to but education to keep their sons on a high social level. And they would not wish to have what might be more readily converted into money, if in any degree it tended to let their children sink in the social scale.[28]

Although argument raged in the reviews over the nation's need for education in science, when it came down to the crucial question of one's own sons, the modernists rarely pushed principle to the point of practice. Isambard Kingdom Brunel (1806-59), the greatest engineer of his generation, sent two sons to Harrow, where they were hardly likely to follow their father's profession; T. H. Huxley (1825-95) sent a son to University College School; Lyon Playfair (1818-98), another leading critic of outdated public school curricula, sent one to Cheltenham; and so on.[29] When science teaching finally arrived in the public schools, it came late, marked by a social stigma and a bias against those aspects that bordered on engineering.

Similarly, the public schools resisted calls for particular training to prepare boys for the expanding professions. Vocational preparation – for law, medicine, or any newer profession – carried the stigma of utility. Edward Thring (1821-87), of Uppingham, a highly successful headmaster, found it "absolutely impossible to direct the studies of a great school to this end [professional education] beyond a certain degree, without destroying the object of a great school, which is, mental and bodily training in the best way, apart from immediate gain."[30] Thring was stating a platitude against which it was extremely difficult for gentlemen to take a stand. One exception was Dean Farrar (1831-1903), who observed that a scientific education would be useful.

> And no sooner [Farrar wrote] have I uttered the word "useful" than I imagine the hideous noise which will environ me, and amid the hubbub I faintly distinguish the words, vulgar, utilitarian, mechanical . . . Well, before this storm of customary and traditional clamour I bow my head, and when it is over, I meekly repeat that it would be *more useful* – more rich in practical advantages, more directly available for health, for happiness, for success in the great battle of life. I for one am tired of this "worship of inutility." One would really think it was a crime to aim at the material happiness of the human race.[31]

Thring's view remained pedagogical gospel. The weight of prejudice was heavily against the compatibility of liberal education (increasingly *the* mark of a gentleman) and utility. Yet if the public school produced exceedingly few scientists, and even fewer engineers, they did send forth increasing recruits to the growing ranks of professional men. As landed society entered its decline, and public schools expanded and increased in number, they became the nursery of professionals. Their disparagement of specialized and practical studies reinforced the traditional content of the professional ideal – the imitation of the leisured landed gentleman – at the expense of the modern role of the professional as expert.

If the technical skills necessary for professionalism were discouraged at public school, the world of business was openly disparaged.

Pre-Victorian public schools had been little more than finishing schools for sons of the landed gentry, with an admixture of farmers' sons and a few town boys. Aristocratic values were unchallenged, and trade despised. Arnoldian reforms retained – even deepened – the low valuation of commerce. In *Tom Brown's Schooldays*, that testament of gratitude to Dr. Arnold, Thomas Hughes spoke scornfully of England's previous "twenty years of buying cheap and selling dear." When Tom Brown, son of an idealized country squire, wishes upon leaving Rugby to "be at work in the world, and not dawdling away three years at Oxford," he is set straight by a master. Nothing was a greater vice to Arnold or Hughes than "dawdling," but there was work and there was work:

> You talk of "working to get your living" and "doing some real good in the world" in the same breath. Now, you may be getting a very good living in a profession, and yet doing no good at all in the world, but quite the contrary, at the same time. Keep the latter before you as your only object, and you will be right, whether you make a living or not; but if you dwell on the other, you'll very likely drop into mere money-making.[32]

Despite Thomas Hughes's assertion of the sovereignty of individual character "apart from clothes, rank, fortune, and all externals whatsoever,"[33] no children of businessmen were in evidence at Tom Brown's Rugby, and none of the characters so much as contemplated a commercial career. In a later and very popular novel about Harrow, Horace Vachell's *The Hill* (1905), a businessman's child arrives at school, but under a cloud of suspicion. Though rising by ability to captain of the cricket team, he remains an outsider, and ends by being expelled for dishonesty. "One is sometimes reminded," another boy typically comments, "that he is the son of a Liverpool merchant, born in or about the docks."[34] Given this stigma, it is hardly surprising that one of the most successful means of resisting the introduction of modern subjects was to associate them with the world of business. When the Taunton Commission was told by the inspector of schools for London that "I have been assured by several men of business that few things would please them better than a successful attack upon classical studies," a potent weapon was handed to the opponents of curricular change.[35]

The public schools gradually relaxed their entrance barriers. Boys from commercial and industrial families, however, were admitted only if they disavowed their backgrounds and their class. However many businessmen's sons entered, few future businessmen emerged from these schools, and those who did were "civilized"; that is, detached from the single-minded pursuit of production and profit.[36] "Somehow or other," the zealous founder of public schools, Nathaniel

Woodard (1811-91), had written the bishop of Manchester in 1871, "we must get possession of the Middle Classes ... and how can we so well do this as through Public Schools?"[37] Although Woodard's ambitious scheme for a vast network of boarding schools to embrace the entire middle class did not go far, the success of the public schools on a more modest and indirect scale gave a new lease on life to traditional social values. Their very physical environment held the urban industrial world at arm's length, and evoked the life of the old landed gentry. Disproportionately, whether new or ancient, they were distant from cities and industrial regions. Southern England had a very high proportion of the most prestigious public schools.[38] New schools were placed, whenever possible, deep in the countryside. Older schools sited in the cities moved out, like Charterhouse to the Surrey Hills. Every public school acquired, or sought to acquire, an estate to ensure its undisturbed rural character.[39] In this endeavor they were ironically assisted by the economic difficulties of the landed aristocracy; particularly after the First World War many large country houses were taken over by old and new public schools.[40]

The ethos of the schools, in keeping with their surroundings, exalted the careers colored by the aristocratic ideals of honor and public leadership – the military, politics, the civil service, and the higher professions. Public school boys made excellent administrators of a far-flung empire, but the training so admirably suited for that task ill fitted them for economic leadership.[41] The public schools nurtured the future elite's political, not economic, abilities, and a desire to maintain stability and order far outweighed the desire to maximize individual or national wealth.

During the second half of the nineteenth century the public schools took a central place in the life of the English upper classes. More than this, although less than one in twenty Englishmen ever passed through them, they became an archetypal national institution. "When we are criticizing its products," noted a typical defender in 1929, "whether by way of praise or blame, it is really to a great extent the English character that we are criticizing."[42] The public schools, observed Roy Lewis and Angus Maude (not unsympathetically) as late as 1949, enjoyed an "invisible empire" among the middle classes, who avidly read the new genre of public school literature.[43] Those who could afford it, sent their sons; those who could not, sought a grammar school as close as possible to the public school model. This latter quest was made easier after 1902, as a state system of secondary education was developed by public school men committed to public school ideals. Soon after it was established in 1899, the secondary school section of the Board of Education came under the control of the Headmasters' Conference.[44] Public school standards became the standards of the section and its officials. The chief official, Sir Robert Morant (1863-1920), who wrote and administered the Education Act of 1902 (for a prime minister with two public school headmasters in his family), "believed," a critic complained in Parliament many years later, "that the best form of education was that which had been given to him at Winchester," and consequently sought to replicate that education as far as practicable throughout the upper reaches of the state system.[45] Supported by nearly all the civil servants involved, this effort succeeded, and the new secondary schools developed a curriculum, an outlook, and forms of organization in line with the ideals of the education of the gentry. This molding of state education, affecting every inhabitant of Britain in one way or another, was a legacy equal in importance to the continued direct education in public schools of the bulk of the country's elite.[46] Through one or the other route, the late-Victorian public school outlook continued to shape British attitudes and values in the twentieth century.

The later-Victorian ancient universities present much the same picture as the public schools. Socially of less significance (most public school boys did not go on to university), they too witnessed a "conservative revolution" beginning in mid-century that revivified them and increased their contribution to the life of the nation, while preserving the essentials of traditional gentry culture. In the eighteen-fifties and sixties, "modern" subjects were scarcely in evidence in the Oxbridge curriculum. Sixteen years after two royal commissions had urged reform, T. H. Huxley could relate to a parliamentary committee the following experience at an Oxford dinner party: "I asked whether it would be a fair thing to say that any one might have taken the highest honours at the university, and yet might never have heard that the earth went round the sun? and all the gentlemen present ["very distinguished university men"] with one consent said 'Yes.' "[47] As with the public schools, very few undergraduates came from business backgrounds. Oxford and Cambridge, even more than the public schools, were precincts reserved for the sons of gentry, clergy, and the more distinguished professions.[48] Both curricula and admissions were widened during the rest of the century, but, as in the public schools, within the context of a reinvigorated ideal of liberal education and the role of the don that perpetuated many attitudes of the past. The "new model" don was reminiscent of the new public school master, a "moral gentleman" who sought to form the character of students; the new ideal of giving moral and spiritual leadership to a materialist society through liberal education was consonant with the ideals of the great headmasters. The ethos of later-Victorian Oxbridge, a fusion of aristocratic and professional values, stood self-consciously in opposition to the spirit of Victorian business and industry: It exalted a dual ideal of cultivation and service against philistine profit seeking.[49] Businessmen were objects of scorn and moral reproval, and industry was noted chiefly as a despoiler of country beauty. Whenever the subject of business arose at Oxford between Tom Brown and his friend Hardy, it was denounced: Hardy despised Carthage as a trading nation and feared that England was going the same way.[50] Well into the twentieth century, undergraduates were regularly discouraged from pursuing commercial careers, and alarms were sounded against the infection of these rarified precincts by vulgar influences from without. The defeat of proposals to abolish compulsory Greek at both universities in 1904 and 1905 revealed, among other things, a continuing determination to suppress the wishes of vulgar commercial elements. So deeply rooted was the disdain for the values represented by commerce and industry that, as Sheldon Rothblatt concluded, "numerous dons and non-resident M.A.'s decided the worth of an academic subject by its usefulness to commerce and industry. In their view almost no subject which could be turned to the benefit of business deserved university recognition."[51]

Like the public schools, later-Victorian Oxford and Cambridge provided a common formative experience for much of the British elite, and at the same time came to represent a *national* way of life. Like the public schools, they became the model for other institutions of education. The civic universities represented an exception to this rule, for they set out to provide a more modern and practical education. They had their successes, but never threw off the lower status that went with their task. Even they frequently imitated Oxbridge practice. Indeed, the post-1960 "Plateglass" universities, the first to seriously challenge the social supremacy of Oxbridge, were closer in many ways to the ancient than to the Victorian foundations. Despite their self-conscious modernity, largely expressed in a great emphasis on the social sciences, they by and large shared Oxbridge's lack of interest in technology and business. The "Plateglass" universities, significantly, were located away from large centers of population, in the cathedral town-country estate setting that had become typical of elite schools. In these cases, physical form followed social and psychological function – the embodiment of an ideal of "civilization" bound up with preindustrial, preurban models – forming an amalgam of an idealized medieval church and a similarly idealized eighteenth-century aristocracy.

Oxbridge institutionalized Victorian resistance to the new industrial world. As Rothblatt reflected, "the disdain of *homo oeconomicus* in Cambridge [and Oxford] was altogether too complete."[52] Oxbridge trained a political leadership with a minimum of interest in or knowledge of the industrial world. Recruits to the higher civil service, for many years predominantly graduates of these two universities, were, Oliver Macdonagh concluded, "almost without exception lacking in scientific, mechanical, technological or commercial training or experience."[53] If Oxbridge insulated the sons of older elites against contact with industry, it also gradually drew sons of industrial and commercial families away from the occupations of their fathers, contributing to a "hemorrhage" of business talent.[54]

The educated young men who did go into business took their antibusiness values with them. As businessmen sought to act like educated gentlemen, and as educated gentlemen (or would-be gentlemen) entered business, economic behavior altered. The dedication to work, the drive for profit, and the readiness to strike out on new paths in its pursuit waned.[55]

Thus, revivified public schools and ancient universities furnished the re-formed and cohesive English elite with a way of life and an outlook that gave little attention or status to industrial pursuits. This development set England apart from its emerging rivals, for in neither the United States nor Germany did the educational system encourage a comparable retreat from business and industry.[56] In education, as in the composition and character of its elite, later-Victorian England marked out its own path, foreshadowing its twentieth-century achievements and difficulties.

PART II

A world view

3

A counterrevolution of values

The whole of the island . . . set as thick with chimneys as the masts
stand in the docks of Liverpool; that there shall be no meadows in it;
no trees; no gardens; only a little corn grown upon the house tops,
reaped and thrashed by steam; that you do not even have room for
roads, but travel either over the roofs of your mills, on viaducts; or
under their floors, in tunnels; that, the smoke having rendered the
light of the sun unserviceable, you work always by the light of your
own gas: that no acre of English ground shall be without its shaft and
its engine. . .
—John Ruskin's nightmare vision of the twentieth century
The Two Paths (1859)

The high-water mark of industrial values
The evolution of ideas, sentiments, and values among the "educated
classes" followed a course paralleling that of their social history. A
watershed in this course was formed by the Great Exhibition of 1851.
Here, under the patronage of Prince Albert, were brought together
the latest products of engineering and decorative arts from many
nations. Without a doubt the exhibition was a triumph for British
enterprise and technology. Most of the medals were awarded to
British entries, and the building itself was easily the most impressive
feature of the exhibition. Designed by Joseph Paxton (1801-65), an
outsider to the architectural profession, it was the first structure to
use iron and glass on such a scale, and the first of such size to be made
chiefly of prefabricated units. In seventeen weeks, financed entirely
by private capital, an area four times that occupied by St. Peter's in
Rome was covered by 800,000 feet of glass fastened to a graceful
structure of 3,300 iron columns and 2,300 girders. The achievement
opened a new age in the history of architecture and construction.

The Crystal Palace, as *Punch* felicitously christened the building,
and its contents were a monument not only to British capabilities but
also to the "visibility of human progress," in Asa Briggs's phrase.[1]
Observing the impressive preparations, the *Economist* was moved to

affirm its "full confidence that the 'endless progression', ever increasing in rapidity, of which the poet sang, is the destined lot of the human race."[2] The displays of machinery, "the grand focus of attraction" according to Henry Mayhew, brought home to the visiting throngs, already awed by the building, the novelty and power of their age: "Round every object more wonderful than the rest, the people press, two or three deep, with their heads stretched out, watching intently the operations of the moving mechanism."[3] A decade later, Samuel Smiles's *Lives of the Engineers* appreciatively characterized the man of technology as architect of a "great leap forward" in human welfare, and as the maker of modern England. What was England, he asked, "without its tools, its machinery, its steam-engine, its steamships, and its locomotive. Are not the men who have made the motive power of the country, and immensely increased its productive strength, the men above all who have ... [made] the country what it is?"[4]

Alongside the engineer in the vanguard of progress came the man of business. As the apostle of free trade, Richard Cobden, put it:

> Commerce is the grand panacea, which, like a beneficent medical discovery, will serve to inoculate with the healthy and saving taste for civilization all the nations of the world. Not a bale of merchandise leaves our shores, but it bears the seeds of intelligence and fruitful thought to the members of some less enlightened community; not a merchant visits our seats of manufacturing industry, but he returns to his own country the missionary of freedom, peace, and good government – while our steam boats, that now visit every port of Europe, and our miraculous railroads, that are the talk of all nations, are the advertisements and vouchers for the value of our enlightened institutions.[5]

The Great Exhibition embodied to the world the new ideals that seemed to have become the national ideals of Victorian Britain. Industry was taking on a heroic aura; even a country squire, Sir Walter Trevelyan (1797-1879), could commission in 1856 a pre-Raphaelite from Newcastle to celebrate industrial Tyneside in the last of a series of historical murals for his country house in Northumberland.

Yet the generation of the Great Exhibition was to mark an end and not a beginning. It would see the high-water mark of educated opinion's enthusiasm for industrial capitalism. Planted within the Great Exhibition itself was a core of cultural opposition, represented by Augustus Pugin's Medieval Court. A sharper contrast could hardly be imagined than that between Pugin's Gothic furnishings and their iron-and-glass enclosure; yet they too were an expression of the period. Pugin thought the Crystal Palace a "glass monster," the product of a soulless age. His fellow Gothicists, more polite, thought much the same: *The Ecclesiologist*, the journal of the influential Cambridge Camden Society, called it "engineering of the highest merit . . . but not architecture." Ruskin concluded:

> The quality of bodily industry which the Crystal Palace expresses, is very great. So far it is good. The quantity of thought it expresses is, I suppose, a single and admirable thought . . . that it might be possible to build a greenhouse larger than ever greenhouse was built before. This thought and some very ordinary algebra are as much as all that glass can represent of human intellect.[6]

The Gothic revival was the most visible expression of a broader movement of reaction to the industrial revolution that traced back to the Romantic poets at the beginning of the nineteenth century.[7] Blake, Wordsworth, and many lesser talents had feared the soullessness of urbanism and industrialism and the utilitarian and materialistic habit of mind these conditions represented. This tradition of reaction was on the whole a pessimistic one, as it saw itself as waging a delaying action against an ever-advancing foe. This tone pervaded the classic literary confrontation between Poet Laureate Robert Southey and Thomas Babington Macaulay in 1829-30. Southey called up the spirit of Thomas More to denounce the modern age: "The immediate and home effect of the manufacturing system, carried on as it now is upon the great scale, is to produce physical and moral evil, in proportion to the wealth which it creates."[8] Macaulay replied with contemptuous dismissal of Southey's nostalgic fantasies, confident of the beneficence and inevitability of material advance.[9] The laurels in this clash went to the rising young partisan of progress, and for the next several decades the psychological current continued to flow in Macaulay's direction. Yet, as in society and politics, an accommodation was being prepared. By 1851, the sharp lines of cultural confrontation were blurring and extreme positions becoming a mark of eccentricity. The otherworldly purism of Romanticism was being bridled, but so too was the almost religious pride and confidence of the ideologists of progress. The aesthetic confrontation symbolized by the Crystal Palace and its Medieval Court was to be characteristically resolved in England by mutual accommodation. As aesthetic medievalism was popularized, it was parted from much of its ideological baggage; at the same time, modernism in English architecture and technique ceased to be a major cultural force. England never again hosted an important, innovative world exhibition of technology or architecture after 1851.

The deaths of three of the giants of British engineering – Isambard Brunel, Robert Stephenson, and Joseph Locke – within months of each other in 1859–60 heralded the end of an era. If the Great Exhibition of 1851 had been the high noon of British technological leadership, these deaths hinted of a yet-distant dusk. When Stephenson died in October 1859, the whole nation mourned him. The entire route of his funeral cortege to Westminster Abbey was lined by silent crowds. In his home county, all shipping lay silent on Tyne, Wear, and Tees, all work ceased in the towns, and flags flew at half-mast. "Never again," L. T. C. Rolt reflected in his history of engineering, "would a British engineer command so much esteem and affection; never again would the profession stand so high." To an extent, this was inevitable. As knowledge grew, the profession became more and more specialized, and teams began to replace individuals. But there was more to it than this. "The public," argued Rolt, "began to lose confidence in the engineer so that he began to lose confidence in himself."[10] The trajectory of admiration for material progress had reached an apogee in the eighteen-fifties. After 1851, and especially from the sixties, currents of thought and sentiment began to flow in another direction – not toward the simplistic rejection of the Young England writers or Pugin, but toward the domestication of the industrial revolution.[11]

Middle-class intellectuals and gentry values
Herbert Sussman has observed of Victorian literature that "the decade of the Great Exhibition marks the end of hope in the blessings of the machine."[12] This shift, really more general in subject, went well beyond literature. The new upper-middle-class generation coming of age in the eighteen-sixties and seventies, shaped by the gentlemanly ideal, was, as Mark Girouard has described it, more relaxed, more cultivated, and more detached from economic struggle than its predecessor. "Fathers who had spent their lives reading the Bible and making money with equally dedicated intensity very probably had agnostic children who were suspicious of the effects of money, and of the commercial society which produced it."[13] For their social values and social criticism, members of this generation turned to men like Matthew Arnold – men of letters who were both new-style professional men and social thinkers.

In nineteenth-century England, as is well known, thinkers and writers never formed a detached intelligentsia, but were for the most part closely connected to practical and institutional life by family, occupation, and aspiration.[14] Social thinkers were also professional men, sharing the predilections of that class. Even the great Victorian cultural critics, who might seem to have been at least one source of antiaristocratic ideals, were in fact moving *with* more than against the tide of gentrification. Their criticisms of early- and mid-Victorian England, more widely influential than similar criticisms on the Continent or in America, contributed in a major way to the containment of industrial values and the shaping of a new cultural tradition for twentieth-century Britain.

Despite the immense sweep of personal idiosyncrasy among mid-Victorian social thinkers, their responses to the advancing world of industrial capitalism tended to converge. From our late-twentieth-century standpoint, the critical and the complacent writers appear closer to each other than they would have admitted. The genial novels of Anthony Trollope, for instance, tend to eschew (with one exception) general social criticism. A set of social values is nonetheless present, and occasionally expressed, as in *Doctor Thorne* (1858):

> England is not yet a commercial country in the sense in which that epithet is used for her; and let us still hope that she will not soon become so. . .
> England a commercial country! Yes; as Venice was. She may excel other nations in commerce, but yet it is not that in which she most prides herself, in which she most excels. Merchants as such are not the first men among us; though it perhaps be open, barely open, to a merchant to become one of them. Buying and selling is good and necessary; it is very necessary, and may, possibly, be very good; but it cannot be the noblest work of man; and let us hope that it may not in our time be esteemed the noblest work of an Englishman.[15]

In this novel, indeed, Trollope gave vent to his anxiety that commercial values were infecting and corrupting an older, quasi-feudal society. This concern grew over the years, and led to his one work of bitter social criticism, *The Way We Live Now* (1875), which satirizes the momentary triumph of these values in the career of a shady financial magnate, Melmotte. Until his empire crashed, almost all of society seemed to cry aloud that "there was but one virtue in the world, commercial enterprise – and that Melmotte was its prophet."[16] Though he was taken to task for the bitterness of this novel, Trollope was only expressing in a more extreme form attitudes he had long held through his years of conventionality. These were attitudes not so very different from those of the great cultural critics like Matthew Arnold and John Ruskin, or of Dickens in his later novels, or even of that exemplar of liberal thought, John Stuart Mill.

The politics of these four men ranged across the spectrum; indeed, the views of each of them varied widely at different times and on different issues. Arnold has been called both a liberal and a conservative, Mill both of these and a socialist, Ruskin and Dickens everything from reactionary to socialist or even anarchist and all positions in between. Yet beneath and despite their personal complexities and their differences lay elements of an outlook they shared and which they helped root in modern British life.

Not one of these four was at all simply conservative. Yet all recoiled, with varying degrees of intensity, from the commercial–industrial society that had arisen in their generation. Even those most identified with the course of liberal progress and most critical of the past and of established institutions underwent this reaction, laying the ground-work for the coming English cultural orthodoxy.

Even John Stuart Mill, the foremost "philosophic radical" at mid-century, felt the qualms of a gentleman and a professional man in the face of the material preoccupations of early Victorian England. Mill's economics and politics challenged the position of the landed aristo-cracy, and his philosophy was empirical and utilitarian. All this should have made him the perfect intellectual of the commercial and industrial middle class. To a degree, of course, he was. Yet even Mill, moving away from his upbringing, repeatedly revealed his disen-chantment with capitalist and bourgeois values. G. K. Chesterton later approvingly noticed that "he boasted none of that brutal optimism with which his friends and followers of the Manchester School ex-pounded their cheery negations. There was about Mill even a sort of embarrassment; he exhibited all the wheels of his iron universe rather reluctantly, like a gentleman in trade showing ladies over his factory."[17]

As early as 1829, Mill complained to a French acquaintance, who had introduced him to Saint-Simonianism, of the English worship of the "idol 'production,'" which "lies at the root of all our worst na-tional vices, corrupts the measures of our statesmen, the doctrines of our philosophers and hardens the minds of our people so as to make it almost hopeless to inspire them with any elevation either of intellect or of soul." Industrialists, whom the Saint-Simonians wished to place in power, were at least in England "the very classes of persons you would pick out as the most remarkable for a narrow and bigoted understanding, and a sordid and contracted disposition as respects all things wider than their business or families."[18]

The business of production was not the chief business of life; even the work ethic was not the core of morality, as his onetime friend and mentor, Thomas Carlyle, claimed. In 1850, Mill's objections came into the open in an attack on Carlyle's "gospel of work" in *Fraser's Magazine*:

> Work, I imagine, is not a good in itself. There is nothing laudable in work for work's sake. To work voluntarily for a worthy object is laudable; but what constitutes a worthy object? On this matter, the oracle of which your [*Fraser's*] contributor is the prophet has never yet been prevailed on to declare itself. He revolves in an eternal circle round the idea of work, as if turning up the earth, or driving a shuttle or a quill, were ends in themselves, and the ends of human existence.[19]

Mill's doubts about economic growth as a social ideal were em-bedded in his economic magnum opus, *Principles of Political Economy*.

His chapter on the probable "stationary state" of the future turned that concept, for Ricardo merely an analytical construct, into one of social philosophy. Mill compared the stationary state – what would today be called the "no-growth society" – most favorably with the progressive state of his day, using it to attack economic striving for the sake of striving. He wished to redirect the bias (as he saw it) of classical political economy toward quantity rather than quality, just as he was to attempt to do with Utilitarianism itself. Rather than looking with sadness toward the eventual cessation of economic growth, Mill claimed it would be a "very considerable improvement on our present condition."

> I confess I am not charmed with the ideal of life held out by those who think that the normal state of human beings is that of struggling to get on; that the trampling, crushing, elbowing, and treading on each other's heels, which form the existing type of social life, are the most desirable lot of human kind, or anything but the disagreeable symptoms of one of the phases of industrial progress.

Mill remained enough the political economist to admit that it was a necessary stage out of mass poverty and barbarism – necessary, but preliminary only, to the new age of gold, "when minds cease to be engrossed by the art of getting on."[20]

If Mill was the archetypal "philosophic" radical, the foremost "sentimental" radical of the age was no doubt Charles Dickens. Through his early career, Dickens was a firm believer in progress and the beneficial march of enlightenment. Writing to a friend in 1843, he complained that if "ever I destroy myself, it will be in the bitterness of hearing those infernal and damnably good old times extolled."[21] Part of the march of enlightenment was the progress of industry. Right up to the writing of *Hard Times*, Dickens's magazine, *Household Words*, was full of enthusiastic accounts of the wonders of modern manufacture; in Mr. Rouncewell (*Bleak House*, 1853) he gave northern industrialists an appealing representative. Ruskin, indeed, called him on his death "a pure modernist – a leader of the *steam whistle* party par excellence."[22]

Yet within this progressive Boz lay a powerful ambivalence, and a seed of dissatisfaction with the liberal march of progress that grew with time into alienation. The work of the later Dickens reflected an important shift in the consciousness of the Victorian professional classes, and exerted an ever-increasing influence on the climate of opinion surrounding economic life. In one sense, Dickens became more radical: Some modern critics have portrayed him as moving from "bourgeois liberalism" to a protosocialism, from attacks on particular abuses to ever-fiercer denunciations of the rich that condemned the "capitalist system" as a whole and that doubted its capacity to reform itself.[23] In another sense, Dickens became more reactionary, ever more fearful of popular disorder while contemptuous of parliamentary government.[24] Yet Dickens's drift was less political than cultural. He found himself more and more repelled by the new society of commerce and production that was replacing the "infernal" old times.

In *Dombey and Son* (1846-8), this changing mood first led Dickens to mock the hubris of the age's ambition, as Prince Albert was soon to put it, "to conquer Nature to [man's] uses":

> The earth was made for Dombey and Son to trade in, and the sun and moon were made to give them light. Rivers and seas were formed to float their ships; rainbows gave them promise of fair weather; winds blew for or against their enterprises; stars and planets circled in their orbits, to preserve inviolate a system of which they were the centre.

Mixed pride and anxiety about the onrush of technology underlay *Dombey and Son*'s description of the construction of the railway through Stagg's Gardens. The railway represented an awesome new power, wonderful yet frightening, for it could carelessly sweep over all other human aims and desires. The bearer of universal improvement was also "the power that forced itself upon its iron way – its own – defiant of all paths and roads, piercing through the heart of every obstacle, and dragging living creatures of all classes, ages and degrees behind it."[25]

As Dickens's uneasiness about technological progress mounted, he found himself unable to respond to the enthusiasms of 1851. "I have always," he confessed to his assistant Wills, "had an instinctive feeling against the Exhibition, of a faint, inexplicable sort."[26] In *Hard Times* (1854) Dickens associated all the things he hated most with industrialism. The mention of industrial towns was henceforth likely to call up the grim picture of his ugly Coketown and its dehumanizing work.

Wealth, Dickens now insisted over and over, could be created at much too high a price. Indeed, the creation of wealth – economic growth – as a social goal increasingly appeared to him to be a moral cancer, claiming – and promising – ever more of life, poisoning natural and essential human values. The creed of money making is summed up by Pancks in *Little Dorrit* (1855-7): "Keep me always at it, and I'll keep you always at it, keep somebody else always at it. There you are with the Whole Duty of Man in a commercial country."[27] By 1864 Dickens's disgust with the creed of economic success culminated in the bitter portrait of the entire commercial upper class in *Our Mutual Friend*. All the successful, or those aspiring to success – Podsnap, the Lammles, the Veneerings, and their circle – are utterly repellent, hollow human beings. The pursuit of wealth stands condemned.

What alternative ideal did Dickens turn to as his disgust with the scramble for wealth deepened? One critic has found the essential development of Dickens's social thinking in "a rejection of the self-made man, towards an affirmation of a gentlemanly ideal which has been purged of its associations with class and social ambition."[28] In *Our Mutual Friend*, this critic has pointed out, the self-made man and the gentleman are brought into confrontation, and, unlike in earlier works, all Dickens's sympathies now lie with the gentleman. Bradley Headstone's powerful will, ambition, and energy all stand condemned as pathological, akin to the inhuman world of Veneering and Podsnap. The traditional gentleman becomes an ally in Dickens's campaign against money values. Eugene Wrayburn, educated in the public schools, can confess to lack of purpose, joke about earnestness, and question the value of energy: "If there is a word in the dictionary under any letter from A to Z that I abominate, it is energy."[29] Dickens was to carry this shift of allegiance still further. About his last and unfinished novel, *The Mystery of Edwin Drood*, Angus Wilson remarked, "England has shrunk to a cathedral town and its classes to the [public-school-educated] upper-middle, professional class." Wilson argued that Dickens here "arrayed what he felt to be the dependable, good, manly (or womanly) and above all healthy part of English society" against the evil of the criminal villain, Jasper.[30] In the end, Dickens turned away from the values of industrial capitalism, not to take up some protosocialist stance, but to join in the renovation of older gentry values. His fictional world led from the Old England of John Bull and stagecoaches through the feverish new urban and industrial society to end in a cathedral town among public school men.

The rejection by Mill and Dickens of commercial society was taken up more explicitly and fervently by the younger writers, Arnold and Ruskin, who in this harked back to the Romantics of the generation before. Arnold's consistency was questionable. On the one hand, he advocated a more "modern" system of education, warning his countrymen that the preservation of their position in the world demanded the cultivation of intelligence; public schools that taught chiefly "cricket and a gentlemanly deportment" were not answering the needs of the second half of the nineteenth century.[31] On the other hand, he propagated traditionalist prejudices against the class whose energies drove the modern world (with which he anxiously urged England to keep up) – industrial capitalists. The existing provision of schools divided the middle class into an upper-professional and a lower-business class; Arnold wished to remedy this by using the state to extend downward the public school type of education. The commercial and industrial middle class was not to be denied the civilizing benefits of an elite education. Certainly, he did not want the intellectual deficiencies of the public schools to be ignored, but it is doubtful whether following Arnold's principles would have brought

England's national education closer to the technical and economic life of the age. Arnold's hostility to the efforts at modernity made by existing middle-class private schools overbore his mild complaints about upper-class schooling. "Lycurgus House Academy," where his archetypal Manchester industrialist, "Mr. Bottles," was educated, was described with withering contempt:

> You are not to suppose from the name of Lycurgus that any Latin and Greek was taught in the establishment; the name only indicated the moral discipline, and strenuous earnest character, imparted there. As to the instruction, the thoughtful educator who was principal of the Lycurgus House Academy, – Archimedes Silverpump, Ph.D., you must have heard of him in Germany? – had modern views. "We must be men of our age," he used to say. "Useful knowledge, living languages, and the forming of the mind through observation and experiment, these are fundamental articles of my educational creed." Or, as I have heard his pupil Bottles put it in his expansive moments after dinner... "Original man, Silverpump! fine mind! fine system! None of your antiquated rubbish – all practical work – latest discoveries in science – mind constantly kept excited – lots of interesting experiments – lights of all colours – fizz! fizz! bang! bang! That's what I call forming a man."[32]

Arnold's social criticism was aimed predominantly at the middle class – his "barbarians" and "populace" receive but a glance in comparison with the steely gaze directed at his "philistines." The "master thought" of his writings, he confessed, was the "bad civilization of the English middle class."[33] With the ever-growing importance of this class, its bad civilization – narrow and materialistic – poisoned the national life. Arnold inveighed in *Culture and Anarchy* against the "worship as . . . fetishes" of economic and demographic growth. Means – and problematic ones at that – had become ends. As he had complained a few years before in what is now an oft-quoted observation:

> Your middle class man thinks it the highest pitch of development and civilization when his letters are carried twelve times a day from Islington to Camberwell, and from Camberwell to Islington, and if railway-trains run to and fro between them every quarter of an hour. He thinks it is nothing that the trains only carry him from an illiberal, dismal life at Islington to an illiberal, dismal life at Camberwell; and the letters only tell him such is the life there.

England had no national purposes or ideals, Arnold believed, other than the instrumental ones of freedom and work: "Freedom, like Industry, is a very good horse to ride; – but to ride somewhere. You seem to think that you have only got to get on the back of your horse Freedom, on your horse Industry, and to ride away as hard as you can, to be sure of coming to the right destination."

More and bigger, Arnold reminded his readers, did not mean better. Indeed, for him they tended to mean worse. John Bright, he complained, cited as evidence of the nation's advance "the cities it has built, the railroads it has made, the manufactures it has produced." But more cities also meant more slums and overpopulation, more railroads brought more rush, more manufactures spawned more ugliness and materialism.

Arnold's descriptions of the life of the successful business class grew increasingly acid-tipped. "The fineness and capacity of a man's spirit," he observed in 1866, "is shown by his enjoyments. Your middle class has an enjoyment in its business, we admit, and gets on well in business, and makes money; but beyond that? Drugged with business, your middle class seems to have its sense blunted for any stimulus besides." By the time of *Culture and Anarchy*, two years later, his disgust was unrestrained:

> [Consider] their way of life, their habits, their manners, the very tones of their voices; look at them attentively; observe the literature they read, the things which give them pleasure, the words which come forth out of their mouths, the thoughts which make the furniture of their minds; would any amount of wealth be worth having with the condition that one was to become just like these people by having it?[34]

Arnold's criticisms of the aristocracy lacked this bite; they were more in the nature of admonitions to members of one's own "side." As he once recognized, he and his class of professional men fell short of their ideal of mental independence. Educated among the aristocracy, aspiring to full social acceptance, they tended toward intellectual deference. They were less critical of aristocratic ideas and values than of ideas and values emanating from elsewhere in British society. In this way, despite his intention to be detached and offer balanced criticism, Arnold's effect was, as Henry Sidgwick pointed out, to reinforce and perpetuate upper-class tastes and prejudices.[35] His biting criticism of the middle class and its way of life sank home, whereas his milder complaints about the aristocracy passed into oblivion. He had hopes for a diminution in inequality, for more intelligence at every social level, and for a more efficient state, but it was a negative aim, "to save the future from being vulgarized,"[36] that called forth his greatest fervor and was to be long associated with him.

Although they differed in many ways, Arnold's contempt for the values of industrial capitalism was shared and amplified by that great thunderer, John Ruskin. A "Hebraist" (in Arnold's sense) unable to look at the world in other than moral categories, Ruskin poured into his sermons on art and society a loathing of capitalism, technology, and industrial society. Ironically, he began writing the second volume of *The Stones of Venice*, his first great denunciation of modern technology and industry, on the very day that the Great Exhibition opened in Hyde Park. Speaking to a meeting of architects a few years later, Ruskin warned them of the modernist fallacy:

> Perhaps the first idea which a young architect is apt to be allured by, as a head-problem in these experimental days, is its being incumbent upon him to invent a "new style" worthy of modern civilization in general, and of England in particular; a style worthy of our engines and telegraphs; as expansive as steam, and as sparkling as electricity.

If this were the case, he continued, perhaps with the Crystal Palace in mind,

> You shall draw out your plates of glass and beat out your bars of iron till you have encompassd us all . . . with endless perspective of black skeleton and blinding square . . . you shall put, if you will, all London under one blazing dome of many colours that shall light the clouds round it with its flashing, as far as to the sea. And still, I ask you, what after this?

Nothing, said Ruskin, but noise, emptiness, and idiocy.[37]

Alongside the false god of technology Ruskin put the "Mammon Gospel," and endorsed Carlyle's challenge as to "whether the Secret of this Universe . . . does after all consist in making money." Instead, he announced, "there is no wealth but life," and "life" was incompatible with the quest for material wealth. An acquisitive society was a debased society, in which achievement was tainted with sin. Ruskin denied that large fortunes could be made without "dishonest acquisition" – without "sacrifice of surrounding lives, or possibilities of life." To remedy the predatory nature of commerce, Ruskin called upon businessmen to model their careers upon the liberal professions. For him, the professions were distinguished by their upholding of the ideals of service over the aim of personal gain. Men of business would "have to discover a kind of commerce which is not exclusively selfish." The proper function of the merchant or manufacturer, he declared, was indeed similar to that of these other professions: "to provide for the nation."

> It is no more his function to get profit for himself out of that provision than it is a clergyman's function to get his stipend. This stipend is a due and necessary adjunct, but not the object of his life, if he be a true clergyman, any more than his fee (or honorarium) is the object of life to a true physician.

Moreover, "providing," for Ruskin, had some of the lofty connotations of spiritual and physical ministration associated with clergymen and physicians. "Your business," he told the Bradford merchants, "is to form the market, as much as to supply it." Thus, if men of business and industry would take for their models the traditional professions, their work would be moralized and they too could assume the honored place in the social order now justly denied them.[38]

In assuming this status, businessmen would have to abandon their unseemly attachment to material accumulation, not merely personally, but collectively. Ruskin time and again denounced the desires for wealth, mobility, and advancement. He denied the "gospel of whatever we've got, to get more" as fervently as that of "wherever we are, to go somewhere else." He urged men in all classes to cease their restless stirrings and remain content where they were, seeking "not greater wealth, but simpler pleasures; not higher fortune but deeper felicity." The rich in particular, he believed, should set an example for the poor by "checking the wing of accumulative desire in mid-volley."[39] Ruskin's ideal businessman was unacquisitive, dedicated to a code of honor instead of a calculus of advantage, and taking as his duty the enhancement of the quality, not the quantity, of life.

How was the quality of life – the keynote of Ruskin's exhortations – to be enhanced? Ruskin's vision of the good life was just what "progress" was destroying: order, tranquility, and harmony. The true satisfactions of human life had not changed: "To watch the corn grow, and the blossoms set; to draw hard breath over ploughshare or spade; to read, to think, to have, to hope, to pray ... The world's prosperity or adversity depends upon our knowing and teaching these few things: but upon iron, or glass, or electricity, or steam, in no wise."[40] England, however, had sold its soul to iron and steam, and bid fair to become "the furnace of the world." Here, vividly presented, were Ruskin's alternatives for his countrymen: stability and contentment or restless change, pastoral contemplation or industrial inferno. His hope for the future was "that England may cast all thoughts of possessive wealth back to the barbaric nations among whom they first arose" and turn instead to the cultivation of noble human beings.[41]

As G. M. Young remarked, "Ruskin evolved, and forced his world to accept, a new set of axioms as the basis" of all future social thought in Britain.[42] He is best known for bringing competition into disrepute. He also, though it has been less noticed, deprived production of intrinsic moral value. Material production for Ruskin's disciples was in itself no virtue, and preoccupation with it clearly a vice. He helped shift concern from production of goods per se to the *manner* of production and the uses to which productive powers were put. An 1885 address of economists and social thinkers to Ruskin lauded him for teaching that "the wise use of wealth, in developing a complete human life, is of incomparably greater moment both to men and actions than its production or accumulation, and can alone give these any vital significance."[43]

Dickens's fiction reinforced these more explicit arguments, and prepared the middle class as a whole to receive them. One legacy of his work was a vivid sense of the horrors of early Victorian urbanization and industrialization. Workhouses, slums, and Coketown – these symbols, given life by Dickens, came to stand for a "bleak age" of transition to city and factory life. One of the most popular history textbooks for children in the interwar years gave over its entire introductory chapter on the nineteenth century to Dickens, quoting his novels to illustrate virtually every aspect of the first half of the century, most of them "abuses" that his "protests" helped remove.[44] Moreover, Dickens's world conveyed an indictment, all the more powerful for being embedded in fiction rather than in formal argument, of the sterility and inhumanity of material ambition. The urgent plea thrust itself upon his reader to temper such ambitions – national as well as personal – with human values.

These Victorian critics influenced the climate of educated opinion in part because it was increasingly prepared by institutional developments to receive their message. Their ideas both shaped and were themselves a part of a conservative revolution in mid- and late-Victorian England that contained the social and intellectual consequences of the industrial revolution. A traditional elite adapted sufficiently to the new circumstances and demands of the age to ward off pressures for a truly thorough upheaval. As the nineteenth century drew to a close, a culture took root in the rapidly growing upper-middle and professional classes – the heirs of the old landed elite – that put the ideals of economic growth and material progress "in their place," a decidedly more limited place than in the world view of Richard Cobden or Prince Albert. Having found a comfortable niche for itself in an accommodation of past and present, this stratum's world view was more and more one of outward acceptance of modernity without inner conviction; new bottles, perhaps, but old wine preferred. Change, for most of these people, had gone far enough, and further change afforded a prospect more disquieting than cheering. Often, they now seemed to echo Goethe's Faust: "Stay, thou art so fair!"

4

The "English way of life"?

I have a cursed hankering after certain musty old values.
—Lord Peter Wimsey in Dorothy Sayers's *Gaudy Night* (1936)

The temperate April sunlight fell through the budding chestnuts and revealed between their trunks green glimpses of parkland and the distant radiance of a lake. "English spring," thought Paul. "In the dreaming ancestral beauty of the English country." Surely, he thought, these great chestnuts in the morning sun stood for something enduring and serene in a world that had lost its reason and would so stand when the chaos and confusion were forgotten? And surely it was the spirit of William Morris that whispered to him in Margot Beste-Chetwynde's motor car about seed time and harvest, the superb succession of the seasons, the harmonious interdependence of rich and poor, of dignity, innocence, and tradition?
—Evelyn Waugh, *Decline and Fall* (1928)

There'll always be an England
  While there's a country lane,
Wherever there's a cottage small
  Beside a field of grain.
—Popular song of World War II

North and South

The cultural conservatism of the re-formed elite was most evident in its conception of what constituted "Englishness." Like the other aspects of its world view seen in Chapter 3, the new national self-image dressed itself in the trappings of an older tradition. One certain sign of the inherent self-limitations within English modernization was the degree to which the increasingly dominant image of the nation denied its chief characteristics – the rise of industry.

This development was not inevitable. An alternative self-image was available to Victorian Britain, one that made the experience of industrialization central. We might follow Donald Horne and speak of two competing metaphors for the nation, "Northern" and "Southern":

> In the *Northern Metaphor* Britain is pragmatic, empirical, calculating, Puritan, bourgeois, enterprising, adventurous, scientific, serious,

and believes in struggle. Its sinful excess is a ruthless avarice, rationalized in the belief that the prime impulse in all human beings is a
rational, calculating, economic self-interest.

In the *Southern Metaphor* Britain is romantic, illogical, muddled,
divinely lucky, Anglican, aristocratic, traditional, frivolous, and believes in order and tradition. Its sinful excess is a ruthless pride,
rationalized in the belief that men are born to serve.

In both metaphors, it was assumed that "Britain is best," but in the
contest as to what Britain was best *at* it was the Southern Metaphor
that won. By the turn of the century, the triumphant Southern Metaphor had led many British to believe that their success was due not so
much to continuing effort as to their unique cultural inheritance. "It
was not for what they did but for what they were that destiny had
rewarded them so lavishly."[1]

The victory of the Southern Metaphor went together with the
devaluation of both the locales of, and the qualities that had made, the
industrial revolution.[2] Such places and such characteristics becar.•:
"provincial." Provincialism in twentieth-century Britain has not been
simply a matter of remoteness from the capital city, as in France. It
has been much more a question of remoteness from one approved
style of life. Working-class and lower-middle-class suburbs might be
provincial, whereas much of the countryside is not. Rural villages, or
ancient cathedral towns that happen to be far from London, are not
provincial. "Things that are rural or ancient," as Horne observed,
"are at the very heart of southern English snobberies, even if they
occur in the North. *Provincialism is to live in or near an industrial town to
which the industrial revolution gave its significant modern form.*"[3]

This outlook was not always simply elitist; it had room for a good
deal of populism. Left-wing intellectuals developed their own variant,
the "English dream" described by Richard Wollheim: an ideal, in
contrast to the American dream of an "affluent and assertive individualism," of a "collective, unalienated folk society," rooted in time and
space, bound together by tradition and by stable, local ties, and
symbolized by the village.[4] This left-wing myth, despite its declared
radicalism, has been closer in spirit to the southern than to the
northern image of England. It has formed an acceptable populist
protest within the southern tradition, attacking the value of hierarchy, but accepting the rest.

"It's an old country"

A central strand of the Southern Metaphor, or English Dream, has
been the pull of the past, seen as tradition. Henry Fairlie (former
Washington correspondent of the Sunday *Times* [London], now living
in America), in a warning to his countrymen in 1976, gave vent to his

exasperation with the pervasive power of this pull of a too-comfort-able past. England had become, he observed, all too much like a family, cozy and secure but also "suffocating": "everyone in his or her own place; everyone doing and saying and being what he or she has always done and said and been." In its decline, the "family" has endless resources to support its sense of familyness: "It can reach for the family album, pull out the family tree, fall back on the richness of its own history." The country, he warned, could not flourish by trying to relive its past. "From this distance, the interest that the English are today taking in their past seems, not merely eccentric, but lunatic."[5]

Even the most exhilarated anticipation did not last. Samuel Smiles could say in 1861 that "everything in England is young. We are an old people, but a young nation. Our trade is young; our engineering is young; and the civilisation of what we called 'the masses' has scarcely begun."[6] As the century wore on, however, shapers of middle- and upper-class opinion, in disenchantment with continual change, turned more and more to the past, and to the elements of the past surviving in the present, as a source of alternative values. The discovery was made that England was, after all, an *old* country, with a precious heritage in danger of obliteration. Concern grew to protect and reforge links with that heritage.

An elite separating itself from the sources of dynamism in existing society and striving to attach itself to an older way of life promoted a change in collective self-image from that of a still-young and innova-tive nation to one ancient and peculiarly stable. Antiquity, real or manufactured, was one of the greatest appeals of the public schools and the prestigious universities, and this extended not only to the curriculum that we saw in Chapter 3, but to the physical buildings themselves. Old buildings were newly treasured as links with the past. Dover College, founded in 1871, typically boasted of its ancient buildings, "which formed part of the old Priory of St. Martin [and] has given to the College from the first the appearance and tone of an ancient foundation."[7]

At first, the appearance of antiquity may have served chiefly to make innovation respectable; the English genius for changing con-tent without changing form, for innovating under the cloak of con-tinuity, has often been praised, but as time went on more and more stress was put on the antiquity of forms, rather than on the novelty of content. The carapace, and fascination with it, became an increas-ingly tighter bond upon the life within.

A shift from the use of the past to make innovation palatable to a preoccupation with the past for its own sake began to become visible in the eighteen-seventies and eighties. These years saw the end of the mid-Victorian boom and the onset of the much-argued-about depression of trade and agriculture. The new elite was ill suited to deal with this new problem of a slowing economy. It had been reconstituted on the assumption of a newly and permanently dynamic economy, and the need to restrain growth, not to restimulate it. The ruling-class style that was just taking shape was "to make big things seem small, exciting things boring, new things familiar."[8] It was admirably suited to damp down social tension, and minimize the disruptive effects of change. It lowered the temperature of society. In doing so, however, it drained prestige from innovation to preservation, from novelty to antiquity, and from change to continuity.

The frequency and popularity of works on local and national history and antiquities attest to a growing public interest in the past. The new urban life of the nineteenth century came to be reconciled with tradition by being placed in a long historical frame. At the same time, as the problems of this new life bore in, civic pride found a distinguished or charming past a refuge. In his study of Victorian cities, Asa Briggs pointed out that, as the century drew to a close, for all but the newest towns, "it was their distant past rather than their contemporary significance which drew most attention from writers." Even some of the newer cities made more of their remote medieval origin than they did of their recent dramatic economic advance. Antiquarians, Briggs noted, "discovered or invented historical pedigrees for new cities with the same enthusiasm that they discovered or invented historical pedigrees for nouveaux riches." "Manchester," Professor James Tait correctly but perhaps misleadingly stressed in 1904, "is a place of high antiquity." "Nottingham," for W. H. Wylie in 1893, was "no creation of the present: it is a growth of ages." The older and less industrial towns, where the past was easily visible and did not have to be insisted upon, began to draw great attention from the reading public. A series of eleven volumes titled "Historic Towns," edited by E. A. Freeman and W. Hunt, and first appearing in the year of the great dock strike, 1889, bore witness to this interest. "The past was to revivify the present," concluded Briggs.[9] It also was to provide a balance to and even a refuge from the present. The quiet cathedral cities were portrayed as much more congenial places that their more dynamic neighbors. The Reverend G. W. Kitchin, for example, typically wrote of Winchester:

> While other centres have leapt forward with feverish speed, and in so doing have trodden out all relics of their ancient state, Winchester lying out of the main streams of English industry and life, has almost stood still . . . Her ancient buildings, her many customs and usages of the past, her tranquil beauty and pleasant neighbourhood, give to the venerable city a right to the undying affection of all whose lot has

fallen to them in such pleasant places . . . No English city has a nobler record in the past, or a life more peaceful in our rushing hasteful age. There it is still given, to those who have the wisdom to know it, to dwell in peace; and there, let us hope, it may still be said with truth that "They also serve who only stand and wait."[10]

Wylie, writing on Nottingham, sought to invest that industrial center with something of this aura: "Amid the unresting roll of our modern machinery and the din of today's business we may hear, if we only listen, the voices of a venerable past."[11] Similarly, the Reverend P. H. Ditchfield, one of the most prolific of the new antiquarians, urged his readers in 1897 to "discover how rich the towns and cities of England are in historical association . . . Let us live again in the past."[12] Whereas the initial urban explosion had drawn attention to the present and the future, by the close of the nineteenth century the old world had been called in to redress the balance of the new – to legitimate, to revivify, and to provide relief from the stresses of the present.

"Pilgrimages" in search of the past became a feature of literary culture. The late-Victorian Poet Laureate Alfred Austin (1835-1913), whose fondest subject was "the older and simpler modes of our national life, when still unmenaced by displacement by less comely and more mechanical conditions,"[13] made such a trip through England in 1901, and published a widely sold account of it entitled *Haunts of Ancient Peace*. Austin's aim in traveling through the country was to find, as he put it,

> *Old* England, or so much of it as is left . . . I confess I crave for the urbanity of the Past . . . for washing-days, home-made jams, lavender bags, recitation of Gray's *Elegy*, and morning and evening prayers. One is offered, in place of them, ungraceful hurry and worry, perpetual postmen's knocks, an intermittent shower of telegrams.

In his travels the poet laureate happily found "Ancientess . . . in abundance," and concluded his book with the reassurance to his readers that Old England still lived. The nation as a whole was yet a "haunt of ancient peace. May it ever remain so!" he rhapsodized.[14] Austin's trip was to be followed by an ever-increasing number of similar trips as the automobile made the countryside more accessible to town dwellers. Yet if scale altered, the character of perception did not: By the turn of the century, writers like Austin had helped establish a mental framework for domestic tourists – the quest for "Old England."

The present character of England, a variety of writers insisted, was rooted in the national past; in the face of the uncertainties of modernity, it was time to rediscover these roots. As the Reverend Sabine Baring-Gould (best known for penning "Onward, Christian Soldiers") argued, since the Reformation the English had increasingly disregarded their ancestors; yet "we owe to those old people more than we suppose ... If we have good in us, if we are scrupulous, honest, truthful, self-controlled, it comes to us in large measure along with our pure blood from honest ancestry."[15]

These sentiments were expressed among radicals as well as among Tories and Liberals, sometimes with even greater fervor. William Morris (1834-96) found the "leading passion of my life" in a "hatred of modern civilisation." Both Morris's early romanticism and his later socialism drank deeply of the revulsion. His well-known poem, "The Earthly Paradise" (1870), began:

> Forget six counties overhung with smoke,
> Forget the snorting steam and piston stroke,
> Forget the spreading of the hideous town;
> Think rather of the pack-horse on the down,
> And dream of London, small, and white, and clean.[16]

Both early and late, Morris looked back to medieval England to find the closest realization of a good society. In his socialist romance, *A Dream of John Ball* (1887), his narrator left behind the "hurried and discontented humanity" of Morris's age for the slower, smaller-scale, more beautiful, and more humane life of the fourteenth century.

With a declared "passion for ... the past," Morris treasured the sense of continuity with earlier generations. The history of England, he conceded as a good international socialist, was not objectively more important than the histories of other nations, "but to us who are come of the actors of it and live amongst the scenes where it was enacted it has a special interest which consecrates it." The products of this past life were still visible: Echoing Tennyson, he affirmed that "no dwelling of men has ever been sweeter or pleasanter than an ancient English house." And not only houses: Near his country house at Kelmscott, in the upper Thames Valley, Morris found within a radius of five miles "some half-dozen tiny village churches, every one of which is a beautiful work of art, with its own individuality."[17] These survivals of an earlier England seemed to bear witness to a vital popular culture that present-day England could not equal. They embodied for Morris, as for Tory writers, a vital reserve of social values for the nation.

"Our England is a garden"

As the new elite adopted many trappings of the past, it also took on a peculiarly rural guise. It was in the same years in which the economy was losing its dynamism, E. J. Hobsbawn has noted, that the widespread "pretence that the Englishman is a thatched-cottager or country squire at heart" took root.[18] If England was, after all, an *old* country, it was also, at heart, *country*. The traditions that seemed more and more appealing were essentially rural traditions, and had survived most purely in the countryside. As Ditchfield remarked in 1889:

> In most of our large towns the old features are fast disappearing; historic houses have been pulled down to make room for buildings more adapted to present needs, and everything is being modernized; but in the country everything remains the same, and it is not so difficult to let one's thoughts wander into the past.[19]

Idealization of the countryside has a long history in Britain. Until the nineteenth century Britain was still a rural civilization, whose rulers based themselves in country estates. With the great exception of London, towns played a relatively small part in English history. In Tudor times, visiting Italians were struck by the absence outside the capital of the kind of urban life with which they were familiar.[20] Given the comparative openness of the English upper class, such rural dominance was self-sustaining. From the Middle Ages on, the pull of the country upon successful townsmen was strong and steady: It was a common and feasible ambition for a flourishing merchant to aspire to possession of a country estate. Once in possession, his family would over time merge with the local gentry.

By the late eighteenth century, however, the English upper class was becoming ever more "urbane," spending more and more time in London and the major provincial towns.[21] Then came industrialization and the explosive growth of cities, which seemed destined to sweep away the rural tradition. By 1851, more than half the population lived in towns, and England had become the world's first major urban nation. As "the age of great cities" (as Robert Vaughan put it in 1842) opened, a long chapter in national history was drawing to a definitive close. Vaughan and others rushed to proclaim the imminent demise of "feudalism" and "rusticity." Yet, in the realm of cultural ideals, this was not to be; the triumph of urbanism was incomplete, to say the least. Out of the midst of the new urban society "ruralism" rose up reborn.

Explicit antiurbanism in England has generally been seen as a temporary reaction to rapid urbanization, fading away with the eventual adjustment to urban life. Though there is much truth to this view, it yet misleads. It is important to distinguish *two* types of antiurbanism in the Victorian period. On the one hand, there was a powerful current of distaste for cities and resistance to their growing economic and political predominance on the part of the country dwellers, especially the lesser heights of the landed interest. At its most straightforward, this reflected the inevitable clash of divergent economic interests: agrarian versus industrial, food producers versus food consumers. This kind of ruralism sprang from and rationalized a defense of material interests, and declined as farming became less important in the national economy.[22]

However, there was a *second* variety of Victorian antiurbanism: the criticism of city life by those whose way of life was essentially urban. This phenomenon owed little to economic interests; its explanation must be sought in less obvious social and psychological realms. This type of antiurbanism did not diminish with the establishment of urban predominance in national life; indeed, a strong case can be made for just the opposite development. Raymond Williams has acutely observed that "there is almost an inverse proportion in the twentieth century between the importance of the working rural economy and the cultural importance of rural ideas."[23]

Underlying the growing cultural importance of the country was a peculiar social situation. England in the later nineteenth century presented the striking picture of an immensely powerful and wealthy landed elite presiding over a waning rural economy. It was an elite powerful and wealthy enough not to feel critically menaced by the decline of agriculture. The English aristocracy was already well established in the cities, and was drawing increasing proportions of its income from ownership of urban, mining, and industrial land.[24] It could afford to let agriculture fend for itself, even if badly, in the world market – and did so, when other European states were throwing up tariff walls. Moreover, rural society in England (though not yet in Scotland or Wales) had long since been integrated into national life. The compact size of the country, its early political unification, and the early spread of a market economy into the countryside, along with the destruction of the peasantry brought about by enclosures and the concentration of landholding, meant that by the middle of the nineteenth century there was no longer a rural society distinctly different from the "national" society based in the cities.[25]

By contrast, agriculturists in America and continental Europe held up their numbers much better, and thus retained much of their social and political weight. Conflicts between landlords and tenants, and between bankers and farmers, as well as between rural and urban economic and political forces, remained live issues. In this way the countryside was "contaminated" with real peasants and farmers, and real clashes of interest, sometimes bloodying the rustic landscape and sometimes menacing urban interests. French peasants, German agriculturists, and American farmers were all major political forces to be reckoned with, and were not usually friendly to the "advanced" elite culture based in the cities.[26] Furthermore, on the continent of Europe the countryside was only now being integrated into national life. The long movement to close the Middle Ages, to "civilize" the countryside, and to unify rural and urban culture was just nearing completion.[27]

Rural society was only now on the verge of giving up its historic role as an obstacle and threat to "civilization." The countryside on the Continent was consequently tainted by its "barbarism" and "idiocy" (in Marx's terms) in a way that had no English counterpart. More than elsewhere, in England the later-nineteenth-century countryside was "empty" and available for use as an integrating cultural symbol. The less practically important rural England became, the more easily could it come to stand simply for an alternative and complementary set of values, a psychic balance wheel.[28] As the editor of *Country Life* remarked in 1924, "The villages in days gone by earned us the title of 'Merrie England.' Now the towns have made us 'Wealthy England,' but, were it not for the villages, [they] would smother us in our riches."[29] There was no significant English parallel to either the Parisian contempt for the rustic provinces and for the peasant or the German use of ruralist myths as instruments of political reaction. The countryside in England played a far more positive and less divisive role in the "psychic economy" of the middle and upper classes.

In the course of the nineteenth century, the social location of rural fantasies in the towns shifted. Attitudes that had first been most noticeable among the working classes, recently displaced from the country, appeared increasingly among the middle classes. While the working classes were adjusting to their new life, rural myths were finding a new audience. Novelist Ford Madox Ford, writing in 1906, saw that the new interest in "the return to the land" was largely confined to "the comparatively well-to-do. For the poor and the working-classes of the towns never really go back. One in five hundred may be attracted by a 'good job', but perhaps not one in a hundred goes seeking, however unconsciously, a country spirit."[30] It was the comparatively well-to-do who formed the vanguard of suburbanization and "exurbanization." They also formed a new reading public, which was ready to respond to a literature that offered an escape from the psychic strains of modern life.[31]

"Country writing" has a long and varied pedigree, and was much developed by the Romantics. In the hands of mid-Victorian Poet Laureate Alfred Tennyson, it was given a new life, both as a comfortable form of escapism for city dwellers, and as means of redefining "Englishness." The poems Tennyson called *English Idylls*, which conjured up charming, changeless rustic scenes, drenched in romance and history, were among his most widely read.

From Tennyson on, the appeal of country writing mounted steadily, until it came to form a distinct literary genre. By 1902 the *Daily News* greeted Alfred Austin's book, *Haunts of Ancient Peace* (whose title was taken from Tennyson), in terms that were becoming clichéd: "Under

its spell we lose for a time the brick-and-mortar civilisation that sometimes seems all-pervading, and gladly fly with the writer . . . to the
green lanes and fields outside our prison."[32] The poet Edward
Thomas recognized that the rapidly growing market for "country
literature" was among city dwellers seeking to escape, if only in
imagination, the life around them. "The city," he observed, "becomes
our scapegoat."[33] Much the same could apply to many of the writers
of country literature. Edward Shanks, a Georgian poet, later recalled
that his fellows were "men whose centre of life was in the great towns
and who did not like it."[34]

A "deep vein of rural nostalgia," as Malcolm Bradbury has seen,
ran through art and sensibility in the later nineteenth and early
twentieth centuries.[35] Literary historians agree that there was a striking increase in the number and popularity of novels, poems, and
essays on country subjects in the last years of the century.[36] The new
wave of rural writing usually claimed to reveal the "true" England. A
popular literary image of England took shape that gave a central
place to the countryside. But not an equal place to all English country:
The truly typical England was usually seen to reside in the historic
and comfortably domesticated rusticality of the South. As John
Davidson's poem, "Romney Marsh" (which became an anthology
favorite), began:

> I heard the South sing o'er the land;
> I saw the yellow sunlight fall
> On knolls where Norman churches stand.[37]

There were variants of ruralism to suit all political inclinations.
Most commonly, it was the life of rural England's upper-class inhabitants that received most attention. The squire, in particular, was
lovingly portrayed as the central figure of rustic life. Indeed, not of
rustic life only, but of English life: His class, above all others, was the
one that had given England its character.[38] As the squire was seen as
the human focus of country and national life, his manor house was
portrayed as its physical focus, and "the most delectable of possible
dwelling-places."[39] The country houses portrayed again and again in
twentieth-century popular fiction have been, like the houses seen
week after week in *Country Life*, "mellow, dignified, creeper-clad,
lawn encompassed, and bathed in perpetual sunshine."[40]

An alternative form of rural myth was available for those of more
democratic bent: In place of the squire, one could idealize the peasant
of old; instead of the country house, the village community and its
cottages. Despite his realistic awareness that the working classes were
every day more thoroughly urbanized, Ford Madox Ford could yet
trace the English character to the country, and, within the country, to
Hodge: "The real heart [of England] is the cottage." "The life of old

England," typically claimed Charles Masterman in 1904, "is the life of the village." "The English village is what is left of England," Hilaire Belloc declared in 1913. The traditional village community was seen as the cell from which English society had been built up, remaining, through its decline, the "fly-wheel" of national life.[41] In the late-Victorian years this populist ruralism was a minor counterpoint to the feudal version, but after 1900, with democracy making squirearchical romanticism less tenable, the idealization of the village came into its own.

In country sleep

Attitudes toward cities and countryside are frequently a key to attitudes toward much else. In America, Henry Nash Smith, Morton and Lucia White, Leo Marx, Roderick Nash, and Donald Fleming have all shown how such attitudes have reflected general values.[42] Such has also been the case in England: What the Victorians said about cities, Asa Briggs observed, "illuminates what they thought and felt about much else."[43] Cities have often served as symbols of modernity, and have attracted praise and blame through this association.[44] The countryside has also served as a symbol, although what its new devotees found there was not identical with what its old rulers had valued. The English countryside was no longer the scene of the first capitalist revolution; even the old symbol of John Bull – tough, crude, assertive – was now too jarring, and was consequently softened. A common characteristic of rustic visions was their stress on stability and tranquillity, on a state of being, which was wistfully conveyed in a poem by Edward Thomas: "all of us gone out of the reach of change."[45] Just as the city embodied change, the countryside seemed to offer release from the tyranny of time's movement. "Nowhere in the world, so much as in England," wrote the novelist Ford Madox Ford in 1906,

> do you find the spirit of the home of ancient peace; nowhere in the occidental world will you find turf that so invites you to lie down and muse, sunshine so mellow and innocuous, shade so deep or rooks so tranquil in their voices. You will find nowhere a *mise-en-scene* so suggestive of the ancient and enduring as in an English rose-garden, walled in and stone pathed, if it be not in an English cathedral close.[46]

As one socialist militant put it, one could lie back in the country, be enveloped by "the permanence of the loveliness of England," and know "the transience of modern civilization."[47]

Rural England in the late nineteenth century was of course already changing, an integral part of modern society. Yet it was rarely seen for what it was. Instead, as Raymond Williams put it, "A triumphant urban and industrial economy remade the countryside . . . in its own compensating image."[48] The country was to be all that modern life was not, a psychic balance and refuge.

Often this need for an imaginative resting place was reconciled with the facts of present change by a kind of catastrophism: A changeless rural order had only very recently been invaded by destructive forces from without. Pastoral retreatism then blended with nostalgic lament. In this mixture a major ingredient was drawn from the work of Thomas Hardy. Despite his intentions, the country aspect of Hardy's writings received, from the beginning, disproportionate notice. About his first novel, *Desperate Remedies* (1871), Hardy remarked to his publisher: "The rustic characters and scenery had very little point, yet to my surprise they were made very much of by the reviews."[49] *Far From the Madding Crowd* (1874), Hardy's most purely "country" book, became his most popular novel.[50] Although "an incomprehensible novel," Edward Fitzgerald observed to a friend, "(I tried it on the strength of the title), [it] contains some good Country Life." In a long essay subtitled "The Historian of Wessex" (characteristic of much contemporary criticism), J. M. Barrie assessed Hardy's work in 1889 and joined other readers and reviewers in urging him to forego attempts to extend his range to London "society" and instead to continue his country settings.[51]

Wessex was taken to its heart by the public as a rural haven from contemporary life. "Many persons," Edward Wright pointed out in 1904, "who did not care whether or not the English novel in Mr. Hardy's hands had become a well-knit drama instead of the string of episodes which once it was, appreciated other splendid qualities in his rustic stories . . . he revealed to them the true romance of country life."[52] This response took on a life of its own, escaping Hardy's control. Wessex societies, guidebooks, and "pilgrimages" bore witness to the strength of a virtual popular cult. Hardy himself bowed to public desires enough to revise his novels and add new prefaces making the Wessex he had invented more prominent in the stories and more easily located by pilgrims.[53]

Wessex appealed because its rusticality was of a piece with the national past. Hardy's country characters move in the footsteps of countless generations of predecessors, forming a long chain stretching back over the centuries. He saw the folk of the countryside as the last link with an almost vanished age – "in many cases our peasantry is the sole remnant of medieval England."[54] With the arrival of modern mobility, however, the rural isolation that had preserved the stable culture of past ages was coming to an end. A harvest supper he went to as a boy, he noted, was "among the last at which the old traditional ballads were sung, the railway having been extended to Dorchester just then, and the orally transmitted ditties of centuries being slain at a stroke by the London comic songs that were introduced."[55] Hardy's attitude toward these changes was, as modern critics have shown, ambivalent.[56] He recognized that the material conditions of life had improved, and he also profoundly sympathized with those of his characters, like Jude Fawley, who rebelled against tradition. Yet he also was saddened, as Baring-Gould was, by the "spirit of unrest" that had come over the land.[57]

The tension in Hardy's work between historical continuity and modern restlessness was powerfully attractive. It was a comfort to think that the very faces of country people might bear witness, just as did the ancient buildings they lived among, to the survival of Old England. At the same time, their departure for the towns roused fear of the imminent decay of the national character. Moreover, this departure was stimulated by the growing mechanization of agriculture, which conjured up fearful images of dehumanization – such as that of Tess reduced to serving the "red tyrant," the new threshing machine. Such complex images were simplified in the lamentations of nostalgic essayists like Baring-Gould: "Alack-a-day! . . . the sower, the mower, the reaper and thresher are . . . extinct."[58] The "Wessex worshippers" thus shaped their own version of Wessex and made it into a mythic image for England itself.

Hardy's writing was great, one critic affirmed, because it was based upon one of "the two classes who enshrine what beauty is left in the distracted modern world" – the peasantry (the other class being the old aristocracy). Through centuries of deprivation, the peasant had learned to "despise riches." The true aristocrat had risen above riches; thus, both had escaped "infection" by "the modern desire for wealth," and because of this retained the "soul" surrendered by

> the money-getting bourgeois class – who take thought for the morrow and sacrifice present to future, who condemn vice because it is expensive or may cause a scandal, who make marriages like contracts in business, whose ideals are respectability and material efficiency, in pursuit of which they encrust themselves more and more stiffly with the mud of this planet.[59]

In such ways, Hardy's complex and realistic fiction was reduced to a one-dimensional, repetitious chronicle of an appealingly timeless and nonmaterial way of life under seige. What happened to Hardy was symptomatic: By the end of the century, rural writing, of which there had never been so much, was both idyllic and drenched in anxiety about change.

This blend of idyll and anxiety colored the work of the foremost late-Victorian country writer, Richard Jefferies (1848-87), who was almost to country nonfiction as Hardy was to the rural novel. So compelling was the image of England that he created that a matching myth about Jefferies himself sprang up in the public mind. He was seen as an archetypal countryman, steeped in "the moral importance of the underlying, ageless agricultural pattern."[60] But his life was a more complex combination of rural and urban. His grandfather, a London printer, had moved to the growing town of Swindon in North Wiltshire to be a miller and baker, and his father kept his hand in the family business even though he moved to a farmhouse outside of town. Richard was born there in 1848, but was sent to live with an aunt in the London suburbs when he was four. He visited the farm for a month's holiday every year. When he was nine, he returned to his parents, and was sent to small private schools in Swindon (which was then developing into one of the great railway centers of southern England), where he became a journalist. Like Hardy's Dorset, Jefferies's North Wiltshire and South Gloucestershire seemed on the surface to be Old England itself – a land where, E. M. Forster was to rhapsodize, "the fibres of England unite."[61] Yet by Jefferies's maturity this countryside was coming under the influence of Swindon's rapid expansion.

Jefferies's background was likely to appeal to an urban middle class newly attracted to the life of the countryside. His writings marked a watershed between an older rationalization of the rural status quo, and an emerging urban-centered ruralism captivated by the quaint culture and organic society townsfolk perceived in the country. Jefferies wrote for the urban reader. "For the first time in rural writing," his most recent biographer observed, "one is regularly conscious of an audience that is to be guided and even coaxed into the countryside."[62]

Jefferies was writing about England as well as the country. His fullest portrait of rural society, *Hodge and His Masters* (1880), was originally entitled *The Heart of England*.[63] There lay the real England; for Jefferies the uncorrupted life of the countryside was vital to the health – psychic as well as physical – of the nation. Quite ready personally to accept change, he could not help insisting on the inner changelessness of country life. Even where change had "intruded," it had not reached the core. "These modern inventions," he remarked in *Hodge and His Masters*, "this steam, and electric telegraph, and even the printing press have but just skimmed the surface of village life. If they were removed – if the pressure from without, from the world around, ceased, in how few years the village and the hamlet would revert to their original condition!"[64]

In this novel Jefferies portrayed a "typical" agricultural district, "Fleeceborough" (based on nearby Cirencester), as an idyllic scene of social harmony – contented villagers in tune with nature and watched over by the benevolent rule of the local resident landowner, possessor of "a truly princely spirit." Both the village community and the squirearchical paternalism stretched back until they vanished into the mists of time. In the fashion of Hardy, Jefferies was fond of calling upon churchyards and registers to testify to the continuity of rural life.

Fleeceborough possessed a "fixed unchangeable character," which, above all else, gave it its interest. Yet now all this was menaced. "Forces are at work," Jefferies warned, "which are constantly endeavouring to upset the village equilibrium." These forces emanated from the city – ironically, the source of most of his readers. Jefferies feared "a party in cities" animated by "rancour" against landlords. These urban radicals had been stirring up the laborers. As a result, "the laborer brings a pressure to bear upon almost every aspect of country life. That pressure is not sufficient to break into pieces the established order of things; but it is sufficient to cause an unpleasant tension. Should it increase, much of the peculiar attraction of country life will be destroyed." The man whom Jefferies had presented earlier as a universally revered patriarch turned out to be "systematically browbeaten all round."[65]

As if this were not enough, the farmers were daily becoming more commercial and more "urbanized" in outlook. "The true old English farmer, and the true old English laborer," he noted while writing *Hodge and His Masters*, were disappearing.[66] Fleeceborough had changed its colors: Rather than a typical rural district described with reportorial accuracy, it turned out to be an ideal. Neither Jefferies nor his imitators ever quite brought these two images into complete focus. As with defenders of the "southern way of life" in the United States before the Civil War, the assertion of Arcadia as reality coexisted uneasily with the polemical defense of a besieged order.

The myth of an England essentially rural and essentially unchanging appealed across political lines both to Conservatives and Imperialists, and to anti-Imperialists, Liberals, and Radicals. Imperialists and "patriotic" writers rarely saw industrial progress as an appropriate source of inspiration. When Imperialists thought of England, they saw a historic countryside filled with country houses and public schools, where officers and gentlemen were bred.[67] Conservatives drew comfort from a picture of an unchanging England in the countryside to set against rising social unrest and foreign threats. Toward the end of the century, a group of self-consciously Tory poets appeared, and wrote in this vein. William Watson, Alfred Noyes, Henry Newbolt, and Poet Laureate Alfred Austin all idealized the same rustic Old England. Austin's poem "On Returning to England," typical of this group, is entirely about hedgerows, cottages, and village spires.[68] We have already watched the poet laureate setting out from London in 1901 to search for "haunts of ancient peace" in rural England. Seemingly everywhere he found "rustic inns, rectories and alms-houses, honest and not ill-paid labour, happy-looking cottages, a kindly and contented people."[69] In the country, cottager and gentleman lived happily together, nestled in the soft embraces of history and nature. So it would in future be, he reassured his readers. As he had written a few years earlier, "the foreign froth that foams against our shore" would beat in vain, and the true England, seated in the country, would survive. Village bells would continue to "chime sweet and safely." Therefore, he concluded,

> Let hound and horn in wintry woods and dells
> Make jocund music though the boughs be bare,
> And whistling yokel guide his teaming share
> Hard by the homes where gentle lordship dwells.
> Therefore sit high enthroned on every hill,
> Authority! and loved in every vale;
> Nor, old Tradition, falter in the tale
> Of lowly valour led by lofty will;
> And, though the throats of envy rage and rail,
> Be fair proud England, proud fair England still.[70]

The assertiveness here gave the game away: It was clearly of great importance that rural change be denied or, more commonly, conjured away by rhetorical flights. Just as we have come to see the large defensive or reactive element in late-Victorian Imperialism,[71] so we should be alert to these notes in the orchestration of Imperial themes in literature and in "factual" writing as well. One promise held out by Imperial expansion was that of escape from the pressure of unwelcome social change at home, and the recreation of "traditional" English life overseas. Parallels were often drawn between English country life and the open-air life in overseas possessions, and both were contrasted to the decadent life of modern cities.[72] Rural life was the repository of the moral character of the nation. It could *not* change, or England itself would be in mortal danger.

After the turn of the century Imperial anxieties fostered explorations of this repository of the national character. Rudyard Kipling, worrying that England's days of predominance were numbered, turned for reassurance from the overseas settings of his Imperial stories and verse to the contemplation of England's own rural past. In 1902 Kipling bought an early-seventeenth-century Sussex manor house, and settled down in what he saw as an England of down shepherds, a happily "primitive peasantry," and old-fashioned landed gentlemen.[73] He wrote to an American friend that "we discovered England . . . and went to live in it. England is a wonderful land. It is the most marvellous of all foreign countries that I have ever been in. It is made up of trees and green fields and mud and the gentry, and at last I'm one of the gentry."[74]

At last an Old English country gentleman, Kipling gave himself up to the spirit of the past. "Behind his outward championship of modern progress," noted an admirer in 1925,

> he loves the unalterable, untouched something in the Sussex people. He has been careful to safeguard Sussex medievalism by refusing to install the telephone at "Bateman's," and where it has been possible has preserved the ancient customs and traditions on the farms. To this day, therefore, all the gates at Bateman's are "heavy-hatches," just as they were in Saxon times . . . Mr. Kipling is a great lover of the wood fire . . . He spends many an hour with his pipe by the great open wood fire in his Elizabethan living room . . . It is a room where the centuries mingle and fade away with the mist in the high roof.[75]

Kipling's literary Sussex evoked Hardy's Wessex. But what had been implicit in Hardy, and only drawn out ideologically by others, was now explicit. Kipling was his own ideologue, and his Sussex was the product of a self-conscious quest for the national identity. The same desires that led some to create a cult of Wessex led Kipling to shape a similar vision of Sussex. His poem "Sussex" and two stories from these years, "An Habitation Enforced" and "My Son's Wife," embody this cosmopolitan intellectual's discovery of roots in a part of England where the past still lived.[76] After establishing himself on long-inhabited English soil, Kipling presented his personal identification with the English past in two books ostensibly for children (but "meant for grownups").[77] *Puck of Pook's Hill* (1906) and its sequel, *Rewards and Fairies* (1910), collections of loosely connected tales set usually in Sussex in various periods of English history, were very widely read by both children and adults. Their subject was the making of England and the English character. Their hero, ultimately, was old Hobden the Hedger, the peasant who carried in his bones and spirit the whole history of the English race.

> His dead are in the churchyard – thirty generations
>   laid.
> Their names were old in history when Domesday
>   Book was made;
> And the passion and the piety and the prowess of
>   his line
> Have seeded, rooted, fruited in some land the Law
>   calls mine.

While Kipling was writing *Puck*, another leading Tory poet was engaged in a remarkably similar enterprise. Henry Newbolt (1862-1938), best known for "Clifton Chapel," had turned his pen to a historical romance about England. *The Old Country*, published the same year as *Puck* and also widely read, was planned as "a story which would exemplify two things. One was the magical power of the English landscape, the other the similarity, at many times during the past centuries, of the way in which the English character has reacted to the same national difficulties or dangers."[78] The slow, humiliating effort of the Boer War had drained away Imperialist exuberance, and turned men like Kipling and Newbolt back from the turbulent frontiers of empire to the quiet English countryside in nostalgic contemplation.

Attraction to the changelessness of rural England, however, was by no means confined to Imperialists or Tories. The socially critical novelist George Gissing, for example, found in rural England the antidote for all he feared and detested in modern life. Time and again in his novels he contrasted urban materialism and rural spirituality. His characters sooner or later attempt to escape into the countryside, sometimes succeeding, as in *Demos* (1886), sometimes failing, as in *The Nether World* (1889). His last and most popular book was a wish fulfillment: *The Private Papers of Henry Ryecroft* (1903) recorded a writer's retreat to a country cottage and his meditations on modern life. "Has the century of science and money-making," he pondered, "sensibly affected the national character?" For reassurance, he looked at the country. He asked himself what "the most noteworthy things in England" were. "Those old villages, in the midlands or the west, which lie at some distance from a railway station, and in aspect are still untouched by the baser tendencies of the time." Such villages were England's greatest achievement and most precious treasure. There England was still true to itself. Gissing's autobiographical character, Ryecroft, concluded, "The last thought of my brain as I lie dying will be that of sunshine upon an English meadow."[79]

Such a vision of the country as a shelter from the winds of change turned up on many occasions in the nineteenth and twentieth centuries in expressions of left-wing attitudes. Rural myths took two distinct forms among progressives and socialists: "accommodationist" and utopian. The first served to undercut the radicalism nominally being put forth by the speaker: John Davidson, for example, who could write passionately of the sufferings of the poor in "Thirty Bob a Week," could write another poem of social realism, "St. George's Day," and midway through it declare "Away with spleen, and let us sing the praises of the English spring," and go on to "drown his social realism . . . in a flood of birdsong."[80] In this way, the rustic South "singing over the land" could take the edge off social criticism and soften potential political conflict. The political appeal of this sort of emollient, patriotic ruralism upon an overwhelmingly urban electorate was to be exploited in the nineteen-twenties and thirties by Stanley Baldwin and Ramsay Macdonald.

At times, the myth of the changeless country supported a fervent utopian radicalism. Kipling's reality ("our England is a garden") was William Morris's hope (to become again "the fair green garden of Northern Europe."). An ideal of pastoral tranquility would be set against the hated present. Such an ideal would be set in the past or in the future, or in both at the same time. Two related messages would be conveyed: first, that present society represented a fall from an earlier demi-Eden; and second, that the good society of the future will have escaped from the pressures of modernity, identified with capitalism – simple instead of complex; in harmony with nature, not alienated from it; cooperative instead of competitive; and tranquil, peaceful, and stable instead of restless and ever-changing. As J. H. Plumb perceived, the "dream of an Elysian [rural] England . . . has haunted English radicalism" ever since William Cobbett inveighed against enclosure and urbanization.[81] This tradition of utopian ruralism found its greatest prophet in William Morris, the foremost intellectual the British Left has produced.

Morris was both a revolutionary Marxist looking forward to a new society and, as we have seen, a nostalgic romantic seeking to revive the traditional rural English way of life. He joined zeal for revolution with a social ideal for which the countryside was the necessary locale. His classic utopia, *News from Nowhere*, was significantly subtitled *An Epoch of Rest*. In it were juxtaposed the "hurried and discontented humanity" of late-Victorian England and the relaxed, peaceful inhabitants of his future pastoral world after the revolution.[82] His utopia is a world without cities and without change. Morris embraced revolution – a short, distinct time for radical change – in order to end, once and for all, the ceaseless, unsettling change that disturbed him. An apparent paradox, but not when we appreciate the power of the desire to escape from change and the growing appeal of "rest" as a social ideal to so many in the English middle classes, whether they professed conservatism or radicalism.

Anti-Conservatives and anti-Imperialists also laid claim to the legacy of Old Rural England. By the Edwardian period, many Liberals and Radicals were arguing that in fact Imperialism had betrayed the "true" England. As Lord Bryce observed, the Boer War presented the spectacle of a "clash of civilisations" – a cosmopolitan industrial society versus a traditional, rural "folk" society.[83] Which was really closer in character to Old England?

Soon after the close of the Boer War, a young literary and social critic, C. F. G. Masterman (1873-1927) (to be a Liberal MP from 1906, and a member of Asquith's cabinet in 1914), complained that the literature of Imperialism had "neglected and despised the ancient pieties of an older England, the little isle set in its silver sea." Greatness had become equated with bigness. In contrast, Masterman discerned the rise of a new literature that was anti-Imperial yet not cosmopolitan – a literature of "nationalism." This development had begun, he argued, in the nineties, but during the heyday of Imperialism its exponents, like the poets William Watson and W. B. Yeats, had been voices in the wilderness. The balance had shifted with the South African War. Masterman saw other writers now adding their voices to the new spirit – H. W. Nevinson, G. K. Chesterton, and Hilaire Belloc. Taking this new literature as a signpost, Masterman anticipated the character of the coming *zeitgeist*: "It will proclaim always a particular concern in the well-being of England and the English people; a pride in its ancient history, its ancient traditions, the very language of its grey skies and rocky shore"; it would be democratic; and it would be social, concerned with restoring the moral and material health of English society, which had been undermined by the new dissolvents of the nineteenth century: urbanism, industrialism, and cosmopolitanism.[84]

This complex of attitudes about England was set out in a symposium by Masterman and others, published in 1904 under the title *England: A Nation*. Edited by Lucien Oldershaw, it was subtitled *The Papers of the Patriots' Club* (referring to a group formed during the Boer War).[85] Contributors included, besides Masterman, a number of other important young Liberals: G. K. Chesterton, R. C. K. Ensor, H. W. Nevinson, J. L. Hammond, and Reginald Bray. They united in putting forth "patriotism" as the true liberal and democratic alternative to Imperialism. "Is there anyone today," asked G. K. Chesterton, "who can reasonably doubt that what led us into error in our recent South African politics was precisely our Imperialism, and not our Nationalism? – was precisely not our ancient interest in England, but our quite modern and quite frivolous interest in everywhere else?"[86]

The contributors to *England: A Nation*, and others of similar disposition, set out in the prewar years to define the character of the "little England" to which they gave their allegiance. That England was ancient, domestic, and rural. Facing the first page of Oldershaw's volume appeared a poem by George Bartram:

> Old England, gracious wielder of the spell
> of pastoral beauty, janitress benign
> Of green Arcadian temples, matron-belle
> Robed rich of rustic glory, it is well,
> Yea, past all boasting, to be son of thine.
>
> Foul fall such ingrates at the spell proclaim
> A charm outworn, and in their lust of gold
> Deem thy swift conquests of sublimer fame
> Than this that shaped them – English such in name,
> Yet aliens utter both in heart and mould.
>
> Stay thou green England, fill thy loins with store
> Of peasant manhood, sow thou plenteous seed
> Of such grim valour as was thine of yore,
> Be thy strong philtres aye and evermore
> The broad green woodland and the wind-swept mead!

England was to be found deep in the counties, just as Kipling and Newbolt were discovering. The historian R. C. K. Ensor explained: "The human wealth of a populous countryside in which all classes lived, and could live, at peace, for centuries – that is our arch-achievement as a nation, the source and condition of our other great-nesses, the base on whose fragments, 'majestic though in ruin,' we can still found, if not our loudest, at least our most legitimate fame."[87]

As one of these new Liberals, Frederick Shaw, later insisted, England was naturally neither capitalist nor Imperialist: "Capitalistic Impe-rialism is a feature of an age, not of a place; the fact that we have established a stronger capitalism than most and a wider Empire than any other nation is at least as much due to our insular position as to any special national instinct." Instead, he found a true national in-stinct in "love of the open air and all that it implies, so much older than all our industries and Imperial greatness."[88]

The old rural life that was the real foundation of England was best explored by another Edwardian Liberal, George Sturt (1863-1927). Sturt's books on rural life, *Change in the Village* (1912) and *The Wheel-wright's Shop* (1923), were later given a new circulation by the praise of F. R. Leavis. Sturt despised much of modern life; writing a friend in 1911, he explained: "I don't like England as she is – industrial, over-capitalized, where the Struggle to Live is so sordid, and success means motor-cars and insolence."[89] As an alternative, having inherited a wheelwright's shop in Farnham, Surrey, Sturt set himself to record the "home-made civilization of the rural English," which seemed to be passing away before his eyes. As were these other Edwardians, he was seeking England. Listening to his gardener (another Hodge or Hob-den), Sturt felt that "in his quiet voice I am privileged to hear the natural, fluent, unconscious talk, as it goes on over the face of the country, of the English race."[90] These voices of England spoke to him of an organic community, in which all men had a place, shared stable values, and lived intimately with nature. Although compared to many writers on old English country life Sturt was a realist, aware that traditional rural life had been far from idyllic, he yet contrasted the present most unfavorably with his image of the past, and saw change as loss in human terms.

The Liberal novelist E. M. Forster felt much the same. The Im-perialist, to him, was "a destroyer. He prepared the way for cosmo-politanism, and though his ambitions may be fulfilled, the earth that he inherits will be grey." In his novel *Howards End* (1910), Forster celebrated Little England, whose heart lay in the countryside. The old country house of Howards End embodied the historic continuity of England, menaced by the "inner darkness in high places that comes with a commercial age" in the persons of an Imperialist business family, the Wilcoxes. Visiting the house, the heroine, Margaret Schlegel, was deeply moved: "Here had lived an elder race, to which we look back with disquietude. The country which we visit at week-ends was really a home to it . . . In these English farms, if anywhere, one might see life steadily and see it whole."[91]

Even the fiery D. H. Lawrence felt the tug of the myth: Of Garsington Manor, the Morrells's country house, he wrote a friend in 1915: "Here one feels the real England – this old house, this countryside – so poignantly . . . it is in its way so beautiful, one is tempted to give in, and to stay there, to lapse back into its peaceful beauty of bygone things, to live in pure recollection, looking at the accomplished past, which is so lovely. But one's soul rebels."[92]

Few others fought off the temptation. Even a cosmopolitan writer like Ford Madox Ford, editor of the *Transatlantic Review*, was, as we have seen, obsessed with identifying and recreating the essential spirit of England, to be found in the past and in the country. He wrote ten volumes of historical novels colored by patriotic affection. In *The Heart of the Country* (1906), part of a three-volume exploration of the contemporary English character, Ford wistfully contrasted, much as Sturt was doing at the same time, the old peasant folk consciousness with the urban-commercial-industrial consciousness that was banishing it.

Maurice Hewlett (1861-1923), a country neighbor and friend of Henry Newbolt, gained much attention for his historical romances, most notably *The Forest Lovers* (1898). Hewlett also saw his work as a quest for the meaning of England, which he found in the traditions of peasant life. His last major work, an epic poem entitled *Song of the Plow* (1916) (which he called "The English Chronicle"), had as its hero Hodge, the archetypal Englishman, carrying on his way of life through the centuries. Hewlett's view of English history was very close to that of Chesterton: antimercantile yet also antiaristocratic, "radical yet favoring the customs of the country, egalitarian but conservative."[93]

Similar in outlook to Hewlett were the poets represented in Edward Marsh's collections entitled *Georgian Poetry*, which sold unusually well for new poetry – between ten and twenty thousand copies of all but the last. The Georgians were generally on the political left – most, indeed, were socialists.[94] Their leftism was not friendly to material progress. Typical was Rupert Brooke's reaction in 1913 to Fiji: He lamented that the happy natives would soon be made over in the image of the West. How depressing to contemplate the whole world becoming "replicas of Denver and Birmingham and Stuttgart!"[95] The socialism of most Georgians was, as Brooke described his own, of "a William Morris sort."[96] The hallmark of the Georgians was pastoralism, an absorption in the English countryside. But they were not really nature poets; rather, they found in the country something of great value: One might there "lie ... until the centuries blend and blur."[97] David Daiches defined their common preoccupation as the "the search for certainty in a disruptive world, combined with the conviction that certainty must be salvaged from the past rather than born again in the future." This shared outlook was summed up in the concluding lines of Brooke's "The Old Vicarage, Grantchester," which Daiches called "the motto of the Georgian poets":[98]

> Say, is there Beauty yet to find?
> And Certainty? And Quiet kind?
> Deep meadows yet, for to forget
> The lies, and truths, and pain? ...oh! yet
> Stands the Church clock at ten to three?
> And is there honey still for tea?

The question being asked by Brooke was "Stands England where she did?" The answer given by the Georgians was yes – if one went away from the cities and suburbs, out into the as-yet unchanged heartland.

By the time of the First World War, nostalgic visions and utopian dreams centering on the country had been blended in literary and, beyond that, in middle-class culture. Martial horrors made this rural myth more appealing than ever. As one writer remarked in 1915, "the soul of England must not be sought in the city but in the countryside."[99] During the war, at the request of the YMCA, Ernest Rhys, editor of the Everyman's Library, put together for the use of soldiers an anthology of writing on England, entitled *The Old Country*. In this volume, which the YMCA distributed widely, patriotic inspiration was drawn, as in the prewar poems, from a highly selective portrait of "home." The urban and industrial England that was providing the men and materials for the conflict was scarcely noticed; in its place was evoked the England of Alfred Austin and Rupert Brooke – "O England," E. V. Lucas's title poem sentimentalized, "country of my heart's desire, land of the hedgerow and the village spire." Sir Arthur Yapp, of the YMCA, spoke in his introduction of the average soldier in France: "In imagination, he can see his village home."[100] The East End of London, Leeds, Wolverhampton, and their counterparts, of course, were far more common "homes" of these soldiers, but there was no place for them in Yapp's image of England despite the fact that his organization did most of its work in such places. Sometimes escapism was explicit. "Within the England of my heart," wrote Edward Hutton in this anthology, "there is no industrial city such as infests, ruins and spoils other lands."[101] A very similar poem had just appeared in the second volume of *Georgian Poetry*. James Elroy Flecker, himself a socialist, wrote in "The Dying Patriot" of a soldier recalling as he lay dying an entirely pastoral and historical England.[102]

Grantchester, where the clock had stopped at teatime, seemed more truly England than restless, industrial Manchester.

Architecture: the myth made tangible

The conservative movement of elite culture in the second half of the nineteenth century also extended to architectural opinion and work. From the Gothic revival through the spread of Old English styles and the simultaneous rise of preservationism, architects gave changing cultural values physical form.

The Gothic revival laid the groundwork. Pugin and the other fathers of the Gothic revival were High Tories, and their movement was hostile to an industrial and capitalist society. They made an appeal to the Middle Ages, and rejected the contemporary world of the nineteenth century. It was a cultural counterattack of an old elite against new forces and new men. Alexander Beresford-Hope (1820-87), son-in-law of the Marquis of Salisbury, chairman of the Ecclesiological Society, and a leading patron of the revival, dreamed of church buildings that would domineer "over the haughty and Protestantized shopocracy."[103] The revival succeeded; Gothic became the most characteristic High Victorian style. Yet it triumphed not against, but with the cooperation of the new "shopocracy," as shown by such buildings as the Manchester Town Hall and the Bradford Wool Exchange. The triumph was by no means complete: Purist versions were usually rejected in favor of a more "contemporary" adaptation.[104] Yet the middle-class acceptance of the Gothic style in the eighteen-fifties marked a watershed – the cresting of the new culture of the industrial revolution, and the beginning of a yielding by its new men to the cultural hegemony of the old aristocracy. High Victorian design, to one of its most recent and perceptive interpreters, reveals the sort of ambivalence that one would expect to follow immediately upon such a watershed – "the expression, very often simultaneously, of material optimism and spiritual disquiet."[105] It exhibited a precarious balance, which began to tip in the sixties and seventies.

The new generation of architects then set out to rediscover the English countryside, and, bound up with the countryside, the English past. Motivating them (as Mark Girouard has pointed out) was dissatisfaction: "Dislike of the present led them to the past, dislike of the town to the country. As an antidote to the present they recreated the past as an ideal world of preindustrial simplicity, at once homely and Arcadian. Adjectives such as 'quaint' and 'old-fashioned' epitomized this world to them and were applied with . . . enthusiastic approbation."[106] The second half of the nineteenth century saw a number of closely related architectural movements and styles flourish – "Old English," "Queen Anne," "the vernacular revival" – all developing out of Victorian Gothic and all expressing a continuation and intensification of the containment of industrial culture begun by the Gothic revival. But if they were extensions of Gothicism, why were they felt necessary? Why not simply hold on to Gothic, as *the* un-industrial, uncapitalist style, as Pugin had seen it? By the sixties, Gothic was exhibiting several drawbacks to the younger generation of architects and aesthetes. It was, for one thing, too fiercely religious. For another, ironically, it had been too successful in becoming a modern vernacular, and in the process became thoroughly urbanized and commercialized. This generation was seeking a style that was preindustrial and "national," yet harmonized with its increasingly secular outlook; Gothic clearly would not do. It was also seeking a style not corrupted by urban industrial capitalism, a style that spoke forth of other values. Once Gothic had been this par excellence, but now "at every corner they saw Gothic shops, Gothic warehouses, and even Gothic public houses." Gothic was flourishing in partnership with industrialism in towns like Manchester and Bradford; commercial Gothic seemed to have absorbed everything they disliked about contemporary society.[107] Morris, for example, began as an ardent Gothicist, but gradually lost hope of a genuine medieval revival in the debased society of industrial capitalism. The Gothic style was being turned into merely another commodity, a window dressing for a repellent reality. Morris characterized the prosperous districts where his patrons lived as "architectooralooral." Style had failed to redeem substance. "I doubt," he later told a group of Glasgow socialists, "the applicability of your old Celtic style to the amenities of joint-stock money-grubbing."[108]

Morris's generation of architects found what it was looking for in an adaptation of English domestic building styles between the late Middle Ages and the Hanoverians, particularly as seen in the country. Their model became the rustic farmhouse or cottage. The essence of the new style was a national self-preoccupation (the Queen Anne movement, as P. N. Furbank has observed, was "above all . . . an idealization of Englishness")[109] and a generalized historicity and rusticity – the purpose of which was to convey a feeling of Old Rural England, rather than to adhere to any particular and consistent style. It was the architecture of Thomas Hardy and Richard Jefferies, of ruralism and nostalgia. From the eighteen-sixties, as Girouard has described, "the whole English rural tradition began to seem increasingly precious and threatened, and it was seen that this tradition included not only medieval churches and barns, but sixteenth- and seventeenth-century farmhouses, red brick early Georgian houses in the market places and back streets of country towns, in short the whole English vernacular tradition."

The new architectural movement emerged with Richard Norman Shaw's (1831-1912) house, Leys Woods, built in 1868 for the managing director of a shipping line. When Shaw exhibited a drawing of the house at the Royal Academy in 1870, it caused a sensation. Leys Woods was immediately seen as "quaint," and, as Girouard remarked, "It suddenly became clear both to City businessmen looking for a quiet corner to commute from, and to prosperous artists anxious to invest their Academy winnings that quaintness was what they wanted."[110] Under the blanket of "Old English," the design incorporated elements from a variety of periods and types. Yet as a whole the plan was new and tremendously appealing. Old English had been put on the map; and Old English meant not the imitation of a style, but the creation of an atmosphere.

The atmosphere was rustic, historic, and "humble" – "cozy," small-scale, antiheroic, evocative of folk life. To be up-to-date, now meant to look as old as possible; not just antique, but gradually and irregularly aged. This was true even among the aristocracy, where "humility" did not appeal. Paul Thompson has noted that the (comparatively few) new houses built for landowners after the Agricultural Depression "no longer boasted their novelty, as had those of their mid-Victorian predecessors. They were discreet, irregular, looking as old as a new house could." Land had ceased being a major source of wealth and the country house was now valued more as a symbol of ancestry than of economic power. "Old walls were thus more fashionable than new."[111] Country houses now sought to blend into, rather than to dominate, the landscape (this is quite clear in the highly influential work of C. F. A. Voysey (1857-1941), particularly in such houses as Broadley's, built in 1898, and The Orchard, built for himself in 1900).[112] Massiveness and grand effects were shunned as foreign: "Everything English," insisted Warrington Taylor, one of the pioneers of the new style, "excepting stockjobbing London or cotton Manchester, is essentially small, and of a homely farmhouse kind of poetry."[113] Suburban villas emulated this turn of upper-class taste, evoking farmhouses and yeoman's cottages. The new planned garden suburbs (from Bedford Park to Hampstead and beyond), public housing estates (as at Becontree in London), and private speculative suburbia all came to reflect this ideal of quaint, aged rusticity. The ideals of the garden-city pioneers like Raymond Unwin (1863-1940) and Barry Parker (1867-1947) included a renewed attention to the importance of tradition, nostalgia for the Middle Ages, and a devotion to the village as the symbol of the "natural" life they sought to restore.[114] In the interwar years the Old English mode moved out from the elite to become a mass style as large-scale private developers took it up in minimal cost versions, and "Bypass Tudor" with its "yearning for roots in the past" proliferated with the suburban explosion.[115] This architectural fashion spread elsewhere, most notably to the United States, but lost strength in so doing. It dominated domestic building nowhere to the extent it did in England, its spiritual home.

Paralleling the rise of Old English stylism was the birth of the preservationist movement. Led by many of the same individuals, preservationism and Old English design drew upon a common fund of ruralist and nostalgic values. Both were apparently aesthetic movements, but were more truly historicist, as they sought to hold onto or recapture the spirit of an earlier England. As Old English meant not a definite style but the creation of an atmosphere, preservationism meant a primary commitment not to beauty but to age.

Preservationist sentiments began to take shape within the Gothic movement itself. As new Gothic design became commercialized, and at the same time began to become boring, Gothic revivalists became uneasy about contemporary Gothic alterations to older structures. Even Sir George Gilbert Scott (1811-78), the dean of restorers, began to warn against excessive restoration. In 1864 he lamented how "a barbaric builder, a clerk of works, or an over-zealous clergyman" could get carried away and "meddle" with everything in an ancient church, ending with "the whole thing *radically re-formed* from top to tow . . . One *perfectly longs* after an *untouched church*." Scott argued that repairs should be made "in a *tentative* and *gradual* manner; first replacing the stones which are entirely decayed, and rather *feeling one's way* and *trying how little will do* than going on any bold system." Scott acknowledged his own guilt. "I do not wish or expect to exempt myself from equal blame where I deserve it. *We are all of us offenders in this matter.*" But it was "high time that some public protest be made" and he called for local vigilance committees that could guard against overrestoration.[116] The suggestion was not picked up, and, ironically, it was to be his own scheme for the restoration of Tewkesbury Abbey thirteen years later that provoked, in reaction, the creation of a national "vigilance committee" that went well beyond his own conception.

After a visit to Tewkesbury in 1877, William Morris wrote an angry letter to the *Athenaeum* calling for the formation of an association to fight against such obliteration of the past. "Our ancient buildings," he declared, "are not mere ecclesiastical toys, but sacred monuments of the nation's growth and hope."[117] From this letter arose the Society for the Protection of Ancient Buildings, the first preservationist pressure group.

Morris's call struck a responsive chord; architects and artists, professional men, and a number of aristocrats of a variety of political persuasions rallied to the cause of the SPAB. In the first years Morris was secretary, and remained afterwards the leading spirit on the committee, but the society was quite nonpartisan. Its influence grew steadily; within five years over a hundred cases were being handled every year, and by 1889 the committee could note with gratification a changed attitude among the educated public toward restoration.[118] By the turn of the century it was common for officers of the society to note the changed climate of public opinion; they were now rowing with rather than against the current. The SPAB eventually assumed the status of a national institution; in 1920, Thackeray Turner, retired from several decades' work as secretary, could observe that "we practically now have no opposition."[119]

After the SPAB came other preservationist bodies, sometimes as direct offshoots, and preservationist legislation soon followed. Preservationism became an ever more powerful and widespread impulse in British public life. This movement was at first seen as aesthetic, and Gothic in particular; in fact, as we shall see, its overriding criterion was rarely beauty itself, but rather antiquity. Buildings "of all times and styles," in Morris's phrase, that were far enough removed from the present were fought for.[120] John Ruskin, the intellectual godfather of the movement, had given forth the dictum that "the greatest glory of a building is not in its stones, not in its gold. Its glory is its Age." In Ruskin, who revered historical continuity in a fashion reminiscent of Burke, the conservative impulse underlying the movement is made plain. "I am," he admitted in 1856, "by nature and instinct Conservative, loving old things because they are old, and hating new ones merely because they are new." It was for him "no question of expediency or feeling whether we shall preserve the buildings of past times or not. *We have no right whatever to touch them.* They are not ours. They belong, partly to those who built them, and partly to all the generations of mankind who are to follow us."[121] Morris reprinted these words in the initial manifesto of the SPAB, and they became a source of inspiration to countless protectionists, whatever their politics. "Our greatest possession," the Reverend Stepford Brooke told the SPAB in 1879, "[is] this feeling of reverence and care for the work and the spirit of those who preceded us."[122]

At first, Gothic was preferred, and most preservationist effort went to protecting medieval, and especially Gothic, buildings. Ruskin and Morris rhapsodized over Gothic, and disparaged most Renaissance and post-Renaissance style. Yet, even in the early years, and increasingly over time, historicity would override taste. The SPAB superficially appeared to be enthusiastic about the Gothic style, but as architect Robert Kerr pointed out in 1884,

> on closer acquaintance this impression is not confirmed. For it declines emphatically to be considered representative of Gothic alone, or, indeed, we may say, of Gothic at all. Its object is not even artistic, but historical; to preserve what is left of the past in the most indiscriminate way; whether good or bad, old or new, preserve it all, so that the reverie of the wayfarer may have not only something authentic, but everything veritable to dwell upon, even when the light of life, perhaps never a very bright light, has quite gone out. This, I need scarcely repeat, is not an enthusiasm of art – indeed,

scarcely one of archaeology; and it has become identified with architecture only because buildings are the most conspicuous relics for such a form of patriotic reverence.[123]

As tastes altered, the initial association with particular past styles faded, and the criterion of age became ever clearer. Out of the SPAB came the Georgian Group, and from it the Victorian Society; protectionist sentiment eventually reached the Edwardian period. The early preservationists generally despised most Victorian buildings, yet as time went on the wheel turned full circle, and the objects of Victorian preservationists' scorn became precious to their successors. Taste changed, and, more important perhaps, time passed, casting the magic of historicity over once-contemporary structures. Even the railways and factories that early preservationists ritualistically pilloried became, once time eroded their functions, subjects of preservationist fervor.

Preservationism carried with it two intertwined attitudes that link the movement to broader currents in later-Victorian culture and society. First, a loss of confidence in the creative powers of one's contemporaries and an elevation of the past over the present; and second, a highly critical view of industrial capitalism and its "materialistic" ethos. Many of those activities that roused the ire of preservationists were not in fact activities of restoration, but of modernization. Such activities were of a piece with those of almost all earlier architects, who were convinced of the merit of their own work in relation to all that had gone before. It was, Robert Macleod has pointed out, "the preservationists who were introducing the radically new idea . . . that their own time, as opposed to all previous in history, was incapable of contributing to the story of architectural development."[124] The SPAB, with profound cultural pessimism, declared it impossible to treat churches "as living things, to be altered, enlarged, and adapted as they were in the days when the art that produced them was alive and progressive." These buildings were now solely "*documents*, which to alter or correct is, in fact, to falsify and render worthless."[125]

The urge to preserve went hand in glove with disparagement of the possibilities of the present era. As the Reverend T. W. Norwood told the first meeting of the SPAB, "It is indeed shocking to think that we who have no style of Architecture, and so little art of our own, should have thus ruined the priceless relics of that one individual living and growing art of our ancestors."[126] Nor was much hope held out for developing a satisfactory new style. If preservationists were horrified by restoration, they were just as hostile to boldly modern efforts. Morris hated most of the innovative constructions that foreshadowed twentieth-century architecture. When he visited the Crystal Palace in 1851 he sat down and refused to go round, declaring it "wonderfully ugly." His attitude never changed: Thirty years later he characterized modern engineering as a "horrible and restless nightmare," and disliked plate-glass windows because they let in too much light. Toward the end of his life he called the Forth Bridge, with its (to a modern eye) powerful, sweeping lines, "the supremest specimen of all ugliness."[127] Morris spoke for most preservationists, in whose vocabularies "new" and "modern" became synonyms for "bad." The high cultural ambitions of their predecessors were abandoned; the best the present age could aspire to was to minimize the damage to its heritage by leaving old buildings alone, and building new ones as simply and unpretentiously as possible. Architects in Morris's circle found the cardinal virtue to be humility, and turned to the old vernacular tradition of building, with its lack of aesthetic ambition. "I never begin to be satisfied," Philip Webb insisted, "until my work looks commonplace."[128]

Preservationism was a professional and gentlemanly activity, and its ethos reflected that fact. Because it would interfere with the rights of private property, it was controversial, and antagonized many political Conservatives.[129] Its radicalism, however, was Tory at root, willing to infringe the individual control of property in the higher interest of protecting the historic continuity of the nation. The material progress that had produced the Great Exhibition no longer seemed to produce much except a concomitant restlessness, a lack of cultivation, and a blatant materialism. The reservoir of value that the past represented was being depleted. Every day, P. H. Ditchfield complained, witnessed the destruction of yet another physical bequest of past generations. Sometimes it was a building, sometimes a scenic view, that yielded to factories, railways, or "mechanical" modern houses without "memories" – such was the "penalty we pay for trade, progress, and the pursuit of wealth."[130]

A meeting of the SPAB rarely went by without some disparagement of "an age when money alone is the sign of worth,"[131] and of those who devoted themselves to the acquisition of such a mean standard. Professor Sidney Colvin, Slade Professor of Fine Arts at Cambridge, entertained the first meeting of the society with a discussion of the vulgarity of restoration. Restorers, he noted, delighted in the brightness and newness of their work.

> The more spick and span the work is, the greater the happiness of all the army engaged in the work of restoration. It is like the satisfaction of the tradesman in the new brass plate displayed in front of his shop window [a laugh and hear, hear] with all its letters sharply cut. Whereas to us every item which is spick and span and new ... is something which requires an apology [Hear, hear].[132]

Businessmen could not be trusted with the care of the nation's continuity. Ditchfield, who decried "the commercialism and utilitarianism of our latter-day civilization," lamented over the kind of persons usually elected to town councils:

> worthy men doubtless, and able men of business, who can attend to and regulate the financial affairs of the town, look after its supply of gas and water, its drainage and tramways; but they are absolutely ignorant of its history, its associations, of architectural beauty, of anything that is not modern and utilitarian. Unhappily, into the care of such men as these is often confided the custody of historic buildings and priceless treasures.[133]

Material prosperity itself was a menace. "It is the wealth of the country," observed Stanley Leighton, MP, a Tory squire, "and not the poverty of the country," that enabled men to tear down old buildings and replace them with uninteresting new ones. The SPAB noted in 1890 "the growing, ever-increasing, power of money to injure and falsify, what want of means had not destroyed."[134]

An upper-middle-class idealism harking back to Arnold and Ruskin characterized the SPAB and preservationism in general. Its target, whether the shafts came from Left or Right, was the low aims of a life dominated by trade and industry. Lord Bryce, a distinguished Liberal, was encouraged by what he interpreted as "the growth of reverential feelings" toward ancient buildings among the public. Such sentiments, he affirmed, speaking for the society, "rescue [men] from that worldliness which comes of mere material prosperity and growth of wealth. Man does not live by bread alone," but requires "all those subtle yet potent ties which bind the present to the past."[135]

Such sentiments were subscribed to both by Imperialists and socialists in the movement. H. E. Luxmoore, a public school master, offered an Imperialist rationale for preservationism:

> The lower forms of human society have, one knows, their own rough efficiency and use; but of a people that is born to, and is worthy of, the heritage of a great history, more is required. Their life is not limited to struggle for more material needs, they do not live by bread alone.[136]

The socialist illustrator, Walter Crane (1845-1915), complained passionately that

> some of us appear to be trying to turn England into another America – for ever scheming railways where they are not wanted, cutting down trees, and clearing away old dwelling places, and insulting even the green fields with advertisements. Anything that interferes with extra percentages is as dust in the balance to such.

Commercialization had already eroded much of Old England: "We might still be happy," he declared,

> were it not for the whirlwind of trade, and the whirligig of fashion ...Happily they leave some quiet corners unswept...or we could never have known what the homes of our ancestors were like. But

how many still does England hold of those delightful places full of
the pathos of old time, where each dumb thing of wood or iron, or
copper, each fragment of faded tapestry seems to have the speech of
romance?[137]

When something new had to be built, the architectural style
favored by most preservationists was usually some variant of Old
English. In this way, change would be fit into an old pattern, and
make the least possible disruption. The Southern Metaphor had
triumphed in the realm of the tangible, as it had in that of the
intangible.

The staying power of the Southern Metaphor
Fascination with old country life, real and imagined, spread throughout the middle class after World War I. Rarely had a triumphant class
come into its inheritance with more diffidence, more readiness to
adopt as its own the values of the class it replaced. E. M. Forster captured the spirit of his own class in 1939 when he observed that, having
"strangled the aristocracy" in the nineteenth century, the middle class
remained in the twentieth "haunted by the ghost of its victim":

> It has never been able to build itself an appropriate home, and when
> it asserts that an Englishman's home is his castle, it reveals the precise
> nature of its failure. We who belong to it still copy the past. The
> castles and the great mansions are gone, we have to live in semi-
> detached villas instead, they are all we can afford, but let us at all
> events retain a Tradesman's Entrance...Our minds still hanker
> after the feudal stronghold which we condemned as uninhabitable.[138]

Evidence of this hankering could be found in the increasing
popularity of country homes. Living in the country was more and
more frequently discussed in papers and on the BBC.[139] An imitation
of traditional rural life-styles became fashionable – either that of the
gentry, if affordable, or, if it was not, or if one's politics barred
identification with the landed upper class, that of the peasantry, with
its rough edges smoothed away. Ersatz countrymen proliferated.
Before the war, writers like Kipling and Rider Haggard had set a
pattern by turning themselves into pseudosquires, whereas affluent
radicals, like Mrs. Charlotte Wilson, first a Fabian and then an
anarchist, began to take up residence in country cottages. Mrs. Wilson
was a trend setter of radical chic: At her insistence, her husband, a
stockbroker, gave up their comfortable London house and bought a
cottage. "It is a charming and quite idyllic little farm," Edith Nesbit,
another middle-class radical, wrote after a visit in 1885:

> They have two rooms – study and kitchen. The kitchen is an *idealized*
> farm kitchen, where of course no cooking is done – but with a
> cushioned settee – open hearth, polished dresser and benches, and

all the household glass and crockery displayed mixed up with aesthetic pots pans curtains chairs and tables – a delightfully incon-
gruous but altogether agreeable effect.[140]

The interwar years saw the proliferation of what Osbert Lancaster
labeled the "cultured cottage"[141] as opinion makers began to emulate
Mrs. Charlotte Wilson's return to the "simple old life" of the countryside. This exodus was made convenient by the motorcar, but it was
animated by an implicit acceptance of the Southern Metaphor.

Though retirement to a picturesque village became fashionable,
there was of course no mass exodus from the cities. The exodus was
chiefly one of sentiment. A boom market developed in books about
the national character, traditions, and antiquities, usually to be found
in the country. Several publishers began series on these themes in the
late twenties and early thirties. Among major publishers, Longmans
led off in 1929 with an "English Heritage" series, with volumes
dedicated to English humor, folk song and dance, the public school,
the parish church, wild life, and so on. This series carried an introduction by Stanley Baldwin and a commendation by Ramsay Macdonald. The following year Batsford started its series titled "English
Life," with volumes on the countryside, Old English household life,
inns, villages, and cottages. Other publishers joined in in succeeding
years. Notable among these efforts was a series of twenty-three
broadcast talks, produced by the BBC at the depth of the depression
in 1933 and early 1934, on what was called the "national character."
These talks aimed to reassure the BBC's vast audience that the events
of the twentieth century were only superficially bewildering, and
even, it would seem, required no wrenching change in national aims
or behavior. Old England still lived and much had to be rediscovered
and affirmed.

The new interest in national traditions was officially sanctioned by
the appointment in 1930 of John Masefield as poet laureate. Masefield,
a popular as well as a serious poet, usually set his verse in the past and
dealt with one or another English "type." He was almost obsessed with
history and with defining the national character through it. "The
nation's past," he later reflected, "is the poet's pasture," and his work
was a collection of gleanings from a rather idealized historical meadow
in which the industrial revolution figured only as an alien blight.[142]

Roy Lewis and Angus Maude, in their 1949 survey of the English
middle class, pointed to the "back-to-the-land" cult evident after
World War I. This cult, being essentially romantic, had little practical
effect on agriculture, the chief business of the land. Instead, it found
its main expression, they observed, "in the buying of books about
farming and the country-side."[143] A mass market for country books,
both fictional and nonfictional, now existed, and publishers rushed to

satisfy it, their lists spawning ever more titles each season. No pocket of rural tranquillity escaped loving description. Batsford emerged as an important publisher on the strength of its beautifully illustrated books on rural scenery and old country life. Newspapers and weeklies sprouted "Country Notes" features, and illustrations of "typical" English scenes, almost all rural, appeared regularly. The tide of pastoral print washed high enough to move Ivor Brown, writing in 1935 on rural England, to protest that "in praise of the English Village so much has been said, and with such lavishness of sentiment, that further ecstatic essays on the rose-clad porches and the ivied cottages are certainly not wanted."[144] Nonetheless, on they came.

The number of novels set in the countryside continued to grow. These works nearly always romanticized rural life and, as one student of them noted, "reacting against industrialism . . . [they] linger[ed] nostalgic[ally] over the past." They tended to be about not the contemporary countryside, but former times colored by childhood recollections, which gave them "a stability and permanence which never exists in real life."[145]

Over the airwaves, too, a rural vogue was entrenched: From "Our Bill," an immensely popular series in the thirties that centered on a Cotswold gardener, to innumerable talks on the beauties, traditions, antiquities, and everyday life of the countryside, the programming of the BBC reflected and reinforced this interest.[146] More than that, the BBC, as part of its self-defined role under Lord Reith of guiding and elevating public opinion, actively promoted appreciation of rural England. The *Listener* pointed proudly in its first volume to the fact that "the countryside and its interests are receiving special care and attention in the Corporation's educational work."[147] Why should they? A 1937 leader provided an answer: Devotion to the countryside "lie[s] at the core of all that is best and soundest in our national life."[148]

The *Listener* knew its readers. During 1941, when the cities were facing destruction, Mass Observation, a pioneer polling organization, asked people living in all parts of the country: "What does Britain mean to you?" One would expect expressions of affection for the threatened towns. Instead, the picture that "Britain" called to mind was for the great majority one of generalized rural scenery, or of particular, familiar country places. Those who thought of urban life did so to contrast it with the "real" rural Britain.[149] Again and again in the twentieth century this point was made. "What does England mean to the ordinary Englishman?" one writer asked rhetorically in 1946. He answered: "just the ordinary things that have always been dear to the simple folk of this island – the ancient traditions, the old churches, the winding roads, the wayside inns, the leafy woodlands, the green meadows."[150] All this was confirmed in 1955 by the anthropologist

Geoffrey Gorer, who analyzed the results of one of the largest surveys of public attitudes yet conducted and concluded that "although England is so overwhelmingly urban, it seems as though most English people picture their country as rural."[151]

Appropriately, after World War I a new body of popular literature flourished – books "in search of England." The most successful of these was H. V. Morton's 1927 work of that title, which first appeared as articles in the *Daily Express* and which went through twenty-three editions by 1936. Morton, and his many successors, went to the countryside to find England. A great number of writers followed in Morton's steps, echoing and underlining his observations, as did Arthur Bryant on the BBC.[152] Opening the BBC's series of talks on the national character in 1933-4, Bryant set the theme: The character of England had been set long ago by "the yeoman farmer . . . the common ancestor of nearly every Englishman." The essential values of this character – spiritual and moral – had been marred but not effaced by industrialism:

> Most of us to-day are town-dwellers, yet there are very few of us whose great-great-great grandparents were not country folk, and, even if we have no idea who they were or from what shire they hailed, our subconscious selves hark back to their instincts and ways of life. We are shut off from them as it were by a tunnel of two or three generations – lost in the darkness of the Industrial Revolution – but beyond is the sunlight of the green fields from which we came. [153]

In the midst of the abdication crisis in 1937 the well-known journalist Philip Gibbs insisted that

> England is not to be judged only by the monstrous ant heap called London or by the tabloid press which panders to the lowest common denominator of mob psychology. There is still the English countryside, where life goes on traditionally in old farmsteads and small villages. There are the cathedral cities where time stands still, and where there is tranquillity of mind. In the old market towns the young farmers who come in with their sheep and cattle belong to Hardy's England, and their minds follow the same furrows. Their blood is the same. Their character has not been changed much by modern fretfulness and "nerves."[154]

What was England? F. J. H. Darton, author of several popular books on the countryside, had asked that question in the late twenties. For an answer he had looked to history. England's past, he insisted, "is a better guide to its future than a number of chaotic cries in the present." "When I am in doubt about any central life in this welter of England I go back to the country . . . there is an England you still cannot kill. It has all sorts of new things in it, but it is authentically the same always." Enraptured, Darton pictured the English village through past centuries, all immanent in the village of the present. "It is the place itself which has mastered Time, and made him stand still. Thus far, and no further."[155]

"I cannot think of [England]," admitted Edward Shanks, chief leader-writer for the *Evening Standard* (London), in 1938, "without remembering all her past . . . Every English landscape is full of ghosts." "So many things . . . have happened in England, that all we English are in a sense strangers who have to come back to our country and learn the traditions of our ancestral house. But, when we do, we are surrounded by ghosts that are friendly as well as heroic and polite."[156] It became a cliché to insist that, as Christopher Hussey put it, "though during the past hundred years we have been forced to live in cities, we are still a country nation."[157] That all this went far beyond an expression of a Tory "country" outlook is obvious from the bipartisan character of such outpourings. Progressives like E. M. Forster, as we have seen, also waxed lyrical about Old Rural England and the national character. In the thirties, Forster wrote two outdoor pageant plays on the theme of the long continuity of English life in the country, and its threatened destruction. In the first he exhorted the audience:

> Houses, houses, houses! You came from them and you must go back to them. Houses and bungalows, hotels, restaurants and flats, arterial roads, by-passes, petrol pumps and Pylons – are these going to be England? Are these man's final triumph? Or is there another England, green and eternal, which will outlast them?[158]

This insistence was repeated even in commercial advertising. Worthington brewers ran a series of advertisements in magazines between 1936 and 1939 entitled "This England . . ." Under pictures of rustic scenes, Worthington stressed the traditional, rural character of their ale, and characterized it as part of the English heritage.

> The men of the cities [as one of the first of these advertisements put it] yearn for the things of the country . . . old turf, quiet valleys and abiding peace. There do they find themselves nearer the heart of their race, nearer the source of honest kindly things . . . To them in their canyons of stone and steel comes Worthington brewed in the age-long English tradition, redolent of the countryside, friendly and shining clear as the English character itself.

In the country, the past was continually available. "How easy it is," another advertisement remarked,

> in this England to step aside into some small pool of history, to be lapped awhile in the healing peace of a rich, still-living past. For this people – more perhaps than any other – carries tradition and old usage into its daily life.[159]

Throughout this three-year series of advertisements, every cliché on the national character – characterizing it as rural, traditional, or slow but profound – was hauled out. Worthington sought to identify its beer with what the company's writers perceived as a national self-image of great appeal.

To go to the country was to recapture an England that could guide one through present uncertainties. The crisis of 1940 vividly impressed this, stimulating as it did national historical consciousness and a concern for agricultural life. H. V. Morton observed with satisfaction in 1942 that the war had brought back the rural, self-contained "atmosphere of the seventeenth century," restoring roots to the English populace. "We have without realizing it tapped wells of satisfaction which had begun to dry up."[160] Journalist C. Henry Warren lovingly described life in his East Anglian village during the early months of war – a story of community, the continuing importance of the squire, and closeness to the past and to the real things of nature. Warren insisted that "this is England, though 90% of her population dwells in the towns; for here the first condition of life is not gain but service – service of the land that feeds us and gathers us at last into its fecund darkness. Here men work creatively." As war intensified, Warren's village portrait took on the aspect of a dream, but "a dream that must be kept before our waking eyes when the horrors that sought to blind us are past. For it is from the ashes (if such must be) of the Larkfields of England that our phoenix strength shall rise."[161]

Whereas Nazi Germany was being portrayed as an industrial society run amok,[162] England was seen as just the opposite: humanely old-fashioned and essentially rural, the world of *Mrs. Miniver* and P. G. Wodehouse. Consequently, the war was seen as a test of the new world versus the old. Even a young intellectual like Rex Warner, enraged at the smug, slothful inequities of interwar England, recognized the clearly worse alternative of dynamic, machine-worshipping inhumanity. In his allegorical story, *The Aerodrome* (1941), England is a village, steeped in traditional inequities and inefficiencies, and Nazism is represented by a newly constructed air base. In the end, the Air Force and its "new order" are defeated. In the same year that Warner's novel was published, C. Henry Warren was similarly declaring that "England's might is still in her fields and villages, and though the whole weight of mechanized armies rolls over them to crush them, in the end they will triumph."[163] In this spirit, Arthur Bryant offered the hope in his weekly column in those grim days of 1941 that the enemy "will presently collapse. For a nation that has lived so long at so violent a pace, lacks the reserve of accumulated energy that can only come from calm and peaceful living."[164] Thus would frightful dynamism prove its own undoing, and English tranquillity be vindicated.

The pastoral dream remained very much alive in post-World War II England. It continued encapsulated within the ancient universities.

John Vaizey has recalled his Cambridge college of the late nineteen-forties and early fifties as an "idealized country village...with its squirearchy, its young squires, and its peasants...[an] idyll of rural England."[165] For a wider public, programs like *The Archers*, an immensely popular radio serial set in a village, expressed a similar, if more populist, vision.[166] In his last effort to examine the state of the nation, Anthony Sampson found that one of the things that had not changed was the "basic fascination of town-dwellers with the land."[167] Ronald Blythe was drawn to study "the national village cult" in his book, *Akenfield*. He noted that

> the townsman envies the villager his certainties and, in Britain, has always regarded urban life as just a temporary necessity. One day he will find a cottage on the green and "real values." To accommodate the almost religious intensity of the regard for rural life in this country, and to placate the sense of guilt which so many people feel about not living on a village pattern, the post-war new towns have attempted to incorporate both city and village – with, on the whole, disheartening results.[168]

"Country notes" continued to flourish in newspapers, *Country Life* and *The Field Bedside Books* sold well, and cottages and farmhouses suitable for modernization commanded ever higher prices. Angus Wilson, noting that "there can be few countries where private patrons have done less for modern architecture," traced it to the continuing prestige of tradition and landed-upper-class style of life, the "lure of the old country house for sale."[169] A literary reviewer observed in 1969 (as he could have anytime in this century) that "a foreigner reading some recent English verse might imagine that we spend most of our time behind the plough or tickling trout, and that the town is still alien to us."[170] As philosopher Stuart Hampshire noted in 1972, "The pastoral dream, the dream of bygone crafts, the dream of traditional quietness is evident in houses and gardens everywhere in Britain."[171] The village in particular continued to serve as a focus for middle-class English dreams. "There is some corner in the English mind," David White reflected in 1974, "that is forever Ambridge; that half-real radio village." He went on to note that "rightly or wrongly, the village represents an ideal living state. Maybe also a resting place, an Elysium. An important feature of Churchill's funeral was the progress of his body from the city of London to the country churchyard at Bladon."[172] That same year – in fact, during the week of the most bitter postwar general election – one could find the *Daily Telegraph Magazine* featuring a cover story entitled "The English Village: The Perfect Microcosm?" "As a system of living," the article declared, "it may be unsurpassed."[173] Martin Green sympathetically observed not long ago that for many years villages have been in England "not agricultural communities so much as places of retirement," where "a middle-class idyll" can be lived.[174]

In the late sixties Paul Jennings, a leading journalist, described the "revival" of the village as a spiritual homecoming for the English people, a return from the Imperial and industrial consciousness of the nineteenth century. The contemporary village was shaped by the intermingling of traditional countrymen, commuters, and "refugees" spreading out from the cities. "What drives them," he noted approvingly, "is a racial memory of rural England which, however obscured, is revived by every weekend trip to the country." Here were Englishmen returning to the ancestral home. The village life they joined was, in Jennings's description, an oasis of tranquillity, a bulwark against the stresses of the modern world. "Villages are the fine flower of what can be produced by many generations being in one place, and there are still a lot of people living in villages who are tying things down and hope to be left quite a lot when the gale of change dies down a bit and we can hear ourselves speak."[175] More and more English people in this century have, as Martin Green put it in 1977, "chosen village values."[176]

"Village values" could be perceived as an alternative to the worship of efficiency, the domination by machinery, the materialism that seemed part and parcel of industrial society. Such a choice was presented directly by J. B. Priestley in a 1949 play, *Summer Day's Dream*, which summed up this middle- and professional-class outlook. Priestley presented an England a quarter century in the future, devastated by a nuclear war. Its remaining population had happily returned to a simple, slow-paced life of farming and crafts. World power had been divided between America and Russia, who vied with each other for material advance. The action of the play revolves around the visit of an American and a Russian to this English backwater. Although they are on a mission to set up international factories for synthetic products, they fall under the spell of the village's strangely satisfying life and, though they cannot stay, abandon their plans to modernize it.[177] "We return," Margaret Drabble noted critically in 1973, "to the Jane Austen view that people who live in the country are good and those who live in the town are bad: that manufacturers are bad: that homely simplicity is better than expansion."[178] It is questionable, though, whether most of the English middle and upper classes had ever abandoned that view. One of the most striking features of modern British cultural history has been the resilience, the staying power of this view of the nation and of the good society.

In this way, the English countryside became a social and cultural force. The abundance of historical associations and natural beauty with which the English countryside had been endowed by previous centuries was not an unmixed blessing for the nation. Like the ex-istence of a vast overseas empire, it encouraged English opinion to retreat into a less demanding world. Like the fixed industrial capital created by early economic success, the impressive cultural capital embodied in the scenery and buildings of the country helped to commit Britain to its past and to an essentially antique self-image.

5

The wrong path?

England certainly saw in recent centuries a progress in the sense of a process . . . it was imperial in a mercantile manner; it seems now to be ending in [a] paradise of plutocrats . . . But anyone attempting to show that this process affecting England actually was England, has to face and answer [the] very arresting fact . . . that every great Englishman with the gift of expression whom the world recognizes as specially English, and as speaking for many Englishmen, was either in unconscious contradiction to that trend or (more often) in furious revolt against it.
  —G. K. Chesterton

By now it should seem clear to the reader that the vision of a tranquilly rustic and traditional national way of life permeated English life, and that any understanding of British economic development must take account of that fact. Nonetheless, the other facts could not be denied; the vision was not secure. Industrialism had of course been born in England; there was no wishing that fact away. But the legitimacy of that birth could be denied: Industrialism and the industrial spirit could be seen as not *truly* English, and, indeed, as a profound menace to the survival of "Englishness." A cultural polarity gradually emerged between Englishness, identified with the pastoral vision (the "green and pleasant land"), and industrialism (the "dark satanic mills"). The vision was felt to be precarious, being eroded bit by bit by the advance of industry. The power of the Machine was invading and blighting the Shire.

Industrialization reappraised
In the middle years of the nineteenth century, Samuel Smiles could portray the industrial and agricultural revolutions as the greatest achievements of English history, a point of view that would gradually become eccentric:

England was nothing, compared with continental nations [he declared], until she had become commercial . . . until about the middle of the last century, when a number of ingenious and inventive men, without apparent relation to each other, arose in various parts of the kingdom, and succeeded in giving an immense impulse to all the branches of the national industry; the result of which has been a harvest of wealth and prosperity.[1]

By the later nineteenth century, such a view no longer evoked the enthusiasm it once had. The new industrial system was looking less and less morally or spiritually supportable. As Bernard Shaw observed in 1912, the later Dickens was showing newly sensitive readers that "it is not our disorder (as the Victorians thought) but our order that is horrible."[2]

The era of the industrial revolution, which had established the order of Victorian England, was ripe for reevaluation. Disenchantment with industrialism encouraged historical reinterpretation of the origins of the machine age. Beginning in the eighteen-eighties, both scholarly and popular historical accounts of the industrial and agricultural revolutions were intertwined with the recasting of social values. This historical writing was not only hostile to unregulated capitalism, but also questioned the value of technological advance, and the pursuit of economic growth itself. Through this writing there was fixed upon the English mind a strikingly negative image of what was, in the long perspective, perhaps the most decisive contribution of England to the history of the human race.

The reevaluation was begun by Arnold Toynbee, an Oxford don and a disciple of Ruskin. Toynbee saw the previous hundred years as blighted by a false philosophy of life that centered on the set of "intellectual superstitions" known as "Political Economy." It was a philosophy that subordinated all considerations to the overriding goal of increased material production. Increased production had been necessary: The mass poverty of Old England could form no basis for a good society. Now, however, he argued, it was time to turn from obsession with production to concentration on distribution and, even more crucial, the quality of life. At the Bradford Mechanics' Institute in 1880 he pointed out:

> It is not merely a question of the distribution of wealth, it is a question of the right use of wealth . . . High wages are not an end in themselves. No one wants high wages in order that working men may indulge in mere sensual gratification. We want higher wages in order that an improved material condition, with less of anxiety and less uncertainty as to the future, may enable the working man to enter on a purer and more worthy life . . . we desire [high wages] for the workman just in order that he may be delivered from that engrossing care for every shilling and every penny which engenders a base materialism.[3]

On another occasion Toynbee took pains to show the "utter separat[ion]" of English radical socialists from continental socialists because of "our abhorrence and detestation of their materialistic ideal."[4]

At the back of his account lay the question, What went wrong? Toynbee's picture of the age of the industrial revolution was somber: It was "a period as disastrous and as terrible as any through which a nation ever passed." Why? Because it unleashed the impulse of greed. The result was that

> side by side with a great increase of wealth was seen an enormous increase of pauperism; and production on a vast scale, the result of free competition, led to a rapid alienation of classes and to the degradation of a large body of producers.

Some benefited; more suffered. Working people frequently endured a fall in real wages, but even more commonly were subjected to an involuntary uprooting from the land, a worsening in the conditions of labor under the factory system, and the insecurity of "those sudden fluctuations of trade, which, ever since production has been on a large scale, have exposed them to recurrent periods of bitter distress." The effects of industrialization on the inner life especially were "terrible." "Cash-nexus," in Carlyle's phrase, replaced "the old warm attachments." The history of the industrial revolution proved to Toynbee that "free competition may produce wealth without producing well-being."[5] As a radical, he recognized this experience to be a step, perhaps necessary, on the path toward a freer and more democratic society. Yet he could only lament the price paid, and condemn this period of unparalleled economic growth as a shameful episode.

After Toynbee, the industrial revolution was seen as the spread, over a green and pleasant land, of dark satanic mills that ground down their inmates – an image sharpened by the contemporary growth of industrial discontent and social criticism. The agricultural revolution was similarly seen as the spread of enclosures, purported to have ruptured the bonds between classes, destroyed village community, and erased what the Tudor era had left of peasant proprietorship, forcing much of the rural population off the land and into the new mills. A Liberal MP, Charles Milnes Gaskell, in an essay that helped to revive interest in that champion of Old England, William Cobbett, wondered if Cobbett had not been right after all in his opposition to the two revolutions:

> Sixty years of struggle and aspirations [since Cobbett] have brought us nearer to what we conceive to be the light. Our hope is that it is no *ignis fatuus*, no dancing meteor of the marshes that we follow ... In spite of all the luxuries of our lives we have chill prospects on every side to tell us how little our vaunted improvements are worth, and how thin the veneer is of civilization.[6]

Tories also took up Toynbee's jaundiced view of industrialization, seeing in it a joint decline in the quality of life and in national character. One of Toynbee's students, the Imperialist Alfred Milner, came to see the industrial revolution as having shattered the old social system, leaving a legacy of "chaos." Milner regretted its effects upon the mass of ordinary Englishmen, who were pushed off the land and into blighted factory towns, where they lost their physical strength and moral values. He came to advocate vigorous state intervention to remedy the national degeneration that unguided industrialism had brought.[7]

Milner's close friend, Rudyard Kipling, collaborated with the historian C. R. L. Fletcher in 1911 on a history of England for school use that reflected the new Establishment's disdain for the industrial revolution. The account gave only brief mention of industrialization, for its story was the traditional one of the political triumphs of England, domestic and foreign. When they did touch upon the industrial revolution, it was to complain – first, that it had depopulated the countryside, where the national character had been formed and nourished; and second, that by undermining agriculture it had placed the nation's security in the hands of foreign farmers and fleets.[8] An "artificial" urban existence, resting precariously on open sea lanes – such was the legacy of industrialization pictured by prominent Tories in these years, adding to the indictment drawn up by Toynbee.

The transformation of national life was seen in a still darker light by a very widely read Edwardian who fused conservatism and radicalism, G. K. Chesterton. In *A Short History of England*, "probably the most generally read of all his books,"[9] he presented a story of national decline that began with the Reformation (which ushered in oligarchic capitalism). Modernizing oligarchs performed the twin "experiments" of agricultural and industrial revolution upon a helpless populace, driving them from their land and into the mills. The nadir of national life was reached, in this account, in the nineteenth century, the heyday of the improving landlord and the driving manufacturer.[10] Chesterton had earlier sketched out the story:

> The ordinary Englishman [was] duped out of his old possessions, such as they were, and always in the name of progress . . . They took away his maypole and his original rural life and promised him instead the Golden Age of Peace and Commerce inaugurated at the Crystal Palace . . . [The rich] forced [the poor] into factories and the modern wage-slavery, assuring them all the time that this was the only way to wealth and civilization.[11]

Chesterton's friend Hilaire Belloc marked out "three great stages in the worsening of our social standard": first, the acquisition of the land by a few; then, the growth of manufacturing capitalism "as a consequence of this and based upon it"; and lastly, "abstracted cosmopolitan finance directed by a handful." Each stage was more evil than the last: "The first was evil, but it remained national and human. It gave us the squires and the impoverished but still healthy and normal English peasant." The second had less to balance its evil; the third nothing. Together, they constituted "three great steps downwards into the abyss."[12] However little headway they made for their remedy of peasant proprietorship, Chesterton and Belloc (far more popular than professional historians) helped cast the economic innovations in England from the Tudors to the coming of factories and railways in a disreputable light.

The most important successor to Toynbee was the politically radical husband-and-wife team of historians, J. L. and Barbara Hammond. The Hammonds' books, though thoroughly professional history, became best-sellers. *The Village Labourer* (1911) was reprinted eleven times into the nineteen-sixties. *The Town Labourer* (1917) had a similar record. Other volumes also sold remarkably well for serious history.[13] The Hammonds did more than anyone else to form the public image of the era of the industrial revolution. Their imprint can be found in textbooks, popular essays, political speeches and writings, and, later, radio talks, and still later, television productions. What Toynbee had initiated, the Hammonds brought to completion – a new, and dark, picture of the age of the industrial revolution.

The Hammonds indicted the nineteenth century for – along with increasing inequality – making a fetish of production, reverencing wealth as a standard of success, and refusing to brake the reckless pace of change. Wealth in itself, individual or national, meant little to them. Like Toynbee (and like the foremost radical historian of the early twentieth century, R. H. Tawney), they had been educated at Oxford, and for cultural ideals they looked to classical Greece and Rome: preindustrial societies, materially poor and technologically unprogressive. They were deeply attracted by the simple way of life of the peasant farmers on the Isle of Axholme (whose fields had escaped enclosure): "The people," they pointed out, "are very poor respecting money, but very happy respecting their mode of existence."[14] "A poor man," they later stressed, "under one system of life, may be happier than a man who is less poor under another."[15]

A system that made material production the focus of life was to them inherently subversive of both human happiness and civilization in the broadest sense. The Hammonds began *The Town Labourer* with Macaulay's exclamation on man's new "dominion over matter," only to turn it on its head. The liberator had become a new enslaver: "The Industrial Revolution," they declared, "had delivered society from its primitive dependence on the forces of nature, but in return it had taken society prisoner." The "vicious monomania" of maximum production degraded all aspects of life; the new industrial town, for instance, "was not a home where man could find beauty, happiness, leisure, learning, religion, the influences that civilize outlook and habit, but a bare and desolate place, without color, air or laughter, where man, woman and child worked, ate and slept." England during the industrial revolution "had turned aside from making a society in order to make a system of production."[16] Indeed, the provisional title of their later volume, *The Rise of Modern Industry*, was *The Spell of Production*.[17]

Production, through the capitalist system, meant profit, and profit had become the touchstone of activity – in that period, tragically, "everything was sacrificed to profit." Wealth was worshipped "as the only standard of success," and the result was a Dickensian nightmare:

> Thus England [the Hammonds charged] asked for profits and received profits. Everything turned to profit. The towns had their profitable dirt, their profitable smoke, their profitable slums, their profitable disorder, their profitable ignorance, their profitable despair. The curse of Midas was on this society: on its corporate life, on its common mind, on the decisive and impatient step it had taken from the peasant to the industrial age.[18]

The novel possibilities of production and profit had "swept . . . the English people . . . off its balance." The "reckless" and "impatient" economic leap was both a cause and a consequence of social disorganization; England, they believed, would have been far better off if "industrial power had advanced with slower stride." The industrial revolution, they concluded, brought "confusion that man is still seeking to compose, that he is still seeking to subdue to noble purposes."[19]

The Hammonds' work merged with other currents of thought – in literature, and in social and political writing – to foster in the twentieth century both the middle-class feelings of "guilt" for the social evils of industrial capitalism cited in 1949 by Roy Lewis and Angus Maude,[20] and nostalgia for a simpler, apparently more satisfying time. We have only to look at the two best-selling histories of England in the nineteen-forties, neither politically radical, to witness the workings of these feelings of guilt and nostalgia. *English Saga, 1840-1940*, by Arthur Bryant, a historian and Conservative publicist, was a Book Society choice that went through fifteen editions between late 1940 and 1948, and twenty editions by 1967; it sold over a quarter million copies. It was described by Sir John Squire as "a sketch of the industrial revolution and its diseases."[21] It traced England's current plight to its adoption in the early nineteenth century of the goal of untrammeled growth. The result was a nation dependent on imports of food, crowded and vulnerable to air attack, divided by class and by the scramble for profit, and worst of all, nearly having "lost its soul" and sense of purpose. Preindustrial England shone through Bryant's book as a secure, spiritually satisfying community.

Even more popular and influential was G. M. Trevelyan's *English Social History* (published in the United States in 1942, and in Britain in 1944), which sold 400,000 copies by 1960.[22] This work represented the culmination of Trevelyan's thinking about English history over four decades, and its themes were prefigured in his previous work. His characterization of the era of the industrial revolution repeated in most essentials the views of the Hammonds: The age had witnessed a breakup of the village community, and loss of a more natural way of life and of rural beauty, for which money alone could not compensate. *English Social History* was an elegy to a vanished rural nation. J. H. Plumb has noted in Trevelyan's work "a deep regret for a world that is fading – the world of manor houses, country pursuits, the rule of liberal and tolerant gentlemen – these things, Trevelyan knew, were being destroyed by the accelerating Industrial Revolution."[23]

Trevelyan saw the census of 1851 as "ominous" in its finding that half the population was urban: "John Bull was ceasing to be a countryman, and a farmer; when once he was wholly urbanized or suburbanized, would he any longer be John Bull, except in the cartoons of *Punch*?" By the twentieth century he found the process more or less complete: "The modern Englishman [he warned in 1931] is fed and clothed better than his ancestor, but his spiritual side, in all that connects him with the beauty of the world, is utterly starved as no people have ever before been starved in the history of the world."

"Agriculture," Trevelyan argued in *English Social History*, "is not merely one industry among many, but is a way of life, unique and irreplaceable in its human and spiritual values." The city life that had come in its place was "a deadening cage for the human spirit ...the stage is set for the gradual standardization of human personality."[24] The great achievements of English history celebrated in Trevelyan's work were fundamentally those of an older England, and were chiefly spiritual and political, not economic. Through his account of modern times ran a sad sense of spiritual loss, coupled with a hopeless nostalgia. Trevelyan had remarked to his brother as early as 1926, "I don't understand the age we live in, and what I do understand I don't like." By 1939, while writing *English Social History*, he could watch the coming of war with detachment: "The 'world' that is threatened," he wrote his brother, "is not my world, which died years ago. I am a mere survivor."[25] Yet this survivor of the eighteenth century produced the best-selling account of English history of his time.

In the aftermath of the Hammonds, Bryant, and Trevelyan, it became common for writers to look back, as did Jacquetta and Christopher Hawkes – searching in 1947 for "the character of England" – to "the eighteenth century, that lovely, poised moment ...the noise and fume of industry still very much in the background, and England still deeply and splendidly rural." What happened then? "Faster and faster, relentlessly...blindly...the Industrial Revolution put an end to the eighteenth century rural order...workers massed like swarming bees round those areas where iron and coal and other minerals lay beneath the surface...ending with ourselves lost in conurbations."[26]

The American specter

The industrial revolution was thus not only revalued, but also redefined as a characteristically un-English event. Industrial values – the worship of machinery, efficiency, and material wealth – had never conquered (many insisted) the inner sanctum of the English character. "Most of us English," J. B. Priestley approvingly noted (summing up a long tradition),

> still cherish an instinctive feeling that men come first and that machines should come a long way afterwards. It is true we were the first machine people, partly because we enjoy inventing machines – and still do – but the idea of serving machines did some injury to the English psyche. Yes of course the wages, the hours, the conditions were terrible, but there was something else, an instinctive resentment, that completed the black bitterness. *And it is with us yet.*[27]

If industrialism were not natural to the English spirit, to whose was it? In the second half of the nineteenth century, an answer seemed to emerge. English writers began to identify the way of life associated with industrialism with the new American nation. Just those characteristics anxiously perceived in the rising new element in English society – the northern industrial middle class – were in this way projected across the Atlantic, where they could be more safely disparaged and repulsed. J. S. Mill had asked in 1840 whether "the American people as a whole, both in their good qualities and in their defects, resembled anything so much as an exaggeration of our own middle class."[28] Matthew Arnold agreed, but saw little beyond the defects, complaining in 1865 that "to be too much with the Americans is like living with somebody who has all one's own bad habits and tendencies." America, he observed some years later, was "just ourselves, with the Barbarians [aristocracy] quite left out, and the Populace nearly" – in other words, a giant, unrestrained replica of the nineteenth-century English middle class.[29] Disparagement of the "American way of life" – seen as the idolizing of technology and wealth – could, from this standpoint, help exorcise these spirits from English culture.

Henceforth, critics of the industrial spirit from various points on the political spectrum homed in on the United States as a warning. Arnold pronounced the country's soil unfriendly to the growth of culture as a result of its obsession with money making.[30] William Morris pictured the place in *News from Nowhere* as a man-made waste-land, "a stinking dust-heap."[31] Even Herbert Spencer, the apostle of progress (but also a professional man), felt the psychic costs of American devotion to material advance, and argued thus with Andrew Carnegie:

> Absorbed by his activities, and spurred on by his unrestricted ambitions, the American is . . . a less happy being than the inhabitant of a country where the possibilities of success are very much smaller . . . I believe on the whole that [the latter] gets more pleasure out of life than the successful American and that his children inherit greater capacities for enjoyment. Great as may be hereafter the advantages of the enormous progress America makes, I hold that the existing generations of Americans, and those to come for a long time hence, are and will be essentially sacrificed.[32]

By the turn of the century, such sentiments had become clichés of educated opinion. An Arnoldian Liberal of the next generation, G. Lowes Dickinson, in the United States in 1901 on a lecture tour, wrote (one senses almost automatically) to C. R. Ashbee, a leader of the Arts and Crafts Movement:

> The two things rubbed into me in this country are (1) that the future of the world lies with America, (2) that radically and essentially America is a barbarous country . . . It is a country without leisure, manners, morals, beauty or religion – a country whose ideal is mere activity, without any reference to the quality of it; a country which holds competition and strife to be the only life worth living.[33]

The widely read left-wing intellectual C. E. M. Joad (1891-1953) (unrestrained by the fact that he had never been to America) summed up this tradition of cultural criticism in 1926 in his popular book, *The Babbitt Warren*, which pictured a machine-ridden, work-and-money-mad land. Two years later, for an American audience, he returned to the theme. Explaining why "the English dislike America," he focused on "the American's worship of size, speed, mechanism, and money." America offered the least resistance to the dehumanizing tendencies of modernity; it had sold its soul to industrialism. This transaction menaced Europe as well because, however misconceived as a path to human satisfaction and civilization, it did bring power. America was the future, he pessimistically concluded, and would eventually swamp European civilization in a tide of materialism.[34]

The snares of economic growth

Even English economists, though popularly seen as "materialists," shared to a surprising degree the general cultural climate of distrust of material progress. Predominantly educated, like leading historians, at Oxford and Cambridge, economists in later-nineteenth- and twentieth-century England tended to take a lofty, "civilized" view of the actual world of business and industry, maintaining a certain distance from its contaminations, or hoping to educate its participants to a wider conception of life.[35] A recurrent theme in the main tradition of British economic thought, originating with Mill, has been (as Donald Winch had noted) a "disdain for personal ostentation and riches, which expressed itself in the low priority, or purely instrumental value, attached to the pursuit of material gain."[36]

The greatest economist of the later-Victorian era, Alfred Marshall (1842-1924), followed Mill in his dissatisfaction with the values of industrial capitalism. Keynes later observed of Marshall that "it was only through Ethics that he first reached Economics." Marshall hoped to encourage the spread of a higher motive – what he called "economic chivalry," in a phrase reminiscent of Ruskin – among the nation's business elite. Money making would then become incidental to the satisfaction gained from performing difficult tasks well.[37] "Marshall," his student F. Y. Edgeworth recalled with admiration, "valued improvement in physical surroundings chiefly as rendering it possible for the many to lead a noble life." He envisaged the gradual development of a social order that would "greatly surpass the present" in, among other things, "the subordination of material possessions to human well-being." Marshall's dedication to elevating economic motives and subordinating them to the enhancement of the quality of life (in which he was unlike his classical predecessors) came out clearly in a remark he made near the end of his life: "If I had to live my life over again [he confessed] I should have devoted it to psychology. Economics has too little to do with ideals. If I said much about them I should not be read by business men."[38] His work, building upon Mill, marked a decisive shift in professional attention from issues of accumulation and production to those of distribution and consumption.

With Marshall, economists began to focus on questions of actual human wants and satisfactions. This technical reorientation followed naturally from his conviction that England had grown sufficiently "in wealth, health, in education and in morality" to be able to afford policies that placed restraints on enterprise. It was no longer necessary for the nation "to subordinate almost every other consideration to the need of increasing the total produce of industry." It was possible to make a gradual transition toward a society "in which common good overrules individual caprice."[39]

After Marshall, J. A. Hobson, (1858-1940), influential outside if not inside the profession, sought to turn economics into an attack upon "economism" – the equation of material affluence with social well-being.[40] Hobson followed Ruskin (about whom he had written an admiring book) in arguing that "the true 'value' of a thing is neither the price paid for it, nor the amount of present satisfaction it yields to the consumer, but the intrinsic service it is capable of yielding by its right use." Those goods that have a capacity for "satisfying wholesome human wants" are " 'wealth'," whereas those that "pander to some base or injurious desire of man" are not wealth, but " 'illth', availing as they do, not for life but for death."[41] Warnings of relative economic decline seemed to him beside the point: The truly pressing question lay elsewhere. "That Britain is no longer the workshop of the world," Hobson answered the Edwardian industrial Cassandras, "is true, and it would be folly to expect it to be so . . . the world exists for some other purpose than the exploitation of foreign nations by British factory-owners and landlords employing armies of people in monotonous occupations."[42]

The Millite tradition of hostility to the "acquisitive society," and disdain for businessmen, continued strong within twentieth-century British economics. Even John Maynard Keynes, who made large profits for himself and for King's College in the stock market, was steeped in it. From his Cambridge and Bloomsbury background, he maintained a fastidious distaste for acquisitiveness. Keynes has been credited with rescuing capitalism – yet, as his biographer points out, he "was not a great friend of the profit motive; he found something unsatisfactory in the quest for gain as such, and came to hope that an economic system might be evolved in which it was curtailed."[43] The side of Communism that appealed to him in the twenties was not its claim to superior efficiency, which he disparaged, but its criticism of "the love of money," which he saw as *the* "moral problem of our age." Keynes's efforts at making capitalism work more effectively had as an ultimate aim, paradoxically, the supersession of capitalist values by higher and more satisfying ones. As he saw it, the real benefit of the almost inevitable advance of abundance was that it would dethrone wealth and material possession as dominating ends of life. Emerging from the "tunnel of economic necessity, we shall be able to afford to dare to assess the money-motive at its true value. The love of money as a possession . . . will be recognized for what it is, a somewhat disgusting morbidity, one of those semi-criminal, semi-pathological propensities which one hands over with a shudder to the specialists in mental disease."[44]

In the tradition of Mill, he held a vision of a future stable society with hardly any need for profit or investment. With proper management, he wrote, "we should attain the conditions of a quasi-stationary community where change and progress would result only from changes in technique, taste, population and institutions."[45] Keynes's writings, one revisionist economist argued in 1976, "set the economically literate in Britain on a course where hard work, efficient industrial organization and the employment of a high fraction of the labor force on productive and profitable work were considered to be of only secondary importance."[46]

To the Canadian-born economist Harry Johnson, the social values underlying Keynes's approach to economic questions were typical of the British academic milieu, particularly that of Oxford and Cambridge. Centered around the colleges, which remained in spirit "feudal institutions," this way of life, he argued, encouraged a paternal and static attitude toward the working class. The main social obligation of the authorities (like the college fellows vis-à-vis college servants) tended to be seen as that of guaranteeing employment. The "social problem" was fundamentally that of providing security for the masses. In a similar way, the academic environment shaped the contempt Keynes and other British economists felt for businessmen:

> It would be natural for College Fellows who had trained the business executive class, usually at the lower end of the spectrum of academic capacity and performance, to regard businessmen as a class as rather inferior to College Fellows. These were people for whom some reputable non-academic non-governmental employment should be found, but who should not be rewarded on an inordinate scale for success in their second-rate activities. It would also be natural for such academics to believe that the messes into which the practical world of business and politics got itself resulted from the defect of inferior intelligence, or, alternatively, the lack of a system of corporate decision-taking comparable to that of a College Fellowship body and its Council.[47]

Despite their wide and often contentious differences, insiders like Marshall and Keynes, as well as outsiders like Hobson and R. H. Tawney,[48] were all influenced by the tradition, descending from Mill, of attaching a low priority to the increase of production and the pursuit of material gain. Another economist of Keynes's generation was even more openly detached: Roy Glenday, holding – of all positions – that of economic adviser to the Federation of British Industries in the nineteen-thirties and forties, had a jaundiced view of modern "materialism." Indeed, rather surprisingly for an adviser of industrialists, Glenday disapproved of industrialism's effects upon the national character. He warned in 1934 of the appearance of "a new type – men and women in whom perhaps the self-consciousness of town life or close contact with the machine has quenched all sense of human intimacy with nature; and who seem content to be dazzled by the never-ending variety of the stream of products which the modern machine is able to pour out in such prodigal profusion."

Glenday, like Keynes and Tawney, looked forward to a more tranquil future:

> We are in a world whose rate of movement is destined to slow down rapidly . . . this, to a people accustomed to flashing along the road of so-called progress at vertiginous speed, will for a time seem like calamity. But it will not be viewed in that light for long. When he has properly realised that speeding is not synonymous with living, man will adapt himself to the new life.[49]

When the "steady state" that Glenday and others saw arriving in the thirties yielded instead to the postwar "affluent society," a number of British economists called upon this critical tradition. One Treasury official sought in 1960 to point out the dangers of the new Western interest in growth. Economic advance, he warned, was disruptive:

> The ultimate fruits of civilization are slow growths that need a stable environment . . . the economic motive running loose in circumstances that permit or compel violent economic change must wreck this environment . . . Name a society whose economic advance delights its statisticians and you name one in which the good qualities of its earlier life are decaying and in which no new civilization has emerged. That good will come from this evil is a possibility, but the economist cannot honestly pretend to know that it is more.[50]

The following year E. F. Schumacher, chief adviser to the National Coal Board, began his criticisms of economic growth that culminated in his best-selling *Small Is Beautiful* (1973). In a lecture in India (to whose spiritual values he was attracted), Schumacher argued "that economic progress is healthy only up to a point; that the complication of life is permissible only up to a point; that the pursuit of efficiency of production is good only up to a point."[51]

At the same time, E. J. Mishan, at the London School of Economics, sounded the first trumpet of his onslaught against economic growth in a technical essay examining the limitations of his specialty, welfare economics:

> the things on which happiness ultimately depends [he argued], friendship, faith, the perception of beauty and so on, are outside its range . . . Thus, the triumphant achievements of modern technology, ever-swifter travel, round-the-clock synthetic entertainment, the annual cornucopia of slick and glossy gadgets, which rest perforce on the cult of efficiency, the single-minded pursuit of advancement, the craving for material success, may be exacting a fearful toll in terms of human happiness. But the formal elegance of welfare economics will never reveal it.[52]

Mishan went on in the sixties to launch a full-scale critique of what the Treasury official had anxiously termed "the juggernaut progress of Aggregate Industrial Output."[53] In *The Costs of Economic Growth* (1967), Mishan joined the language of welfare economics and the language of the succession of English moralists from Arnold and Ruskin onward. Post-World War II "growthmania," he argued, had eroded the traditional curbs upon materialism that were essential to human happiness. It had inflamed the tendency of capitalism to foster dissatisfaction and greed, legitimized the efforts of the advertising industry to create ever more factitious needs, corrupted the populace by inculcating the principle that "enough does not suffice," and subordinated all the ways of pleasant and ultimately satisfying living to the demands of incessantly multiplying traffic and industry. In a more popular verison of his book, published two years later, he waxed even more passionate:

> Generations have passed, and, like the woods and hedges that sheltered it, the rich local life centered on township, parish and village, has been uprooted and blown away by the winds of change. Today no refuge remains from the desperate universal clamour for more efficiency, more excitement, and more novelty that goads us furiously onward, competing, accumulating, innovating – and inevitably destroying. Every step forward in technological progress . . . effectively transfers our dependence upon other human beings to dependence upon machines and, therefore, unavoidably constricts yet further the direct flow of understanding, the sympathy between people. Thus in the unending pursuit of progress men are driven even further apart and come to depend instead, for all their services and experiences, directly upon the creations of technology.[54]

Mishan thus called up the image of an Old Rural English way of life – humane, tranquil, and satisfying – disintegrating under the hammer blows of rapid technological and commercial change. Economic growth seemed to carry with it menacing snares that threatened the deepest values of the nation. It was a gift horse that was turning out to be of Trojan manufacture, to be examined warily rather than embraced. In this suspicion and resistance, Mishan was summing up a century-long English tradition in regard to industrialism and economic growth.

PART III

Toward behavior

Introduction

Ideas, we know, have consequences. When the vision of England as a green and pleasant land invaded by a somewhat alien industrialism was taken up by the children of Victorian industrialists, it could not help but affect the world of action. Politics and business in the twentieth century bore the imprint of a divided bourgeois consciousness. The nation that had been the mother of the industrial revolution was now uneasy with its offspring. The class that had reared industrialism almost seemed to wish to deny paternity. The result was two paradoxes, one in the world of politics and one in the realm of business.

The political history of Britain over the past century has usually been seen – in contrast with that of continental Europe – as one of a moderation deriving from what Adam Ulam has called the "saturation with industrial values" of all classes.[1] According to this interpretation, all major political parties wholeheartedly accepted the framework of industrial society, clashing only over the details of its arrangements. No truly fundamental criticisms of this society were allowed into the political arena. Both Conservatives and Labour were moving toward "technocratic" rather than ideological stances.

An industrialist, or technocratic, political consensus has been seen as having established itself by the nineteen-twenties, under the premiership of Andrew Bonar Law, Stanley Baldwin, and Ramsay Macdonald. All of these leaders, it has been argued, believed that industrial advance would largely solve existing social problems. The first two were themselves businessmen. For Macdonald, Bernard Barker has argued, social reform depended upon not class struggle, but "efficiency, planning, organization, science; upon the understanding of economic change and the conscious pursuit of greater wealth."[2]

Political moderation, yes; but the conscious and committed pursuit of economic growth? That is not so evident in twentieth-century British politics. It is not evident because politics was also saturated with another set of values that worked to counter industrial values. Gentry values and the gentry myth of England domesticated industrialism in political thought and action as they did in the wider culture, separating industrial capitalism's "acceptable" face from its "unacceptable" one. The consequences were, on the one hand, the political ineffectiveness of pure antiindustrialism (in contrast with Germany, for instance), and on the other, the absence (until recent years) of commitment by political leaders to the wholehearted pursuit of economic expansion. Politics reflected the general ambivalence about industrial society, and helped in practice to dampen rather than stimulate industrial development.

In business, too, industrial and antiindustrial values were joined. Britain had the world's oldest class of industrialists, who yet were held in lower esteem, and who themselves displayed less self-confidence and class pride, than was the case for most of their foreign imitators. Business itself, like politics, was affected by the cast of general middle- and upper-class culture. Businessmen increasingly shunned the role of industrial entrepreneur for the more socially rewarding role of gentleman (landed, if possible). The upshot was a dampening of industrial energies, the most striking single consequence of the gentrification of the English middle class. In the climate and activities of twentieth-century British government and business, we can see the picture of a nation, and an elite, at war with itself.

6

Images and politics

The history of every people ought to be written with less regard to the events of which their government was the agent, than to the disposition of which it was the sign.
— John Ruskin, *The Stones of Venice* (1853)

Conservatives: Toryism versus industrial capitalism

Many years ago, G. M. Young noted a paradox of the Victorian era. "In a money-making age," he observed, "opinion was, on the whole, more deferential to birth than to money," and "in a mobile and progressive society, most regard was had to the element which represented immobility, tradition, and the past."[1] This deference (and the tension underlying it) shaped the character of English Conservatism. The reconstruction of Conservatism in the Victorian and Edwardian periods was a two-way process. The Tory party shifted its base from the land to property in all its forms, making room for the new middle classes. By 1918, in A. J. P. Taylor's phrase, the party had "caught up with the modern world."[2] Yet only in part. Many of the values and attitudes of Toryism lived on within the reconstituted party, alongside industrial and capitalistic values. The party continued to invoke the rustic spirit of the nation. Conservatism was enamored of rural England, as much an England of the mind as of reality. Conservatives imbued with the Southern Metaphor of the nation tended to look askance at a number of central characteristics of industrial capitalism – its ugliness (or at least untidiness), its "materialism," and its instability. Two historians of the party, T. F. Lindsay and Michael Harrington, have recently noted that "the idea of the free market, with its stress on the sovereignty of the individual consumer, was diametrically opposed to all that Toryism stood for. To the Tory it was obvious that economic forces should be made to accommodate themselves to the established pattern of social relationships."[3] Although Toryism retreated, and the Conservative party altered, the old values and beliefs were not buried, but merely put in the closet. The Conservative party, one scholar observed, "had to make peace with the middle class, yet

Toryism could not cease its protests against making a fetish of profit-making. Commercialism, materialism and profiteering all came under attack."[4] Again and again in the twentieth century, the old values would be brought out by speakers and writers; often, no doubt, only to give political maneuvering the guise of principle, or to provide a venerable covering for what otherwise might appear too nakedly a businessman's party. Yet even rhetoric and rationalization have their significance and influence. The choice of images to appeal to and identify with can tell much about the values of both actor and audience. In twentieth-century Conservative evocations of past standards, it has been observed, "one can see the continuing influence of the Tory tradition, no longer fighting a rearguard action against the emerging industrial society, but drawing on pre-industrial values to humanise, and perhaps obstruct, the process of industrialization."[5] Nigel Harris observed in his study of Conservative industrial policy that "just as Liberal businessmen had crossed to the Conservative party as external and internal challenges awoke increasing anxiety – had, as it were, 'joined the aristocracy' – so others also imbibed the aristocratic defense of a society that had passed."[6]

The cautious terms on which Conservatism accepted the industrial revolution were evident in the failure of Joseph Chamberlain (1836-1914) to capture control of the party on a platform of tariff reform in the first years of the twentieth century. Chamberlain offered an activist, urban, industrial version of Conservatism that promoted economic reform. He recognized before other leading politicians that England had entered a new and more difficult economic era. To prevent national decline, he called for making economic resurgence the central aim of politics. His call was rejected. One historian concluded:

> Chamberlain was demanding nothing less than that Edwardian board of directors should become captains of industry and emulate Abbot Samson of [Carlyle's] *Past and Present* . . . The sacrifices he was asking were far too great. He demanded, in effect, that they renounce the reassuring comforts of the central Liberal intellectual tradition of the nineteenth century, which, whether in terms of Mill or Cobden or Green or Morley or Spencer or Hobson or indeed socialist versions of it as with Morris, offered in one way or another an ultimate reconciliation of forces, involving less and less anxiety, ultimate harmony and repose, an end to strenuous conflict.[7]

Chamberlain's crusade was not only too "strenuous," but it also appeared too purely economic. Lord Robert Cecil disdainfully remarked about the Chamberlainites: "Their whole way of looking at politics . . . appears to me entirely sordid and materialistic, not yet corrupt, but on the high-road to corruption."[8] Landed Conservatism, represented by another Cecil, Prime Minister Arthur Balfour, repelled the challenge of Chamberlain and tariff reform. Following in the steps of his uncle, Lord Salisbury, Balfour led a now-bourgeois party with aristocratic hauteur. In 1891 he had characteristically described his successor as Irish chief secretary as "that *rara avis*, a successful manufacturer who is fit for something besides manufacturing."[9]

When the party leadership was passed to a manufacturer, it was to one of very different outlook and temperament from Chamberlain. Stanley Baldwin (1867-1947) was heir to a successful Worcestershire ironworks business, but he was nonetheless not attracted to industrial life. He continued the business out of "a sense of duty," but, having bought a country house with a small estate attached, he established himself in the public mind as "Farmer Stan" (though he left the mechanics of farming to tenants and his wife).[10] Baldwin returned again and again in his speeches to this self-image and to a corresponding image of the nation. "To me," this self-described "son of the soil" remarked in perhaps his most frequently quoted address, "England is the country and the country is England."[11]

Baldwin inherited from his mother, a modestly popular author of rustic melodrama and a close relation of Rudyard Kipling, a literary tradition that spoke more to him than the industrialism of his father. Baldwin felt himself a novelist manqué, and preferred the company of men of letters to that of men of business. His son described him as a "businessman who . . . wilts in the company of businessmen and cares nothing for the game of success."[12] After he turned to politics, his literary inclinations found their outlet in public speaking. As a "Minister for Public Opinion," a critical observer conceded in 1930, "he has hardly a rival among contemporary British politicians."[13] *On England*, a collection of his addresses, went through many editions, including paperback; his recommendation of Mary Webb's rustic novel, *Precious Bane*, turned it into an enormous best-seller; the *Times* concluded upon his retirement that "he interpreted the essential spirit of England."[14] Baldwin's message to the nation was, as he urged in a 1933 BBC talk, "Let us hold on to what we are." What *were* the English? Rural and reverent of tradition: "The country represents the eternal values and the eternal traditions from which we must never allow ourselves to be separated."[15]

The country with which Baldwin identified the nation was, as he described it in lyrical prose, a place virtually unaltered for centuries. What were the most typical "sounds and sights of England?"

> . . . the tinkle of the hammer on the anvil in the country smithy, the corncrake on a dewy morning, the sound of the scythe against the whetstone, and the sight of a plough team coming over the brow of a hill, the sight that has been seen in England since England was a

land, and may be seen in England long after the Empire has perished and every works in England has ceased to function, for centuries the one eternal sight of England . . . These are the things that make England.[16]

Baldwin was at pains to explain to his employees, remarked his friend J. C. C. Davidson, "that, although they were now working in a factory, they all stemmed from the land, which was really their spiritual home."[17] In difficult moments at Westminster, he claimed to draw refreshment from contemplating the persistence of the old country life, and to cherish the hope of eventual retirement to it. Of his beloved rural Worcestershire, he declared his confidence that

> whatever may happen to England, whatever defilements of her countryside may take place, whatever vast buildings may be completed, whatever disgusting noises may be emitted upon her roads, at any rate in that one corner of England the apple blossom will always blow in the spring and that there, whatsoever is lovely and of good report will be born and flourish to the world's end.[18]

Such realism tended to go together with a complex of other "Tory" attitudes. Maurice Cowling observed of Baldwin and his colleagues that "at a primitive level the Conservative leaders had many instincts in common with some aspects of Labour thinking. There was the same affectation of dislike for the millionaire press. There was the same distaste for the ostentation of wealth. There was the same concern with decency and virtue and a belief . . . that the rich had a duty to be kind to the poor."[19]

Baldwin in particular was guided by a gentry ideal of the purpose of politics. In his speeches, Paul Addison noted, he "identified the chief problem of statesmanship at home not as the raising of living standards or the cure of mass unemployment, but as the preservation of parliament and the British character from extremism."[20] He dealt with the pressing issue of industrial relations – very successfully, in the short run at least – by conceding much of the socialists' criticisms of the inhuman tendencies of modern industry, and by setting forth a lovingly colored picture of his father's slow-moving, patriarchical factory as an alternative ideal. Despite his reputation as a progressive, which stemmed from his sympathies with the grievances of Labour, "in a real sense," Robert Rhodes James perceived, "Baldwin's views were reactionary, in that he constantly harked back to times of gentler industrial and human relations."[21] Asking his followers in the House of Commons to reject a private member's bill to restrict trade union subsidy of the Labour party, he evoked the spirit of his old family firm:

> It was a place where I knew, and had known from childhood, every man on the ground; a place where I was able to talk with the men not only about the troubles in the works, but troubles at home and their

> wives. It was a place where the fathers and grandfathers of the men then working there had worked, and where their sons went automatically into the business. It was also a place where nobody ever "got the sack".[22]

Baldwin was profoundly out of sympathy with the tendency of modern industry to leave behind the comfortable world of his childhood. In this tendency he found the sources of social conflict. He saw modern industry in 1939 as characterized by "alternating periods of feverish activity followed by the throwing-out of armies of workmen into unemployment and despair." The two great economic priorities were reestablishing a humane pace of work and reinstituting a measure of security; the pursuit of efficiency was not only less important, but also could work against these needs. Since the Great War, he reflected, the industrial system

> has been moving and changing more quickly than man can adapt himself to the demands of the machine. Speed and monotony are two aspects of the modern workman's life which demand investigation, not only by employers and employed, but by scientific psychologists, for they are consciously or unconsciously at the bottom of much of the unrest we see around us.

He felt himself to be a representative from "those far-off days before acceleration was regarded as a manifestation of civilization."[23]

For industrial ideals, Baldwin looked to the past. Upon his enrollment as an honorary freeman of the Stationers' Company in 1927, he lauded the guild for its ancient ideals of "honest craftsmanship" and "service to others," ideals that did not flourish in the modern economic climate. "We must be profoundly thankful," he told the stationers,

> [that] you chose your motto at a time when the words "Verbum Domini Manet In Aeternum" rang as a profound truth in the minds of men . . . Had the Company been founded today think what mottoes might have been suggested by some of the great men who are living amongst us at the present moment. You might have had "Push and Go" for your motto, or you might have had "Devil take the hindmost" or "Charity begins at home" or "Blow your own trumpet for no one else will blow it for you" [*Laughter*]. But thank God you have a motto that has come down from the ages and that will live into the ages.[24]

Fittingly, Baldwin's favorite piece of contemporary English fiction was Winifred Holtby's *South Riding* (1936) (made into a film in 1938), a story of a hard-up but honorable country squire who defeats the plans of speculators attempting to turn a dishonest penny on a new housing estate. Ironmaster he might be, but at heart he saw himself and his Conservatism as carrying on the torch of the Tory tradition, as standing up for the values of an older England against the inroads of inhumane and mechanistic commercialism, which was grounded in what he saw as "the greatest peril of our age, the peril of materialism."[25]

In this task he was joined by his intimate friend and colleague, Edward Wood, later Viscount Halifax (1881-1959). A landed magnate, Halifax expressed his desire, while minister of agriculture in the twenties, to shift the aims of agricultural policy away from efficiency per se toward "keeping on the land the maximum population which the land will support." He thought little of the application of machinery, which only accelerated rural depopulation. He feared "those vast aggregations of the population in industrial cities, whose prototype, that 'wen', which Cobbett hated and deplored over one hundred years ago, still threatens the nation and the national character in the London of today."[26] Halifax's first, admiring biographer admitted that his view of rural society was romantic. "For all his efforts to assimilate new social tendencies," Alan Campbell Johnson commented in 1941,

> he gives the impression of being out of his depth in modern technical civilization, almost afraid of it, which may be one explanation of his underlying sympathy with Gandhi. He proclaims a vision of a Merrie England with subsidies which as an ideal and a symbol is the British counterpart of Gandhi's spinning-wheel.[27]

Like Baldwin, Halifax saw Conservatism as an antimaterialist creed, and was fond of reminding his listeners and readers that

> true civilization is surely not limited to the satisfaction of purely physical wants. Running water in every bedroom, the wireless, the telephone, a stud of motorcars – all these popularly accepted signs of the progress of humanity do not in fact add one inch to the national stature . . . they may have precisely the opposite effect, to imperil the character of the people and rob it of its individuality.[28]

Maurice Cowling has remarked that for Halifax,

> "Conservatism" was a flexible, even porous, container which various Cecils and Stanleys had constructed and into which (though not a Conservative) Grey had poured much Whig water immediately after the war. In their cases, decency, idealism and landed virtue had been offered as bandages to industrial society. Halifax's contribution was a [quasi-religious] tone and manner . . . connected with conceptions about the duties and instincts of a "gentleman".[29]

Such a gentry vision of politics was spread by a variety of Conservative politicians and publicists as well. The widely read 1924 book, *The Conservative Mind* by "A Gentleman with a Duster" (journalist Harold Begbie), supported Baldwin's rise by refurbishing the notion of a distinct Tory tradition and identifying it with Baldwin, Halifax, and their political allies. Begbie described a living Toryism carried through the years by landed gentlemen, the men who "created the incomparable beauty of the English countryside" and gave the national character its most admirable qualities. "What radiance now persists," he claimed, "in our dark and troubled industrial existence shines mainly from their tradition."

The true voice of this tradition, Begbie argued, was sounded by paternal, antiindustrial, and antimaterialist landed gentlemen like Lord Shaftesbury. Real English Conservatism had been in revolt ever since against the "economic chaos" brought in by Liberals, against the wrong direction taken in the early nineteenth century. "All the confusions which we inherit in our national life," he asserted, "have descended to us from the days of the Industrial Revolution." Only the landed men who had kept in touch with an older England could clear them away.[30]

This "tradition" was summoned up by many interwar Conservatives. The most precious English institution, reflected Hugh Sellon, a young politician, in 1932, was "our heritage of the beauty of England," for that had nurtured national stability, for which there was the greatest need in the tumultuous modern age. He explained: "If the Englishman is, politically, a more balanced and sane creature than some of his neighbours, he may draw some of his balance and sanity from the fact that his eyes have, since they first opened, rested on a landscape of peace and sober proportions which is found nowhere so perfectly as in England." In a book proposing to set out guidelines for the rethinking of national policy, Sellon observed that "it might well have been better for England if she had never become a great manufacturing country." He saw the disappearing countryman as "the natural guardian of the nation against the spread of false economic doctrines," and consequently made rural revival a key plank of his proposed new Conservatism.[31]

During the thirties, this call for rural preservation and revival was made by other Conservatives, most notably by Lord Eustace Percy (1887-1958). Percy, minister of education in the twenties, enjoying a reputation as "Minister of Thought," linked the national government with the intelligentsia.[32] He was convinced of the superiority of a landed over a restless and materialistic urban society, and urged in books and broadcast talks "the intensive cultivation of our homeland." People should be helped onto the land, and, once there, encouraged to "substitute . . . the idea of craftsmanship for the idea of 'getting on'."[33] Percy interpreted the economic blizzard after 1929 as the onset of "what Victorian economists used to call 'the stationary state'." The previous three hundred years of headlong expansion were abnormal, and had to end. Percy was not very unhappy about this; he saw it as an opportunity to create (or recreate) a more satisfactory way of life. The nation, "which has lived for its stomach," had been attacked by debilitating digestive trouble. This ailment, however, was only a premonitory symptom of a "pernicious anemia" that threatened its very life. It could only save itself by "returning to a simpler and more strenuous way of life. It must work hard to get wealth, but it must be wealth of a kind that dignifies life, wealth that can be enjoyed instead of being merely consumed."

Percy predicted that England would return to "the standards which have always governed societies before they acquired great wealth through trade – societies, for instance, like seventeenth century England before the emergence of the Indian 'nabob'." He argued for the concept of self-sufficiency as both "an economic activity not less socially useful than mass-production for sale, and as a moral ideal more dignified than the worship of industrial efficiency." England, he felt, was specially fitted for this new economic era and was more favorably placed than any other nation except France, as America was more favorably placed for "her more sanguine but surely less noble experiment" of unrestrained growth.[34] "There is nothing," one of the contributors to Percy's symposium, *Conservatism and the Future*, argued, "specifically characteristic of our people either in lending money abroad or in exporting manufactures."[35] A host of other Tory-inclined writers echoed this argument. "Great Britain," Percy insisted, "which has led the world in the ambitions and energies of expansion, can lead it also in the prudent labours of consolidation."[36]

Even the Conservative who most clashed with the Baldwin-Halifax wing of the party, Winston Churchill, nonetheless thought very much in terms of the Southern Metaphor of England. Whereas Baldwin, whose wealth derived from industry, had adopted a rustic way of looking at the nation, Churchill had been born into it. Born at Blenheim, Churchill was immersed in upper-class tradition. A particular image of England and its past was always with him, more than with any other leading politician, even Baldwin. Churchill thought and acted against a backdrop of a specific conception of English history. As befitted Marlborough's descendant, Churchill emphasized in his histories the military triumphs and imperial expansion of England – "Great Britain" as opposed to Baldwin's "Little England." Yet, like Baldwin, his view of national history was archaic and nostalgic, and had little place for the industrial revolution and all the political and social changes that it produced. His England, like Baldwin's, was not the England of modern London or Manchester or Birmingham, but of landed gentlemen, John Bull farmers, and sturdy yeomen. Churchill, in his *History of the English Speaking Peoples*, was as deeply obsessed as Bryant with defining the English tradition. This made him a splendid symbol for a nation under siege, but clouded his vision of the present. As J. H. Plumb remarked:

> The pageantry of a coronation superimposed on the steelworks of Sheffield or the sprawling suburbia of Manchester never struck him as odd; for him the right things were in the right places; embattled they might be, threatened perhaps by the future, but so long as the

Island people rallied round their monarch and their Parliament, the world might be defied.[37]

Twentieth-century gentry Conservatism, as the case of Churchill suggests, had Whig-Liberal as well as purely Tory tributaries. Victorian Whiggism had always been of two minds about the advance of urban industrial society, which was difficult to accommodate in a rural picture of England. Lord Rosebery, the Liberal chairman of the London County Council, confessed in 1891 that

> there is no thought of pride associated in my mind with the idea of London. I am always haunted by the awfulness of London: by the great appalling fact of these millions cast down, as it would appear by hazard, on the banks of this noble stream, working each in their own groove and their own cell, without regard or knowledge of each other, without heeding each other, without having the slightest idea how the other lives – the heedless casualty of unnumbered thousands of men. Sixty years ago, a great Englishman, Cobbett, called it a wen. If it was a wen then, what is it now? A tumour, an elephantiasis sucking into its gorged system half the life and the blood and the bone of the rural districts.[38]

Another leading landed Liberal, Sir Edward Grey, foreign secretary from 1905 to 1916, looked with even more horror on the "hideous cities" and "ghastly competition" of the modern world. If God shared his view, he wrote a friend in 1912, "then the great industrial countries will perish in catastrophe, because they have made the country hideous and life impossible." Soon after his departure from office, Grey confided that "I feel deep in me that the civilization of the Victorian epoch ought to disappear. I think I always knew this subconsciously, but I took things as I found them and for 30 years spoke of progress as an enlargement of the Victorian industrial age – as if anything could be good that led to telephones and cinematographs and large cities and the *Daily Mail*."[39]

Whig detachment from and disdain for the society produced by industrial capitalism was not confined to those with aristocratic family connections. Liberals like G. M. Trevelyan, as we have seen, became ever more nostalgic for the preindustrial England of landed gentlemen and sturdy peasants. There were many men, like the last Liberal prime minister, H. H. Asquith, who accepted the doctrines of economic liberalism but withheld approval of the kind of life they underpinned. Asquith was the son of a Yorkshire woolen-mill manager, but briskly detached himself from his origins as he rose from Balliol College, Oxford, through the bar, and into the Establishment. By the time he came into power, he was contemptuously referring to the new leader of the Opposition, Andrew Bonar Law, an iron merchant who had broken the Tory aristocratic succession, as the "gilded tradesman."[40] C. F. G. Masterman told a story from the early years of World

War I that aptly illustrates the contradiction: The question of large speculative profits being made out of shipping cargoes of food or munitions to England arose in cabinet: "Disgusting," said Asquith:

> A minister at once protested. He declared that this was the normal operation of trade. He declared that if their men had not done it other men would have done the same. He declared that if they had chosen not to bring the stuff to England they could probably have attained as much or greater profit by taking it to neutral or allied countries. "I can see nothing disgraceful," he said, "about the whole transaction." "I did not say disgraceful," said Mr. Asquith, with a characteristic shrug of the shoulders. "I said disgusting."[41]

Taken to extremes, discontent with urban industrialism and nostalgia for Old Rural England could nurture fascistlike political sentiments. What was merely fastidious in Sir Edward Grey could become vicious in others. Lamenting the decline of British power, "An Overseas Englishman" in 1922 blamed "blood-poisoning." The Scots, Welsh, and Jews had taken over the country, and a cosmopolitan urban life was smothering the real nation. Another "ultra," Rawdon Hoare, returning from fourteen years in the empire, found England in 1934 decadent, with pacifism and hedonism rife and Americanization in full swing. The countryside was being destroyed by unregulated urban expansion directed by land speculators, often Jewish. These writers looked to the traditional elements in the countryside for signs that the nation's heart yet beat. "An Overseas Englishman" pointed to "the decorous seclusion of the homes of the real English, who, in hall or hamlet, have somehow managed to keep themselves and their manners, and ideals – aye, and their sorrows, to themselves." One of the main arguments of Sir R. G. Stapledon, a leading agricultural scientist, for encouraging a rural revival was that, genetically, country stock – more purely English – was sounder than town stock. Lord Bledisoe, a leader in agricultural organizations, provided a foreword to another plea for rural resettlement, in which he argued that "contact with Mother Earth is the most powerful antidote to the poison of Bolshevism."[42] Oswald Mosley denounced the transformation of "Merrie England" into a "sweatshop and slum" – "the green beloved country becomes the playground of the stockjobber." Mosley contrasted the "virile country stock" and the "yeomen of England" with the degenerate urban figure of the "long-haired intellectual."[43] Such a "hard," racist version of the rural myth perennially recurred, most notably in Enoch Powell's speeches in the nineteen-sixties. Powell was described by a biographer as a politician "who had earned his reputation for being a coldly logical thinker." Yet he astounded conventional politicians with a series of romantic addresses, beginning in 1964, that blended hostility to the immigration of colored persons with calls on the English people to reclaim the national cultural identity that had existed before Imperial expansion and before industrialization, and to recognize that they were now "once more akin with the old English" of the Middle Ages.[44] Powell's orations were not "sports," but drew upon the myth of England that had come to pervade middle- and upper-class culture. They were drenched in evocations of the beauties and virtues of pastoral, historic England; parodies, almost, of Austin, Kipling, Housman, Masefield, and so many other writers; and first cousins to the speeches of that earlier Tory politician, Stanley Baldwin. In one address, for example, Powell called upon his and his listeners' long-dead ancestors to tell of England:

> What would they say? They would speak to us in our own English tongue, the tongue made for telling truth in, turned already to songs that haunt the hearer like the sadness of spring. They would tell us of that marvellous land, so sweetly mixed of opposites in climate that all the seasons of the year appear there in their greatest perfection; of the fields amid which they built their halls, their cottages, their churches, and where the same blackthorn showered its petals upon them as upon us; they would tell us, surely, of the rivers, the hills and of the island coasts of England.[45]

Although Powell may have been echoing Baldwin, the effect was different. In part, the reason was that the culture was shifting: What was central in the twenties and thirties was beginning to appear eccentric by the sixties (we will address this more closely later). In part, also, the reason lay in the political ideology such flights of rhetoric were decorating: Powell's was an arousing, aggressive, and extreme ideology, at odds with the emollient uses to which the rural myth had generally been put. The language was all too familiar, but the use seemed perverse and dangerous. The mainstream of twentieth-century English politics had seen repeated dipping into the well of the rural myth, but to dress up gestures and policies of conciliation, consolidation, and protection of the status quo.

The rural myth and its associated "gentry" sentiments left their mark on government, not in the extremist forms of Mosley or Powell, but through the respectable center, giving a particular cast to economic policy. The ideals of "gentry England" helped muffle economic competitiveness and innovation. The avoidance of conflict, the warding off of uncertain change, and the minimizing of materialism all became aims of government pronouncements and actions. Just when, after World War I, the role of government was gaining major importance for the national economy, government and politics had become permeated by a mentality that regarded industry as a necessary evil and innovation and competition as risky and not quite reputable.

Baldwin's Conservative and national governments, despite their business composition, in many ways prepared the way for the controlled economy of the nineteen-forties. Indeed, Baldwin has been called "the first of our collectivist Prime Ministers."[46] The Conservative party of his day, it has been argued, "did much to undermine, if not to destroy, the structure of liberal capitalism."[47] His governments' drift toward increasing regulation of the market was partly motivated by the political competition of Labour, but it was also derived from emotional detachment from industrial capitalism. Insofar as they served as bulwarks of the status quo (and of the party itself), business and industry were supported by Conservatism. In their role as a dynamic force, bringing change and upsetting social order and traditional social standards, they were not. The establishment of the BBC, readily approved of by nearly all elite opinion, was an early indication of this:

> Here was a great new field, with limitless potential, from which private enterprise and competition were to be excluded from the very start. The grounds for doing so were purely paternalistic. Competition, it was said, would lead to the domination of entertainment values, trite and frivolous programmes. The fact that competition could result in the preponderance of such programmes only if the consumers wanted them did not seem to count for much. In effect, a small minority of the nation decided that the values determining the character of broadcasting should be congenial to themselves, that they alone knew what was "good" for the rest of the public, who could like it or lump it.[48]

Laissez-faire was, Baldwin declared in 1935, as dead as "the slave trade."[49] The government, dissociating itself from the tainted image of capitalism, encouraged a general industrial movement toward organized market sharing and the fixing of prices and of output. This process was profoundly congenial to many Tory minds. "In place of the extreme rivalry of the nineteenth century," Arthur Bryant noted with satisfaction, "industry is returning to the ancient medieval practice of co-operation and mutual agreement." Harold Macmillan, at the time a leader of the young radicals within the party, also approved, seeing the renewal of "that organic conception of society which was the distinct contribution of medieval thought" to replace "individualism and *laissez-faire*."[50]

By 1939 the prevalent form of organization in the British economy was uncompetitive private enterprise in partnership with the state. The government had gone some way toward restoring the ordered economy that the old Tories had unavailingly defended against the driving individualism of the early industrial era. Moreover, a tenacious pattern of government response to industrial difficulty had been established. The stability so gained had its price, for, Lindsay and Harrington have argued, "by favouring, even to the extent of subsidy, the existing industrial structure, the Government was working against the forces of change and innovation which, though ruthless in their consequences for some old industries and regions, were the main factor working for the steady upward trend of the standard of living."[51]

This pattern in Conservative industrial attitudes continued after World War II. Again, agriculture was extolled not simply as an important part of the economy, but as the soil that the national spirit required to flower. Even Conservatives like R. A. Butler and Quintin Hogg, who were not country landowners, paid homage to the rural myth. At the 1948 party conference, Butler typically intoned: "In saving agriculture we are saving more than our own economy. We are saving a way of life in which the features are kindliness, freedom, and above all, wisdom. These are the qualities of the countryman and countrywoman. They are instinctive with Conservative policy, they are vital to our existence."[52] The year before, Quintin Hogg, a self-described townsman, in his widely read tract *The Case for Conservatism*, portrayed rural life as central to Conservative values and to national welfare: "The Conservative believes that farming is more than a business; it is a way of life, essential for the well-being of the community in war and peace . . . The Conservative believes – and so far science has borne him out – that a purely urban community tends to die out." One of the traditional rural values Hogg saw as inspiration for Conservative policy was the limitation of the profit motive; "good husbandry" meant, in industry as in agriculture, using the profit motive but not permitting it to dominate, "for if it does we shall do violence to the heritage which we have received from of old." A purely profit-oriented economy was the equivalent of American "dust bowl farming"; the antithesis of long centuries of English rural experience.[53]

The postwar Conservative leadership held itself rather aloof from industry, and had surprisingly little direct contact with industrial leaders. This was particularly obvious in the case of Churchill and Eden, who came out of the landed aristocracy, but it was evident even with middle-class men like Butler and Macmillan.[54] Though a large minority of the party's MPs began their careers in business, neither a distinctive "business" nor, especially, an "industrial" point of view was visible among them.[55] It was, on the contrary, usual for leading Conservatives to look with disdain at the vulgar behavior and life-style of nouveaux riche businessmen.[56] The leadership responded to the 1945 Labour victory by widening the distance between Conservatism and industrial capitalism. Lord Hinchingbrooke, representing the Tory Reform Committee organized by thirty-six MPs in 1943, had already announced that

> True Conservative opinion is horrified at the damage done to this country since the last war by "individualist" business-men, financiers, and speculators ranging freely in a laissez-faire economy and

> creeping unnoticed into the fold of Conservatism to insult the Party with their vote at elections, to cast a slur over responsible Government through influence exerted on Parliament, and to injure the character of our people. It would wish nothing better than that these men should collect their baggage and depart.[57]

Hinchingbrooke's view remained influential after the war. Aubrey Jones argued in 1946 that the party should not let itself be identified with industrialism for "the industrial system which arose in Britain in the nineteenth century...was a Liberal achievement to which the Conservatism of the day was rightly opposed...Conservatives... will wish to abate the evil consequences of the industrial revolution, for which they have no special responsibility."[58] Similarly, Quintin Hogg, in *The Case for Conservatism*, claimed for his party the longest tradition of criticizing capitalism as "an ungodly and rapacious scramble for ill-gotten gains, in the course of which the richer appeared to get richer and the poor poorer."[59]

These arguments were echoed at the highest levels. "We are not the Party of unbridled, brutal capitalism," Eden declared at the 1947 party conference, "and never have been." Macmillan had insisted back in 1936 that "Toryism has always been a form of paternal Socialism."[60] But its form of socialism had never, party apologists cautioned, fallen into the error of materialism. *The Right Road for Britain*, the official party statement in 1949 for the next election, announced:

> Conservatism proclaims the inability of purely materialist philosophies to read the riddle of life, and achieve the necessary subordination of scientific invention and economic progress to the needs of the human spirit...Man is a spiritual creature adventuring on an immortal destiny, and science, politics and economics are good or bad so far as they help or hinder the individual soul on its eternal journey.[61]

Churchmen: economic growth versus a moral society

The note of spirituality in the Conservative party statement should remind us of an important world of middle- and upper-class thought, not to be wholly identified with either Conservatism or socialism, that both represented and influenced the general climate of opinion – that of religion, and especially that of the Church of England. Despite its membership decline, the Church of England remained, in the first half of the twentieth century at least, a powerful force in the shaping of public attitudes, behavior, and policy. And in spite of sharp ideological differences within it, one can almost speak of a consensus of gentry values and attitudes held in Anglicanism from Right to Left.

The best-known Conservative churchman of this century was undoubtedly William Ralph Inge (1860-1954), the dean of St. Paul's. Already possessed of a modest renown before World War I as a religious scholar and theologian, Dean Inge leaped into the public eye with the appearance of his *Outspoken Essays* in 1919. This book went into five printings within three months, and, together with a second volume published three years later, eventually sold nearly 70,000 copies. This was an impressive number for collections of essays originally published in periodicals such as the *Edinburgh Review*, the *Quarterly Review*, and the *Hibbert Journal*. Though *Outspoken Essays* contained a number of theological pieces, what appealed to a general audience were Inge's ventures into secular and topical issues like patriotism, the birth rate, and the future of the English race. As soon as laudatory reviews appeared, journalistic offers began to flow in, and the "Gloomy Dean," as he had been tagged by the *Daily Mail*, was launched on a career as public sage to interwar England. Inge wrote regularly for the *Evening Standard*, which had a circulation of a half million, and intermittently for a number of other papers, becoming, as John Raymond has observed, "a characteristic figure of the Baldwin Age."[62]

Despite his reputation for what the archbishop of Canterbury described as "originality and sometimes eccentricity of thought,"[63] Inge was in many ways a thoroughly conventional member of the professional classes – fiercely patriotic, suspicious of left-wing intellectuals, proud of the public schools, and a lover of cricket. As an instructor of the middle classes in the twenties and thirties, Inge was repeatedly disdainful of, and even scolded, the life of business and industry. As early as 1906, he was speaking of the "vulgarity of industrial competition."[64] Among his favorite aphorisms was Wordsworth's "Getting and spending we lay waste our powers." "The passion for accumulation," he announced, lay at the root of the discontent of modern life. The more he inveighed against what he labeled "economism" and "consumptionism," the more copies of the *Evening Standard* were bought in order to catch his latest secular sermon. The dean was repeating, in simplified language, the strictures of the great Victorian cultural critics – Arnold, Ruskin, and others. But his very vulgarization of them signified a widespread disenchantment with the economic faith of many Victorians. Inge summed up this nineteenth-century faith in order to heap scorn upon it: the "myth" that "a nation advances in civilization by increasing in wealth and population, and by multiplying the accessories and paraphernalia of life." The preeminence of economics, he insisted at the end of the thirties, "belongs to the nineteenth century; it created the mentality of the capitalist and of the communist, thereby setting its stamp on western civilization for more than a hundred years. Economism is like a science of the stomach without knowledge of physiology or of other organs."[65]

This scorn was by no means radical, for Inge found the chief present-day embodiment of the vice of economism in the Labour movement, which threatened humane values with its greedy materialism. He was fond of equating old-fashioned capitalists and new-fangled socialists, both morally dangerous products of an unnatural industrial system. The General Strike deeply frightened him; Inge attributed it ultimately to the antisocial and unpatriotic sectionalism "which is the curse of industrial civilization."[66]

Made even gloomier by the Great Depression, Inge, like so many others, came to repudiate the age of England's rise to preeminent wealth and power – the nineteenth century. "The whole episode which made England the workshop of the world," he declared at the end of the thirties, "was alien to the spirit and character of the English people."[67] On another occasion Inge characterized the nineteenth century as a mere "episode" in the history of a country that had been most distinguished as the home of a lofty idealism, "the country of Shakespeare and Milton, of Wordsworth and Shelley, of Tennyson and Browning."[68]

England had been diverted from its true nature by the industrial revolution; it could look forward in the future to returning to itself. "Our little island has had its day of gross material success. Henceforth we must turn our attention to higher things."[69] Inge rather cheerfully accepted the prevailing bleak economic prognosis; his acceptance went well beyond realism to reveal gratification with the apparent failure of materialism. Inge consoled any readers disturbed by his economic pessimism with a prospect of a "higher" national world role: "Intellectually and spiritually we [can] continue to make great contributions to the true wealth of humanity. If we do, we shall receive much more sympathy and admiration from foreign nations than when our rather blatant prosperity made us disliked even more than envied."[70]

Inge's successor at St. Paul's, W. R. Matthews, continued Inge's diatribes against "economism." In a BBC symposium in 1934 called "Whither Britain," Matthews warned against letting the depression turn politics toward materialism. "A nation," he argued, "is far more than an economic unit . . . The government of a nation is not a board of directors and has in its keeping something more precious than material wealth" – "a distinctive character." The "peculiar genius of the British people" had expressed itself in the nation's free political institutions, and their preservation, not economic recovery per se, should be the nation's chief concern.[71]

Alongside writing clerics like Inge were widely read laymen who wore their Christianity on their sleeves. The popular middlebrow paper, the *Illustrated London News*, provided a weekly forum (in a column titled "Our Notebook") for the views, from 1906 to 1936, of G. K. Chesterton, and from 1936, of the historian Arthur Bryant.

Chesterton is the larger figure, but Bryant has also played an important role in modern English culture. We have already encountered him tracing, on the BBC, the national character to the countryside, and writing the history of "the industrial revolution and its ills." Bryant also had taken part in Conservative party affairs, taught at the Conservative "political college" at Ashridge, and wrote speeches for Stanley Baldwin. From 1936 until the seventies, he regularly expounded to a wide audience a personal philosophy that was Christian, Conservative, and critical of industrial capitalist society. "In the spiritual values that raise men above the beasts," Bryant characteristically mourned, "our age and the age that preceded us have been tragically bankrupt." Selfishness, acquisitiveness, worship of efficiency, and material progress – these were the values that had come to hold sway. [72] "The Luddites," he declared, "were right": The machines had enriched the world, but they had also robbed the working man of his livelihood. In general, the industrial revolution "has so far harmed man even more than it has benefited him." In terms of fundamental human needs, the eighteenth-century cottager was probably better off. [73]

Bryant hoped for a return to traditional national values centered on the "quality," not the "quantity," of life. "In the past," he reflected in one of his first columns, "it was one of the boasts of England that we taught the nations how to live. In the seventeenth century we were a people whose claim to greatness was based almost entirely on a certain national passion for the ideal of quality." In the following two centuries, English energies turned to the single-minded quest for wealth and power. "Now the wheel has come full circle again, and the pursuit of wealth and power seems no longer to interest us . . . It may well be that the next fifty years may witness a return to our traditional British role of preaching and practising quality, and of once more teaching the nations how to live."[74]

During World War II, Bryant joined the growing demand for social reform, looking toward

> a world in which men and women make the things they need primarily for use and not merely for profit – the modern, technological equivalent of the world which at its best made the Cotswold barn and the medieval cathedral, instead of the world of Manchester *laissez-faire* and Brummagem cheapness that made the slum, the jerry-built house, and the dole queue.[75]

Inge's and Bryant's antiindustrial Tory Anglicanism was shared by an impressive group of intellectual laymen that included C. S. Lewis and Charles Williams. The most distinguished of these, T. S. Eliot, turned in the thirties from the implied social criticism of poems like

The Waste Land to the explicitness of prose. Drawing upon the writings of other Anglicans, Eliot warned that

> the organization of society on the principle of private profit, as well as public destruction, is leading both to the deformation of humanity by unregulated industrialism, and to the exhaustion of natural resources . . . a good deal of our material progress is a progress for which succeeding generations may have to pay dearly.[76]

If industrial capitalism was not embraced, to say the least, by the Anglican Right, it was even less welcomed by the church's Left. The foremost socialist in church circles was without question R. H. Tawney (1880–1962), who left Inge far behind in attacking "economism." Like so many church Conservatives, Tawney was educated at a leading public school (Rugby) and Oxford (Balliol). His ancestors had been prominent in the industrial revolution, in beer, banking, and engineering, but as far as this famous economic historian was concerned, they might never have existed. T. S. Ashton recalled that when, by chance, the records of the Tawney banking company were given to the London School of Economics and Political Science, "it proved impossible to kindle in the great-grandson even a flicker of interest."[77] "Reverence for economic activity and industry and what is called business," Tawney insisted in 1920, was "fetish worship":

> Like a hypochondriac who is so absorbed in the processes of his own digestion that he goes to his grave before he has begun to live, industrialized communities neglect the very objects for which it is worth while to acquire riches in their feverish preoccupation with the means by which riches can be acquired.
> That obsession by economic issues is as local and transitory as it is repulsive and disturbing. To future generations it will appear as pitiable as the obsession of the seventeenth century by religious quarrels appears today; indeed, it is less rational, since the object with which it is concerned is less important.[78]

Tawney looked with contempt upon postwar concern with the nation's slipping economic position in the world:

> When a Cabinet Minister declares that the greatness of this country depends upon the volume of its exports, so that France, which exports comparatively little, and Elizabethan England, which exported next to nothing, are presumed to be pitied as altogether inferior civilizations, that is . . . the confusion of one minor department of life with the whole of life . . . When the Press clamors that the one thing needed to make this island an Arcadia is productivity, and more productivity, and yet more productivity, that is . . . the confusion of means with ends.[79]

Apalled by such materialistic confusion, Tawney sought through writing, teaching, and politics to "deflect" the pernicious tendencies of the modern economy and to develop "a standard to *repress* economic appetites."[80] His mission was carried on not only in the Labour party, where he came to exert great influence, but also in the Church of England. Tawney was the Anglican layman who most influenced academic opinion within the church in the era between the wars (including, very directly, the views of Archbishop Temple).[81] Tawney built upon an active tradition of Anglican social criticism.[82] From the eighteen-seventies, the church leadership had been growing increasingly critical of industrial capitalism, following the general movement of ideas within the upper-middle and upper classes from which the leaders of the church were drawn. Nearly all educated at the best public schools and Oxbridge, bishops, deans, and dons found it natural to look with distaste and disapproval upon the world of commerce and industry. Such an inclination could flourish in them unchecked by the practical necessity, often forced upon many of their fellows, of making a living in that world. Clerical social attitudes became ever more sympathetic to socialism – indeed, the most radical church leaders also tended to be the most upper-class. This moralistic and antimaterialistic radicalism was part of a wider social attitude, shared by many nonradical clerics like Dean Inge, of detachment from industrial capitalism and its values.

In the interwar years particularly, several groups of social critics flourished in the Church of England; these groups often attacked industrialism itself. The most important was the interdenominational Conference on Christian Politics, Economics and Citizenship (known as COPEC), organized in 1924 by Temple and his allies in the church. COPEC's lay membership was drawn chiefly from the professions and the voluntary social services. Its reports, over the following few years, laid out a wide-ranging critique of capitalism, set in a historical frame constructed by Tawney, a leading member. Nostalgia for the Middle Ages and for the crafts and recreations of an idealized, earlier rural age permeated COPEC.[83]

Still more radical (or reactionary) groups were active, like Conrad Noel's Catholic Crusade (which combined a kind of communism with medievalism and Anglo-Catholicism), the League of the Kingdom of God, and the National Guilds League, which brought together secular and church guild socialists.[84] After the National Guilds League foundered, many of its Anglican activists reappeared in the Christendom Group, a loose organization in the twenties and thirties devoted to working out a fresh Christian social philosophy. Despite mass unemployment – clearly the chief social problem of the time, especially after 1929 – the Christendom Group found little appeal in the question of production. The interests of its members ran in another direction: toward creating a society in which the question of production would cease to dominate. At the core of the group's thinking was the guild idea, the peasant ideal of distributed property and self-sufficiency, and a hatred of "international finance." At meetings and in group publications, attacks were leveled at the spiritual dangers of industrialism, at popular forms of consumption, and at what would later be called "the affluent society." P. E. T. Widdrington, one of the group's leaders, attacked the entertainment industry as a dangerous influence, and regretted that most American families owned a car.[85] Many in the Christendom Group went further: Sir Henry Slesser, solicitor-general in the first Labour government, denounced technological advance per se, arguing that the essence of Christianity lay in the transfer of interest from the material to the spiritual sphere.[86]

The Christendom Group achieved its greatest recognition at the Malvern Conference in 1941, called by Archbishop Temple to consider questions of postwar reconstruction. Its outlook dominated Malvern, and shaped the report of the conference. That year, Christendom Group intellectuals published a book setting forth a new national "vocation": As England had led the world into industrialism, it could now atone by showing the world the way out. It could accomplish this new mission because it had never really given its soul to industrialism; its rustic soul was waiting, like a Wagnerian Teutonic hero, to be recalled by a nation awakened to its peril. Evacuation, these men pointed out, could mark a new national beginning: the end of the dominance of the cities and the revival of the English countryside.[87] Such views are also aired at Malvern, whose report described the war as not "an isolated evil," but "one symptom of a widespread disease and maladjustment" set in motion by capitalist industrialism. "The existing industrial order," it explained,

> with the acquisitive temper characteristic of our society, tends to recklessness and sacrilege in the treatment of natural resources. It has led to the impoverishment of the agricultural community, and is largely responsible for the problem of the "mass man," who is conscious of no status, spiritual or social, who is a mere atom in the machinery of production, and who easily develops the herd psychology, which is automatically responsive to skillful propaganda.

The report stressed that the decline in religion was most apparent in the southeastern urban complex, and deplored the "mechanical thinking" of the new technical classes. It concluded by looking back nostalgically to Old England, when religion was strong and industry yet unborn. The conference called for the revival of agriculture, so as to return the people to the land. Such a return could revive, it declared, "true community, which is possible in a village as it is not in the great cities."[88]

Malvern marked a high-water mark for such ideas. The two pamphlets containing the Malvern proceedings sold, together, more than a million copies. In the aftermath of the conference, Temple's *Christianity and Social Order* sold over 140,000 copies, spreading many of the ideas expressed at Malvern to much wider circles. Although thereafter antiindustrial sentiments within the church began to wane, they were not on the whole replaced by positive sentiments so much as put to one side. The church remained a reservoir of rural romanticism, and of uneasiness with industrial development and economic growth.[89]

Labour: the vision of "Merrie England"

The gentry tradition was of course less potent on the Left than on the Right, but it was by no means absent there. Moreover, its fainter impress was made up for by the influence of the related "peasant" cultural tradition, the populist face of the rural myth. Just as Baldwin and Halifax (and churchmen) had called upon the spirit of William Cobbett and the immemorial traditions of the English village, so did radicals. J. H. Plumb has pointed out this backward-looking, rustic strand in English radicalism, claiming that no one "can understand the development of liberalism and Socialism in England, even the British Labour Party today, without understanding William Cobbett." Ever since his time, Plumb argued, "the dream of an Elysian England of patriarchs, well-fed peasants, contented, if illiterate, craftsmen, and compassionate profit-sharing landowners, has haunted English radicalism."[90] From the late nineteenth century, a broad spectrum of Labour thinkers – like Morris, Carpenter, and Blatchford, and later Tawney and G. D. H. Cole – and politicians – like Ramsey Macdonald and even a cockney like George Lansbury – invoked the memory of Cobbett and the associations of "Merrie England."[91]

Toryism, too, had its influence on the Left. As Cyril Joad remarked in 1946, "Like many other Englishmen of my type, I have Tory tastes and radical opinions and my tastes are often at war with my opinions."[92] Radical impulses have been perennially absorbed by a resilient English society. As Francis Hope noted in 1966, the experience of English radicals has frequently resembled a science-fiction story: "One steps into English society, and finds it is not a spaceship but a stomach; one expects to be transported, and is merely digested."[93] These radicals, like Joad, often found themselves admiring the "landed style." Such admiration revealed itself in odd moments, as when, in the twenties, on a country ramble past a great estate, G. D. H. Cole burst out – to his student Hugh Gaitskell's surprise – with a "panegyric of the English aristocracy"; when Ramsay Macdonald confided similar esteem for her order to the marchioness of Londonderry; when Harold Laski declared that he would much rather have been governed by an aristocrat like Lord Shaftesbury than by Richard Cobden, "by the gentlemen of England than by the Gradgrinds and

Bounderbys of Coketown"; when H. N. Brailsford rapturously praised country gentlemen who turned political critics; and when Richard Hoggart confessed himself drawn to the cozy Trollopian picture of mid-Victorian rural life displayed by Kilvert's diary, for "how much it embodied social responsibilities."[94]

The early prophets of English socialism – Morris, Carpenter, Blatchford – joined idealization of "Merrie England" with denunciation of industrialism and commercialism. Morris's *News from Nowhere* portrayed a future pastoral England in which men were liberated from the thrall of machinery, free to work with their hands on what they enjoyed doing and at their own pace. Machinery still existed, but offstage, virtually invisible, set to work by itself. Further technical development was no longer necessary or desirable. One of his utopians explained: "This is not an age of inventions. The last epoch did all that for us, and we are now content to use such of its inventions as we find handy, and leaving those alone which we don't want."[95]

In his socialist agitation, Morris liked to question such foundations of British economic power as the coal industry: Was this unhealthy and unpleasant work really necessary? "For myself," he told a miner,

> I should be glad if we could do without coal, and indeed without burrowing like worms and moles in the earth altogether; and I am not sure but we could do without it if we wished to live pleasant lives, and did not want to produce all manner of mere mechanism chiefly for multiplying our own servitude and misery, and spoiling half the beauty and art of the world to make merchants and manufacturers rich. In olden days the people did without coal, and were, I believe rather more happy than we are today, and produced better art, poetry, and quite as good religion and philosophy as we do nowadays.[96]

Morris's antiindustrial sentiments were spread widely by what G. D. H. Cole called "the most effective piece of popular Socialist propaganda ever written," Robert Blatchford's *Merrie England* (1894), which within a few years sold a million copies in Great Britain. Blatchford here identified socialism with rural life. He called agriculture the essential basis of a healthy national life, and he minced no words about the factory system: "The thing is evil. It is evil in its origin, in its progress, in its methods, in its motives, and in its effects. No nation can be sound whose motive power is greed." England had to choose, Blatchford declared, citing Ruskin, between the quality of men and the quantity of production. Men's *real* needs were few and simple, and could be met without the spread of factories over the land. There was yet time to turn back:

> The Manchester School will tell you that the destiny of this country is to become "The Workshop of the World." I say that is not true; and that it would be a thing to deplore if it were true. The idea that this

country is to be the "Workshop of the World" is a wilder dream than any that the wildest Socialist ever cherished. But if this country did become the "Workshop of the World" it would at the same time become the most horrible and the most miserable country the world has ever known.[97]

Even among the unromantic Fabians, the quest for material abundance was held in bad repute. Most Fabians were not only institutional reformers but also moralists, intent on bringing about a higher – and perhaps a simpler – life-style. Even to Sidney Webb in 1886, socialism meant "the call to frugal and earnest living."[98] Beatrice Webb, reflecting in her diary in 1915 on "the Ideal that moves me," found it in "the thought of an abstract Being divested of all human appetite." Mrs. Webb's hope was that man would evolve upwards by subordinating his material desires to the intellectual and spiritual side of his nature.[99]

In this way a deeply conservative impulse was implanted within twentieth-century English radicalism and socialism: to erect barriers to economic appetites and to sublimate their force in higher pursuits. As G. M. Trevelyan, a representative intellectual radical of the Edwardian era, argued in 1901, "The natural process of modern economy is on the whole towards evil rather than good, but the way of salvation does not lie backwards in vain regret [though later he was to succumb to just such regret]; it consists in deflecting the Titan forces with which the modern world is armed from purely economic to partly ideal ends." The alternative to such action was "the world growing ever blacker, uglier, noisier, more meaningless."[100] The task of a "progressive" party was set out as the deflecting of economic energies toward moral and spiritual goals.

Such a program not only became the cause of Labour intellectuals like Tawney, but it also was invoked – for different purposes – by politicians, whose outlooks were shaped much more by Carlyle, Dickens, and, especially, Ruskin, than by Marx or Robert Owen.[101] In particular, the note of anti-economism was touched frequently by the first Labour prime minister, Ramsay Macdonald (1866-1937). With Macdonald, the man most responsible for shaping the modern Labour party, condemnation of "economic fetishism" went hand in hand with rural myth weaving to rival his opposite number, Stanley Baldwin. As Baldwin had extended the fabric of the myth of England to embrace the Welsh background of one side of his family, Macdonald brought together England and his native Scotland. These two leading politicians of the interwar period had much in common, and recognized it; Baldwin was to Macdonald "a good type of cultured liberal Conservative," and Macdonald received similar appreciation from Baldwin.[102] Macdonald possessed, as one friend observed, an "intense and abiding sense of the picturesque and a deep love of the ordered and ancient and the hierarchical." Margaret Cole sourly described a visit to the prime minister: "He was obviously delighted with Chequers . . . his first role was that of an inheritor of broad acres, deeply sensitive to the traditions of the countryside." In Macdonald's talks, Lossiemouth filled the role of Baldwin's Bewdley, and simple fisher-folk the role of farmers and farm laborers. Macdonald, like Baldwin, loved to contrast the artificial world of Westminster with the real world of the countryside; sitting on the front bench during debates, he would, as he put it, "return often in imagination to the green roads upon which I had gone but a few days before." He also presented himself as an old-fashioned, pensive countryman, a "true son of the soil" and of the traditional ways of Old England. The head of a party holding up the red flag spent much of his time delivering lines such as "I have gone to meet the Springtime in the sheltered vales and creeks of the West." A political trip through the Cotswolds in the spring of 1929 moved him to pay homage to the superiority of the Old England surviving there: He saw in its stone-grey villages "the England of long past centuries, before the industrial revolution made the power of economics predominant in the life of the people, and when industry was conducted by craftsmen who fashioned beautiful things because they put themselves into the work they were doing." He contrasted this with the "fussy and meaningless life of today."[103]

Arguing within the party in 1927 against the ILP's campaign for an immediate commitment to a national "living wage," Macdonald warned that capitalism "has made us far more than we imagine. It has given us notions of value that are wrong . . . and it itself, being so grossly materialistic and having given economic resources such an important place in life, has misled us when we search for remedies against it." Instead of challenging the materialistic values of the society around them, the ILP militants had implicitly accepted them. Their program, he felt, was at bottom unsocialist, if not antisocialist, as it rested on the essentially capitalist assumption that the object of social action was material enrichment rather than improvement in the quality of life. Under capitalism, Macdonald wrote the next year,

> The poor strive to get what they want so sorely; the rich are afraid that they may lose what they have. And there is no resting on one's oars. One must go on accumulating whether one has £1,000 or £1,000,000. One must make higher and higher demands for wages and more and more provision for public aid lest personal efforts should fail. There is no satisfaction in this sleepless urge, and there-fore there is no end to it. The generations will come and go, but the last will still be pursuing and still be in fear. It is the fear that I emphasize – the fear ever brooding over the insecurity of material possession – the struggle on a purely material plane for something

that in its nature is purely ephemeral and passing – the destruction of all values of being and living by reason of the tragic pressure to possess things.

    That is why ... Socialist politics must always be subordinate to Socialist ideals of life.[104]

David Marquand has pointed out that this side of Macdonald proved a political asset, both inside and outside Labour. Many Labour supporters, he notes,

> had been inspired as much by a revulsion from the ugliness and materialism of late nineteenth-century industrial society as by a hatred of poverty and injustice. It was partly because he spoke to and for this strand in British Socialism, the strand which produced the I. L. P. Arts Guild of the middle twenties and which looked back to Walter Crane and William Morris, that Macdonald was able to capture the imagination of the Labour movement in a way that a narrowly political leader would have found it hard to do.

At the same time, Marquand went on, this rustic nonpolitical image of the wanderer among the moors and dales helped Macdonald appeal more successfully than any other Labour politician to a middle-class public outside the Labour party.[105]

    The Tory dream of a revival of English life on the land was also dreamt by socialists (Tawney was not alone in considering himself "a peasant displaced from the soil"[106]). Frequently summoning up the spirits of Cobbett, Morris, and Blatchford, a number of Labour politicians in the interwar years followed their leader in Baldwinian rhetoric. Noel Buxton, minister of agriculture in the first Labour government, denounced the "oppressive atmosphere of the factory" and its "modern Robots." From this grim scene, his imagination "turn[ed] in relief to the green lanes and running brooks of our English countryside, to the cottages in the valleys nestling in the shadow of great trees, to the pure sky and sweeping white clouds." These old places, tragically emptied over the previous century, still beckoned. "These are the places," he announced, "which I want to see populated with the flower of our race and overflowing with crops of milk and honey." He found it a hopeful sign that all the political parties were realizing that "the neglect of the countryside spells the neglect of the source and springs of the nation's life."[107]

    George Lansbury, a lifelong Londoner and deputy leader of the party, saw throughout his career a solution to unemployment in home land-cultivation. The resettlement of the countryside was more for him, however, than an economic matter; it touched on some of his deepest emotions. "I just long," he wrote in 1934, "to see a start made on this job of reclaiming, recreating rural England. I can see the village greens with the Maypoles once again erected and the boys and girls, young men and maidens, all joining in the mirth and foll of May Day."[108]

Even though the trade union side of Labour was less susceptible to this imagery and its associated values, it was not completely aloof. It is true that (as Susan Howson and Donald Winch have shown) the General Council tended to support the broad ends of industrial innovation and rationalization, rather than "retreating into romantic anti-technology redoubts."[109] Still, in the same year that Macdonald was arguing against the "materialism" of the ILP, his counterpart on the industrial side of the movement, Ben Turner, imparted in a presidential address to the Trades Union Congress his "dream" of a more leisurely society. "We should not," he cautioned the delegates, "make a fetish of work and more work, but aim at the well-being of all, and a more gentle and less nerve-racking life than at present obtains."[110] The year before, the rising trade union leader Ernest Bevin had visited the United States. While picking up ideas for improving home industry, Bevin reacted like a typical middle-class English visitor: "He thought," his biographer has noted, "[American] civilization crude, noisy, boastful, and materialistic." Detroit reminded him, as he wrote in his notebook, of "the Lancashire of the last century ...No culture. Blasé, gaudy, noisy. No one talks to you except in dollars and mass production and the way they boss labour. A very undesirable place."[111] The appeal of the rustic image, too, had penetrated into the councils of the working class: No one thought it strange when, upon receiving a life peerage in 1974, the general secretary of the TUC, Vic Feather, chose to pose for the papers as a sage old countryman, a Hodge come to prominence.

Although World War II and the economic crisis that followed pushed aside such disdain as Turner's and Bevin's for the "fetish" of work and productivity, socialist discomfort with "material values," often tinged with ruralism, by no means vanished. It was most vividly and continually expressed by writers and publicists, the left-wing counterparts of Tories like Bryant and Inge. The most notable of these was J. B. Priestley, novelist, playwright, and essayist, who identified himself throughout his life with the Labour movement, wrote frequently for papers like the *New Statesman*, and indeed was taken off the BBC by Churchill in 1941 for his radicalism. From the thirties on, he became more and more hostile to the drive, which he saw as inherent in modern society, to produce and consume ever more goods. His chief complaint about modern capitalism was the same as Bryant's, despite their opposition in practical politics: not that it made the mass of the people poor, but that it made them unhappy, that it was organized on false moral and psychological principles. From a left-wing stance, he sounded forth with attacks on what Inge labeled "economism" and "consumptionism" and on what Bryant excoriated as "materialism." "We cannot seek grace," Priestley reminded his readers in 1937, "through gadgets. We can be just as unhappy in spun-glass trousers as we were in worsted ones. In a bakelite house the dishes may not break, but the heart can. Even a man with ten shower-baths can still find life stale, flat and unprofitable."[112] Numerous variations on this observation recurred in his writings and broadcast talks over the next four decades.

Priestley first ventured from fiction into social criticism with his *English Journey* in 1934, and became a national figure in 1940 through his broadcast talks. From the start, in *English Journey*, Priestley joined the chorus of denunciation of the nineteenth century: "It had found a green and pleasant land and had left a wilderness of dirty bricks." He went on, however, to express disgust over the more recent developments of twentieth-century England as well. The England of 1933 was an improvement in some obvious ways: "cleaner, tidier, healthier," and more democratic. Yet it was also "standardized" and monotonous. "It is a large-scale, mass-production job, with cut prices. You could almost accept Woolworths as its symbol."[113] The unique national character was fading before the advance of Americanization.

The chief thread in Priestley's writings after the war was an attack upon the "affluent society." He contributed both to the *New Statesman* and to mass-circulation papers, and in 1955 coined the denunciatory term "Admass":

> *Admass.* This is my name for the whole system of an increasing productivity, plus inflation, plus a rising standard of material living, plus high-pressure advertising and salesmanship, plus mass communication, plus cultural democracy and the creation of the mass mind, the mass man ... Most Americans (though not all; they have some fine rebels) have been *Admassians* for the last thirty years; the English, and probably most West Europeans, only since the War. It is better to live in *Admass* than to have no job, no prospect of one, and see your wife and children getting hungrier and hungrier. But that is about all that can be said in favour of it. All the rest is a swindle. You think everything is opening out when in fact it is narrowing and closing in on you. Finally you have to be half-witted or half-drunk all the time to endure it.[114]

By comparison, the nineteenth century began to look better to Priestley as it receded. He recalled his childhood in Bradford, before life had become spoiled by illusions of material salvation, as a satisfying time. Then people were far less barraged by exhortations to acquire ever more products, and consequently they had far less anxiety about money:

> My father never had much money, but then he was not thinking about money but about other and better things ... Probably [his style

of life] would seem to people now ridiculously old-fashioned, narrow, inconvenient, altogether too limited. But if it is states of mind
that are important, and not things, possessions, status symbols,
grabbing and spending money, then that was the good life.[115]

Priestley gave pungent, uninhibited expression to sentiments ob-
servable in leading Labour politicians. Bevan's reactions to America,
for instance, later to be amplified by Priestley, were echoed by
Clement Attlee, who disapprovingly noted on a wartime visit that
American unions were much too materialist in their aims.[116]

Even the architect of the postwar export drive, Sir Stafford Cripps
(1889-1952), accompanied his ritual exhortations to higher production with even firmer and more heartfelt exhortations to austerity in
consumption. The nation, when it understood that moral values came
ahead of material gratification, could learn to do without. A country
landowner from an ancient gentry family, Cripps was an archetypal
Tory socialist who looked to the Church of England rather than to
any political party to provide, as he put it, "the moral force and the
driving power for social and economic development."[117]

The "battle of the dollar gap," he emphasized in a 1947 broadcast to
the nation,

> is not merely a battle for material things . . . There is not one of us
> who does not realise in our heart of hearts that there are greater
> values in our lives than the mere material things of which we may
> now have to go short. The love of our families, the friendship of our
> comrades, our attachment to our homes and our countryside, our
> passionate loyalty to the welfare of our country, all these prove to us
> day by day that our strength and our happiness reside largely in the
> things of the spirit.[118]

The easing of economic pressures in the fifties brought an end to
the zeal for raising production exemplified by Cripps. Both emerging
ideological wings of British socialism agreed that with the end of mass
unemployment, the economic problem had been largely solved. The
leading theorist of revisionism, Anthony Crosland, although attacking
"puritanism" on the Left, argued that the program for economic
growth

> should increasingly be overshadowed by the "social policies" . . . and
> we should not now judge a Labour Government's performance
> primarily by its record in the economic field . . . The pre-war reasons
> for a largely economic orientation [of Socialism] are . . . steadily
> losing their relevance; and we can increasingly divert our energies
> into more fruitful and idealistic channels, and to fulfilling earlier
> and more fundamental Socialist aspirations.[119]

In the other flank of the party, the Bevanites too were turning away
from economics while carrying on Cripp's disapproval of acquisition
and consumption. Aneurin Bevan (1897-1960) himself, his follower

Michael Foot has stressed, "was profoundly critical of many of the most spectacular developments in modern industrial civilization and he was critical in terms which are rarely employed by Socialists who have forgotten or never read William Morris." The man who most profoundly influenced Bevan's thinking (with the possible exception only of Marx), José Enrique Rodo, had put it thus (when speaking of America as the exemplar of modern industrial capitalism):

> An organized society which limits its idea of civilization to the accumulation of material abundance, and of justice to their equitable distribution among its members, will never make of its great cities anything that differs essentially from the heaping up of ant-hills.[120]

Bevan's essential complaint against industrial capitalism was, like Priestley's (and Bryant's and Inge's as well), not material but moral. Indeed, he observed in 1952, "if the destiny of man is merely to accumulate the means of production, then there was no previous system to compare it with." But, he went on,

> it failed in the one function by which any social system must be judged. It failed to produce a tolerable home and a reputable order of values for the individual man and woman . . . Priority of values was lacking because no aim was intended but the vulgar one of the size of the bank balance . . . Efficiency was its final arbiter – as though loving, laughing, worshipping, eating, the deep serenity of a happy home, the warmth of friends, the astringent revelation of new beauty, and the earth tug of local roots will ever yield to such a test.[121]

This polarity of efficiency versus human values was thus readily drawn by as many socialists as Conservatives (not to mention many politically unaligned churchmen). The attitudes that the polarity stood for had indeed become deeply rooted in middle- and upper-class opinion. When Harold Macmillan ventured, uncharacteristically, to tell the electorate in American fashion in 1959 that "they never had it so good," he was disparaged on all sides of educated opinion for this vulgar appeal to materialism.[122] The world of politics was permeated with the values and sentiments of the gentry counterrevolution against industrial capitalism. Consequently, the political elite, like the social and cultural elite of which it was part, both desired and feared technical advance and economic growth.

7

The gentrification of the industrialist

> I believe that the worship of material values is the fatal disease from which our age is suffering, and that, if we do not eradicate this worship, it will inevitably destroy our whole society and not even leave us any business to discuss. We must steadfastly keep on reminding ourselves all the time that material efficiency is only a means and not an end.
> —Samuel Courtauld, address to the Engineers' Club, Manchester (1942)

The image of an essentially rural, traditional England, and the distrust of materialism and economic change that went along with it, had practical effects on business. They kept alive a mental picture of modern, industrial England as a society of "dark, satanic mills," neither appealing nor quite legitimate as an expression of the English way of life. Social prestige and moral approbation were to be found by using the wealth acquired in industry to escape it. This myth of England both diverted talent and energies from industry and gave a particular "gentry" cast to existing industry, discouraging commitment to a wholehearted pursuit of economic growth.

For a century and a half the industrialist was an essential part of English society, yet he was never quite sure of his place. The educated public's suspicions of business and industry inevitably colored the self-image and goals of the business community. Industrialists responded to their mental environment, sometimes by seeking to leave the world of production for more acceptable realms of gentility, and sometimes by striving to adapt their way of life to the canons of gentility. Rarely were these canons challenged, and then only by self-professed "rugged individualists" who had a strong sense of swimming against the tide. As a rule, leaders of commerce and industry in England over the past century have accommodated themselves to an elite culture blended of preindustrial aristocratic and religious values and more recent professional and bureaucratic values that inhibited their quest for expansion, productivity, and profit.

Finance versus industry

An important distinction must be borne in mind at the outset. Nineteenth-century economic development threw up not one but two groups of new businessmen, with differing characteristics and different fates: one based on commerce and finance and centered in London, the other based on manufacturing and centered in the North.[1] Although these classes gradually merged with the old landed elite in the twentieth century, it was the first of these groups that was decidedly richer, more powerful, and possessed of a more distinguished historical pedigree – and was, like the growing stratum of professional men, much more readily accepted by that older elite. In particular, the City, with its centuries-old traditions, its location near the heart of upper-class England, and its gradually woven, closely knit ties to the aristocracy and gentry, enjoyed a social cachet that evaded industry.[2]

The distinction between finance and industry makes more comprehensible the failure of Victorian economic transformation to produce a revolution in social values. As W. D. Rubinstein has pointed out, to accept the centrality of this distinction is "to make the fundamental break which the Industrial Revolution undoubtedly represented less important, and to make the continuities at the top of society between the Old Society and the New stronger and more tenacious." The new elite of wealth, even during that century of industrialization, was, more than has been realized, "traditionalist, Anglican, and, in a very real sense, conservative."[3] New wealth was not as likely, as historians once assumed, to be associated with industry; the new culture of industrialization was consequently limited in extent. In the realm of social structure as in that of values, the impact of the industrial revolution was muffled in Britain. The industrialist was left somewhat isolated, the legatee of an aborted rebellion against the standards of "upper Englishry," standards that refused to take the processes of material production quite seriously.

Such a separation within the upper levels of British capitalism helps explain the aloofness of the twentieth-century City from the needs of British industry. This aloofness can be traced back to the eighteen-seventies, when so much of the social pattern of modern Britain was being fixed. The year 1878, which saw the failure of the City of Glasgow Bank, was, W. P. Kennedy has argued, a watershed for British banking's relation to industry: "A point had been reached where the entire system had either to be reorganized to withstand the greater risks of steadily enlarging industrial requirements or the system had to withdraw from long term industrial involvement. The system withdrew. After 1878, no longer would banks become willingly involved in the long term financing of industry." The capital markets became "deeply biased away from favoring most home industrial projects." Consequently, the development of industry was handicapped, and a vicious circle of declining relative profitability was created that continued through the twentieth century. Insufficient long-term investment hobbled productivity growth, which in turn made such investment ever less attractive, and so on in a downward spiral. Particularly hurt were the new electrical equipment and automobile industries, two of the industries of the "second industrial revolution."[4]

Why did British bankers take that turn away from industry? Domestic industry may already have become less profitable than other opportunities afforded by a rapidly developing world economy. Yet there seems to be more to it than this. That financial watershed paralleled the wider cultural watershed: As Kennedy observed about capital markets, "Institutions successfully created in Britain to ensure the stability necessary to early industrialization were distinctly less appropriate for the problems of sustaining subsequent development."[5] The stability had been achieved; now what was becoming necessary was a radical overhaul of institutions (and values) to actively foster continued development. Instead, stability remained the overriding end; confronted with the choice between safety and maximum growth, the financial system (like the social system as a whole) opted for safety. This pullback from industrial involvement was made more likely by the social separation that already existed between the worlds of finance and industry, and the contemporaneous entrenchment of antiindustrial sentiments in the financial and professional classes.

The existence of two unequal capitalist elites had other less direct, but no less significant, effects upon the economy. It encouraged a pattern of occupational recruitment skewed toward the more prestigious form of business activity, just as recruitment was similarly skewed toward the professions, and weakened pressures for educational attention to the needs of industry. The hiving off of an upper level of capitalists rendered the psychological position of those engaged in running industry still more exposed, for they had to suffer not only the anticapitalist shafts of Labour publicists and politicians, but also the condescension of gentlemanly professionals, civil servants, landlords, and even financiers.[6]

"Industry is a leper"
Anthony Sampson observed in 1971 that it was "impossible to divorce the question of managers' incentives from the climate of society which surround[ed] them."[7] This climate was a chilly one for English

economic enterprise and business pride. As D. C. Coleman complained in his Cambridge inaugural lecture, "The businessman has not simply been one of the more unloved figures of English history; worse than that, he has never quite been taken seriously."[8] For one brief historical moment, when men like Andrew Ure and Samuel Smiles were discovering a moral purpose in industry and finding in its progress the material for a new kind of epic drama, this seemed to be changing. But the moment passed, the purpose grew dim, and the audience turned away. Business and, most of all, industry were pushed aside to the periphery of British social and cultural concerns, to be criticized and disdained. Entries for businessmen in the *Dictionary of National Biography* have been proportionately fewer than for any other major profession, and even the obituary columns have been ungenerous to them.[9]

We have seen how the late-Victorian world of politics and government was less than welcoming to industry. Arthur Balfour and Herbert Asquith, Edwardian Tory and Liberal prime ministers, were hard to distinguish in their condescension. One of Balfour's biographers was struck by his lack of sympathy with industrialists; much the same could be said of Asquith.[10] These attitudes thoroughly permeated the upper echelons of government. Typical of the men who filled these echelons was Frederick Lugard (1858-1945), the great colonial administrator. Lugard's father, a poor clergyman, had a large family, and while at public school in 1875, Lugard was offered a job in the business of his elder half sister's husband. He considered leaving school early to take the job, but was painfully aware that if he did so he would forego any chance of sitting for the Indian civil service examination. He wrote about his dilemma to his younger half sister:

> If I go in for this [the business job] I have to throw overboard the I.C.S. which if I passed it would be an infinitely better thing besides being a thoroughly gentlemanly occupation, and look at it how I may, I can't bring myself to think that an Assistant in a Sugar Factory is such. Of course "a gentleman is a gentleman wherever he is," but still the Lugards have been in the Army and in the Church, good servants of God or the Queen, but few if any have been tradesmen.[11]

Lugard decided for the ICS: He failed the examination and went into the army instead.

This aversion was long-lasting, as Alexander Cockburn illustrated with an anecdote:

> In 1939 a British businessman of my acquaintance was sent by the Department of Economic Warfare to Ankara. His mission was to buy up certain Turkish commodities of strategic value and thus deny them to the Germans. Generously supplied with cash, he went to

work with a will. But be began to find his patriotic labors impeded at every turn by the British ambassador in Ankara, Sir Hughe Knatch-bull-Hugessen, a person subsequently best remembered for having had the misfortune to employ a German spy as his valet. The businessman tried to explain to Sir Hughe the strategic importance of his activities. The ambassador brushed his explanations aside. "Don't speak to me of commerce and finance, sir," he impatiently exclaimed. "It goes in one ear and out the other."[12]

The intelligentsia, so often critical of men like Sir Hughe, was at heart with him in this matter. Harold Nicolson, a successful diplomat who was also an intimate member of the Bloomsbury circle, was expressing the deeply-rooted prejudice of both milieus when he confided his conviction that "really . . . the intelligence of the ordinary Leicester businessman [was] subnormal."[13] As Noel Annan noted a few years ago, "one common assumption" shared by most English men of letters in this century was "that the career of moneymaking, industry, business, profits, or efficiency is a despicable life in which no sane and enlightened person should be engaged; and that indeed such people are unworthy of a novelist's attention." Annan saw how the assumption extended, in Britain more than elsewhere, beyond the literary world, "across the whole spectrum of opinion makers," where the life of industry and business was denigrated. In Britain, as in no other country, he observed, "life began slowly to imitate art. The British began to govern their national life by the classic assumption of the novel." The "propaganda of the intelligentsia" became "the accepted gospel of the country."[14]

A business historian has pointed to the instructive contrast between the American attitude toward Henry Ford and the English attitude toward his counterpart, William Morris (1877-1963), founder of Morris Motors, the ancestor of British Leyland. "Ford is a folk hero," Neil McKendrick argued, "who attracts fame and controversy. Morris has received largely uninformed and unenthusiastic acceptance." He found the differing posthumous fames of the two English William Morrises even more instructive: "For despite leaving one of the most popular cars in the world to bear his name, William Morris is completely overshadowed by his Victorian namesake in the mental reference map of most educated men and women."[15] Such disdain has been a commonplace of educated opinion over the years. A reviewer in the *Times Literary Supplement* could claim in 1969 that "private enterprise business and businessmen are more disliked, detracted and depreciated by the British radio, press, and two out of our three political parties than by all parties and media of public communication in all other western countries." In the same period, a chief executive vented the kind of feeling that rarely saw print, complaining to a business writer that, behind all the public exhortations to industrial growth, "industry is a leper." Not surprisingly, a poll of directors of leading British companies in 1974 revealed that 75 percent thought that television was "biased against business and private enterprise," and 88 percent felt that universities were similarly biased; despite the business gloom of that annus terribilis, not many felt the problem to be new.[16] In fact, it was not new. As should be clear by now, the unattractiveness of the life of industry and trade reflected the predominance of gentlemanly standards, derived in part from the landed aristocracy and in part from the rise of the professions and the civil service – standards set in the course of the nineteenth century.

Education and the image of industry
The uncertain position of industry stands out from the history of education in Britain. Elite educational institutions from the Victorian era on, as we have seen, reflected and propagated an antiindustrial bias. The genteel pattern of the later-Victorian public school was fixed (one level lower) on the new state grammar schools from their establishment by the Education Act of 1902. Similarly, the ancient universities served as a powerful model for state-provided higher education in the twentieth century. The University of Oxford, one science don complained in 1903, "has always ostentatiously held herself aloof from manufacturers and commerce."[17] At the civic universities, strong links with industry were gradually forged, as Michael Sanderson has shown, but only with the stigma of low prestige.[18]

Technological education made slow headway. Manufacturers aspiring to the status of full-fledged gentlemen recognized that engineering was not a suitable career for such a goal. Consequently, they did not seek it for their sons. "It was admitted," Sir Eric Ashby has observed, "that the study of science for its useful applications might be appropriate for the labouring classes, but managers were not attracted to the study of science except as an agreeable occupation for their leisure."[19] Thus, engineering was left to the sons of the skilled working class. Such segregation of the subject by social class indicated the true valuation of technological studies in Victorian and Edwardian England. That Chamber of Commerce speakers and politicians on tour in the North gave ritual genuflections to "the greatness of British industry," "the workshop of the world," and the rest, counted for little against their own hopes that their children would escape the world of industry.

In the interwar years, there was a rise in the number of university graduates entering industry, but this occurred more out of necessity (as a mounting number of graduates confronted a scarcity

of openings in the overseas civil service and the traditional professions) than choice. The better students on the whole found more
gentlemanly employment, and the number of industrialists' and
engineers' sons leaving behind their fathers' sort of life continued to
exceed the number of graduates entering it. On balance, the universities were still, as earlier, an avenue out of, not into, industry.
Yet even so, dons like Sir Ernest Barker deplored the hesitant
appearance of courses of study related to industrial needs. Barker
worried in 1931 that universities would degenerate into "handy"
institutions furnishing "even the world of business" with recruits.
The ancient universities in particular had the duty, in Barker's eyes,
of defending for the rest the "stronghold of pure learning" and
"long time values against the demands of material progress."[20]
When such "demands" were embodied in an actual industrialist
actually impinging upon the university, as most notably in the case
of the Oxford motorcar manufacturer, William Morris, the academic response was more pungent. "How I hate that man," was C. S.
Lewis's dismissive comment on one of the greatest benefactors of
Oxford University.[21]

The Second World War gave the government a direct interest in
the development of technical courses in universities. Yet, as a vice-
chancellor complained in 1958: "The crude engineer, the mere
technologist (the very adjectives are symptoms of the attitude) are
tolerated in universities because the State and industry are willing to
finance them. Tolerated, but not assimilated."[22] During the nineteen-
sixties, the government's attention turned to the technical colleges
founded in the nineteenth century, whose development had long
been hampered by social prejudice. They were "promoted," first to
colleges of advanced technology, then to full universities. In their
wake, the numerous little-known polytechnic and mechanics' institutes were upgraded and merged into "New Polytechnics." It is too
soon to tell whether a fundamental change transpired; educational
shifts require decades to make their full impact on society. Certainly,
however, traditional attitudes were not easily dislodged.[23]

Long-standing attitudes eroded the hoped-for effects of educational reform and expansion. The first wave of new universities – the
small, elite creations led by Sussex – turned out to be as notable for its
continuity with Oxbridge tradition as for its modernity. As A. J. P.
Taylor (a Manchester boy) objected, "They all assert the doctrine that
university education is a way of escape from life, and not a preparation for it." Their founders, remarked one writer, "preferred tourist
sites to turbines." Whereas politicians were raising the call for technologists, the new universities of the early and mid-sixties devoted
most of their resources to the arts and social sciences. Only one of the

seven founding vice-chancellors measured up to the yardstick set by C. P. Snow: more than nodding acquaintance with the Second Law of Thermodynamics. Their potential clientele clearly shared this bias: Unfilled science places appeared by 1967-8, even while the universities were being deluged with applicants.[24]

One new university did stress a "close relationship with industry" – Warwick, the only one placed in an industrial region. Management studies and engineering were rapidly developed, business firms contributed to the endowment of chairs, and the dream of a great Midlands MIT began to take shape. The dream blew up in 1970, caught between pressures from businessmen and an increasingly antibusiness student-movement. The Warwick confrontation, involving sit-ins, publication of files, and a shake-up of administrative policies and personnel, played the international theme of student revolt with characteristic English overtones. Students and faculty radicals struck a responsive chord in the educated public with their charges of commercial corruption of higher national values at Warwick, and potentially everywhere: "It is sobering to realise," the Warwick rebels warned (sounding precisely like J. B. Priestley),

> that the mid-Atlantic of Midlands Motor and Aircraft Industry offers one possible model of a British future. It is a febrile, wasteful, publicity-conscious world, whose prosperity floats upon hire-purchase and the shifting moods of the status-conscious consumer; a brash, amoral, pushful world of expense-account living, lavish salesman-ship, cocktail bars in restored sixteenth-century inglenooks, and of refined managerial techniques of measured day-work; a world of mergers and takeovers, of the unregenerate, uninhibited Mammon of the Sunday business supplements.[25]

If the prestigious new universities kept their distance from industry, what of the universities formed from older technical colleges? Even here, "practical" studies, clear vocational orientations, and close connections with industry were all associated with low status. As their status rose, their emphases tended to alter correspondingly. In becoming universities, the colleges of advanced technology became much more conscious of their respectability and, in the view of one knowledgeable critic, "turned their back on their technical college tradition and embraced that of the universities."[26]

Even the new educational philosophies of the sixties and seventies carried on many of the traditional biases against economic enterprise and technical innovation. John Rae argued in 1977 that "the so-called reforms in British education all have a familiar ring," reminiscent as they were of much of later-Victorian public school orthodoxy in their continuation of a bias against trade and industry. In the Victorian public school the low status given a career in trade and industry did serve a purpose – the empire needed a large, confident, and fairly conventional class of administrators, whereas the economy seemed to be taking care of itself. This situation reversed itself a century later. As the empire disappeared and the economy lagged, the need to reform the curriculum and to destroy "its unworldly bias" arose – and was missed.[27]

By the mid-seventies, little seemed to have changed. The *New Statesman*'s education correspondent could still observe that the engineer's low status "is at the heart of our industrial problem." This observation was warmly seconded by a reader, an engineer with a half century of working experience, who contributed some personal recollections:

> An engineer friend of mine was taken by his bank manager father to luncheon a few years ago, in the latter's club, the exclusiveness of which was impressed upon my friend beforehand. "I don't know," the father said, "how they [the members] will regard an engineer." My friend, I may add, held a responsible position in the design office of a prominent engineering firm. "I got the message," he told me.
>
> An acquaintance spoke of his fiancée's father as one who "does the drains in ———."He was in fact, the borough engineer of that town!

By contrast, on the Continent an engineer was frequently addressed as "Engineer," much as a medical man is addressed as "Doctor." Nowhere in continental Europe, remarked a management consultant, "does one find the extraordinary British split of 'pure' and 'applied' science," one "clean," the other "dirty."[28]

The attitudes of university graduates were slow to change. In the early sixties, the sociologist Ferdynand Zweig observed that "industry [has] . . . failed to captivate the imaginations of Oxford students"; in 1976, Prime Minister Callaghan similarly complained that "many of our best trained students . . . have no desire to join industry." A 1970 survey of student attitudes toward industry found, predictably, a combination of ignorance and distaste. One of the nation's major firms confided anonymously to the *Observer* in 1975 that in university recruiting interviews "it is almost unknown for any interest to be expressed in a career in manufacturing." Even geography helped maintain this low status; the least fashionable parts of the country to live in were the most industrial areas. The pattern Roy Lewis and Rosemary Stewart had found in the late fifties seemed still to be true: They had concluded, after many interviews with graduates, that those who had entered industry had done so mainly for one of three reasons: "family tradition, money, or because, having failed to get the kind of work they want, it is the only alternative to teaching." As one young man told them: "My first choice was the Foreign Office, my second UNESCO, my third the BBC, my fourth *The Times*; then there was nothing left but teaching or business, and as I can't bear little boys, it had to be business." The hero of Margaret Drabble's roman à clef, *The Ice Age*, emerged from university (Cambridge) in the early sixties disdainfully oblivious to the world of manufacturing:

> It must be said that it never once crossed Anthony Keating's mind that he might get a job in industry. Rebel he was, but not to such a degree: so deeply conditioned are some sections of the British nation that some thoughts are deeply inaccessible to them. Despite the fact that major companies were at that time appealing urgently for graduates in any field, despite the fact that the national press was full of seductive offers, the college notice boards plastered with them, Anthony Keating, child of the professional middle classes, reared in an anachronism as an anachronism, did not even see the offers: he walked past them daily, turned over pages daily, with as much indifference as if they had been written in Turkish or Hungarian. He thought himself superior to that kind of thing: that kind of advertisement was aimed at bores and sloggers, not at men of vision like Anthony Keating.[29]

Industry in other developed countries – the United States, West Germany, France, Japan – found it easier to recruit managers and technologists with high qualifications. An economist and a socialist – attempting in 1976 to explain why, in West Germany, a higher proportion of better graduates entered industry, the best of them frequently possessing engineering degrees – saw as "central" the status of industry: "The ideas that industry is not a fitting occupation of a gentleman (old version), or for an intellectual (new version), seem not to have existed in Germany. In West Germany neither making money nor making three-dimensional artifacts are culturally dubious activities."[30] Similarly, in postwar France, the technocrat, combining technical and managerial training and roles, played a powerful role throughout industry and also in government. Engineers, managers, and civil servants did not form separate social categories, but shared a similar background, training, and outlook. The shock of defeat and occupation spurred an ongoing revision in the value attached to economic development, and consequently the stigma that once may have adhered to business and industry became confined, as in West Germany, to narrow circles of disaffected intellectuals.[31] This also happened, in even more striking form, in Japan. There the twentieth century witnessed a dramatic reversal of social values, as the samurai contempt for merchants vanished without a trace, to be replaced by an integration of the businessmen – as businessmen – into the elite power structure, an integration that was even more thoroughgoing than that in France or West Germany. Engineers had perhaps less traditional hostility to overcome, for of course craftsmanship had been esteemed; nonetheless, technological expertise has never been more valued

than in contemporary Japan. Whereas, in Britain, provision for technological education outran demand, in Japan entrance into engineering programs has been highly competitive, more so than for any area
except medicine.[32] In France, West Germany, and Japan, defeat in
war seemed to provide a spur to industrial recovery and advance, and
to the image of industry as a national cause that was lacking in
victorious Britain. For a variety of causes, then, an industrial career
was in the twentieth century less esteemed in Britain than elsewhere.[33]

Industrialists as aspiring gentry
The failure of industry to rise in status in Britain, as it did elsewhere
over the past century, encouraged in Britain a hemorrhage of talent
out of this area, as in the well-known case of Marshalls of Leeds, a
renowned firm that sank as the founder's sons and grandsons took up
the more congenial role of rentier country gentlemen.[34] It also condi-
tioned the outlook of those who remained in or entered industry.
Businessmen's self-images and aims adapted to the climate of opinion. The minister for economic affairs at the U.S. embassy in London
in 1955 was struck by

> a sense of doubt concerning the social utility of industry and the
> legitimacy of profit, a sort of industrial inferiority complex often
> suffered by business leaders themselves . . . In the extreme, some
> British industrialists seem almost ashamed of their vocation, looking
> on their jobs as a necessary evil or – in the case of family businesses –
> an inherited "white man's burden."[35]

British businessmen have been reticent in print about their business
achievements. Despite the appeal of the success story, autobiographies
are scarce. Neil McKendrick blamed this paucity, so frustrating to the
historian, on the desire of successful businessmen in their later years
to downplay their connection with profit-seeking industry and trade.[36]
Businessmen not only tended to be self-deprecatory and apologetic
about their economic role, but they also sought to emulate the one
fully approved standard – that of the gentleman. The most striking
development in the social history of the businessman and the industrialist over the last century was the gentrification of the business
class. What Walter Bagehot called "the rough and vulgar structure of
English commerce . . . the secret of its life"[37] was increasingly smoothed
out and refined. The higher one moved in the British business world,
the more did gentlemanly standards come to prevail. As Peregrine
Worsthorne, associate editor of the Sunday *Telegraph*, has reflected,
the cruder impulses of capitalism and industrialism had been tamed:
"Throughout the rough years of British Capitalism, the distinctively
inhuman or impersonal characteristics of that type of economic
organization were never allowed entirely to supersede the gentle-

manly tradition of human relations or the paternalistic concept of noblesse oblige."[38] It was far more rewarding to be seen and to act as a squire than as a Gradgrind of Bounderby.

The chief agent transmitting these standards was the same institution that first promoted a negative view of the life of business and industry – the educational system, particularly the public schools, developed by the Victorians. Even while the public schools were directing their best pupils away from industry, the spread of the public school model of education ensured that increasing numbers of highly placed industrial managers were public school products. Despite inculcated preferences for professional and bureaucratic careers, these were simply not expanding at a sufficient rate to absorb the rising numbers of public school graduates. Thus, virtually all the leading public schools were sending more and more of their boys into the business world – 6 percent from Marlborough in 1846, but 23 percent in 1906; 6 percent from Merchant Taylors in 1851, but 42 percent in 1891; 9 percent from Clifton in 1867, but 25 percent in 1907.[39] This trend continued in the twentieth century, more, it would seem, out of necessity than choice. In 1951, a sample inquiry revealed that approximately 58 percent of the directors of the larger public companies in Britain had been at public schools.[40] Charlotte Erickson's study of the leadership of the British steel industry showed a steady increase in the proportion of leaders educated at public schools. Similarly, in the early twentieth century, Oxford and Cambridge drew ahead of provincial universities as the favored venues for that minority of steel leaders who went to universities. Most who had been to the ancient universities had read arts, not science. A rising proportion of these Establishment-educated industrialists were sons of men in the industry. The increasing importance of these institutions in the training of future steelmakers was not, therefore, a sign of any major increase in the appeal of an industrial career to the sons of the professional and upper classes. Nor was it, Erickson concluded, so much the result of a conscious recruitment policy on the part of firms as "a reflection of the high degree of family control and the attitudes of these families that education for social status was to be preferred to specific education for an industrial career." By contrast, Erickson found a very different pattern in the Nottingham hosiery industry. Only a few hosiers received an elite education.[41] Operating on a much smaller scale, in a more provincial environment, these men never attained the wealth of the steelmakers, or with it the aspiration to high status. The pattern of steel was repeated in other major industries. As time went on, the larger the business the more likely it was that its leaders had attended public schools or the ancient universities.[42] More and more in the twentieth century, the higher echelons of the larger businesses were dominated by men whose standards had been formed in the gentlemanly mold; these men themselves set a pattern to be emulated by managers lower down the scale of authority.

Within industry, D. C. Coleman has argued, the growing influence of the gentlemanly ideal – the ideal of the educated amateur – helped call forth another ideal, that of the "practical man." This ideal superficially opposed, but in many ways complemented, the first. The "practical man" was the defensive ideal of those who had not received an elite education, and who responded (not necessarily with logical consistency) by disparaging the value of education or formal training for their work – while, at the same time, aspiring to the ranks of gentlemen.[43] The "cult of the practical man" was thus not what it might once have been – an alternative ideal – but a transitional ideology, for managers not yet become gentlemen. As such, it posed no challenge to the growing hegemony of gentlemanly standards, and indeed reinforced its economically inhibiting tendencies.

The twin cults of the educated amateur and the practical man strengthened resistance to science-based innovation. Both parties had a built-in distrust of any theoretically grounded knowledge. "Economics, management techniques, industrial psychology," observed Coleman, "all were frequently looked upon with grave suspicion, for they represented attempts to professionalize an activity long carried on jointly by 'practical men' and gentlemanly amateurs." Furthermore, they bolstered the inclination to place the highest value on stability and order. As they became successful directors, "practical men" became ever more interested in the immediate gratification of social ambitions, in the playing out of certain social roles, than in direct profit maximization or innovational activity. They found their main task in life to be ensuring that they and their heirs behave like leisured landed gentry rather than like the successful innovators they had once been. They thus drew closer in attitude to the gentlemen who sat with them around the boardroom table, who had already been inculcated with "a vague but persistent belief that some things were indeed more important than profits."[44]

The gentlemanly ideal fostered in managers a lack of commitment to their vocation. In 1931, André Siegfried had already noted resistance to making "a job of work": "A gentleman, we must realize, never strives too much; it is not considered the thing."[45] Striving, that is, in his work; a great deal of energy might be expended in rising above it. Nowhere else in the industrialized world, Michael Shanks observed in 1962, "are trade and manufacture regarded to such an extent as means to *better* things – to politics, to land-ownership, to culture, to a position in the City."[46] Managerial activity was seen not only as a way station, but also often as only a part, and not the most important part, of one's present life. Roy Lewis and Rosemary Stewart, comparing American, German, and British managers in the fifties, were struck how the latter,

> lacking the support of public opinion, tends to regard his [sic] work either as only one aspect of his life, or as a rather distasteful way of acquiring the wherewithal to conduct their real life, their private life, according to the civilized and serious ritual which expressed the values that are considered really important.[47]

No wonder, when they had been told thus for decades. Even diligent statesmen would be praised for evidence that they, too, were not slaves to the job. Typically, Arthur Bryant had seized in 1936 upon one of Neville Chamberlain's letters to a paper about bird-watching to anoint him with the mantle of true Englishness. "In a single short letter," Bryant enthused, Mr. Chamberlain "has done more to capture the heart of his countrymen than in all the actions and speeches of a long and highly useful political life." Chamberlain was not, after all, simply a businessman in politics. "We may have become a nation of business men," Bryant argued, "but we are business men in spite of ourselves. We do not like or respect a man merely because he wears black and grey trouserings and sits at a desk all day. What we really like and admire about him is what he does when he gets away from the desk."[48]

Such attitudes lived on in the postwar rise of management education, which assumed in Britain a characteristically gentlemanly form. The Oxbridge tradition of teaching not how to *do* certain kinds of work but how to *be* a certain kind of person inclined the new management education toward, in one consultant's view, "acculturisation for social roles at the expense of work itself." Beginning with Henley, housed on an archetypal country estate, such institutions spread a pastoral, gentry veneer over rising young executives. "We are really in the civilising business here," the head of one such establishment privately reflected. Even the newest, most serious, and most "American" of these institutions – the business schools at Manchester and London – did not entirely escape the pull of this tradition. In London, the school's choice of location and housing was significant: A decade after its founding, Alastair Mant observed in 1977,

> almost the most important man in the London Business School remains John Nash, the creator of its magnificent home. You enter the place round the back, nearest the noise and hubbub of urban London, walking into a humdrum, convex modern shell. A few paces east (or, symbolically, six to ten weeks or one to two years later) you emerge, cradled by the concave Palladian splendour of the old front, into the Regent's Park. "Here," it was said, is "every man a king!" The sensation is more than symbolic; if you happen to work in despised industry and, worse, if you missed university of any kind, not to

mention Oxbridge, then to pass through this building is to press a little closer to the extreme centre of concentric British society. It is not a process to be despised; it is a matter of no little import to British businessmen to be made whole again, to re-enter society more fully from the social outskirts of trade and commerce.[49]

Within industry, the gentlemanly ideal created a hierarchy of status. Bankers' depreciation of industrial managers was mimicked by these managers' depreciation of technicians and salesmen. Marketing went against the grain of gentility, which Harold Laski saw as nurturing "a refusal to consider adequately the wants of the customer; he must buy not the thing he desires but the thing you have to sell." There was, after all, something repugnant about pandering to and even stimulating materialistic mass tastes.[50]

Even more than sales, however, production itself was the Cinderella of British industry. Of all industrial sectors, production was in the twentieth century the worst paid, and the least likely to lead to high management positions. In Germany, Sweden, and Japan, engineers became much more fully represented in the ranks of management. In Britain, areas of training like law and accountancy were more advantageous than engineering for career advancement.[51] "It is as if," Mant observed of this imbalance, "the primary task of industry was laundering money, with production as an irksome constraint on that primary task rather than vice versa."[52] Men of talent who did find their way into production showed, as Anthony Bambridge put it in 1975, "an unseemly haste to get out." He cited a report by the British Institute of Management on business graduates in industry that found that although 17 percent of business graduates were employed in production before going to business school, only 6 percent returned to production.[53] Such behavior was a rational personal response to the prevalent standards of prestige and reward within British industry.

There was one way that production could be valued: if it were separated from questions of utility, and treated as a pure technical problem. At Rolls-Royce, ever since the First World War, commercial values had not been allowed to intrude upon dedication to technical perfection. Its chairman replied to Anthony Sampson's question about profits in 1969: "If you said we're here to make profits, we'd never be making aeroengines: we'd have gone into property years ago."[54] In this special "pure engineering" ethos, the disdain of the gentleman for the descent into the marketplace was reproduced, and obsession with production legitimized. The price was eventual bankruptcy in 1971.

Foreign economic successes evoked an ambivalent response from gentrified managers: envy of the success itself, but distaste for the way of life out of which it sprang. In the nineteen-twenties and thirties, Prime Minister Baldwin had assured both business audiences and the general public that they need not and ought not abandon traditional standards in favor of apparently more successful alien ones. Foreigners, whether German, Russian, or American, lacked the keys to the good life that the English possessed. Such themes were played over and over in all quarters. The *Listener* summed them up in a 1958 leader entitled "The British Way of Life":

> There are those who would root up the past over here and sacrifice everything to the hydra-headed monster of salesmanship. Sometimes one feels there is too much of that about the American way of life, where everything from an academic magazine to a religious service in church has to be pushed and pummelled for fear it will be missed. The truth is surely that both traditional values and modern triumphs need celebrating.[55]

Americans in particular (and more recently Japanese) were perceived by many leaders of industry (as they had been for a long time by educated opinion generally) as narrow people obsessed with the economic side of life, paying for their material successes with the quality of personal life. Even in the largest companies, where international competition was most severe (perhaps *especially* in such companies, given the education of their directors), sophisticated, worldly managers were yet reluctant to emulate the ways of their overseas competitors, seeing them as a threat to a cherished way of life. Given free sway, it seemed, foreign ways would subvert the "English way."

Samuel Courtauld (1876-1942), chairman from 1921 to 1946 of the Victorian family silk firm that had become by his accession the world's leading producer of rayon, feared the growing influence of America. In 1927 he confessed: "I view the so-called 'Americanization of Europe' with the utmost dislike. I doubt whether American ideals of living – purely materialistic as they are – will finally lead to a contented working nation anywhere when the excitement of constant expansion has come to an end." Courtauld admired American technical achievements, but despised what he saw as the American way of life, its business included, and wanted no part of it in Britain.[56] A collector of Impressionist paintings and a friend of literary figures, Courtauld exemplified the new type of gentleman-industrialist. His views came to be echoed by other industrial leaders until they formed an almost unconscious mind-set.

As the need to modernize industry became obvious, the example of foreign models had this mind-set to contend with. Peter Menzies, deputy chairman of Imperial Chemical Industries, Britain's third largest company, told Graham Turner in the late sixties that it would be wrong for British businesses to "take up the American pattern"; the British, he felt, needed to protect consciously their less materialistic way of life. "The Americans," he explained, "are very deep into the rat race and the people of Western Europe want a wider life, they don't just want money to spend. In that sense, we're in something of a quandary – we want to keep our private lives while staying in the first league." "Even the most energetic Englishman," said one managing director, "won't buy this business of total dedication to the company. I feel that in giving myself seventy-five percent of the time I'm doing quite enough." Similarly, Lord Stokes, head of British Leyland, told Turner he wanted to "stay half-way" – adopting certain valuable American management techniques without importing the many unattractive features of their business style.[57] In the seventies, Japan replaced America as the model of economic success, with similar responses from business. Again, worries were expressed about the rat race, the overvaluation of material things, and the threat to one's private life.[58] As one permanent secretary had put it in the sixties: "We want to have the fruits of American society, but we are not prepared to accept the roots."[59] For "American" one could now read "Japanese" or "German"; the attitude was the same. Even a business journalist, trying to make his readers recognize "that industry is the prime force in our national prosperity," prefaced his book with this disclaimer: "I would not regard the emulation of the sort of societies which exist in America, West Germany or Japan as any sort of achievement. We already have a society which American critics believe to be the most civilized in the world."[60]

The English tradition of business was portrayed, in comparison with foreign models, as founded on the values of "humanity," "honor," and "craftsmanship." Back in 1911, the *Engineer* had objected to American ideas of scientific management with the comment that "there are fair ways and unfair ways of diminishing labour costs ... We do not hesitate to say that Taylorism is inhuman."[61] We have seen Stanley Baldwin, in his pronouncements on industry, constantly harking back to a time of gentler human relations (typified by his old family firm, "where nobody ever got the sack") and of "honest craftsmanship." The Institute of Industrial Administration, from its foundation in 1920, propagated a "higher" conception of management than that coming over from the United States. One of the most influential interwar books on management told of service replacing the profit motive, which as a prime industrial goal "becomes increasingly remote and archaic."[62] In a similar fashion, family and military analogies were favored in describing the ideal character of industrial life. The president of the Institute of Labour Management, in a 1943 speech, took as his theme the naval phrase "a happy ship." He said, reported the journal of the institute,

> that the old conception of industry was based on the amount of money to be made out of it, and he suggested that the proper outlook was how much happiness sprang from it; happiness resulting from the efficiency of its human relations and bred of a sense of security and self-respect in all the members of the team.[63]

The purpose of industry was seen less and less as primarily that of producing goods efficiently; industry had overriding social obligations. As Samuel Courtauld put it: "The quality of the workers who leave the factory doors every evening is an even more important thing than the quality of the products which it delivers to the customers."[64]

At the depth of the depression in the thirties, another writer of this mode called for clinging fast to the specially humane and moral English tradition of business. The current world crisis, J. Aubrey Rees (editor of *The Grocer's Year Book*) insisted, demanded more, not less, regard for human values as opposed to material values. Here England could play a uniquely valuable role, as long as it held fast to its traditions:

> At a time when the world seems to have lost its sense of direction, England, true to its age-old traditions, can make its definite contribution . . . In moments such as these . . . the one thing to be preserved at all costs is the traditional honour which has been for centuries the hall-mark of Englishmen in commercial and international relationships . . . To deface this hall-mark is to lose something greater than markets, necessary though they undoubtedly are; to lose something that has grown in the growth of our Empire, developed with the extension of our trade, and become the finest jewel – unpurchaseable – in our trading diadem. Whatever the stress, the circumstance or the difficulty, there must be no retreat from the tradition built up by the men of the past, a tradition that has made us great. There may be adjustments to meet a new situation, but this must not be the twilight of civilization.[65]

Honor, not enterprise, was the core of this tradition. Other writers stressed another facet of the English commercial tradition – dedication to quality over quantity. One such was the economic historian, Ephraim Lipson, who, comparing Britain with America in the fifties, was characteristically repelled by American standardization, and urged British manufacturers to hold fast to their traditional policy of quality and craftsmanship and to not give way to an obsession with lowering the costs, regardless of the sacrifice.[66]

British businessmen in the twentieth century came to accept a dual orientation – what one business school professor called "the British mission – to combine business with humanity."[67] As Sir George

Schuster, a director of the Westminster Bank and of several other firms, hopefully asked in 1947, "Can we, the nation of shop-keepers and money-makers, show the world how to put money-making in its right subsidiary place in the scale of values, without ceasing to perform well all the varied – and vital – functions which underlie the process of money-making?"[68]

A gentlemanly economy
These aspirations to gentility imparted a particular tone to business behavior in Britain. But its consequences were not the same throughout the business world; finance was not hampered as industry was. The milieu of finance, as we have seen, was not all that different from the traditional world of the aristocracy. It was already wealthy and socially established in the mid-nineteenth century, when the cultural counterrevolution was gaining momentum. It was "clean" – well removed from the actual processes of production. It involved the extraction of wealth by associating with people of one's own class in fashionable surroundings, not by dealing with things and with the working and lower-middle classes, in perhaps grimy and ugly and certainly unfashionable locations. The life of finance was readily reconcilable with the gentry ideal, could recruit the best talent, and could call forth its energies without apologetics or the debilitation of a collective inferiority complex. There was no hemorrhage of ability out of finance: Families like the Barings, the Barclays, the Smiths, and the Rothschilds remained active over generations, becoming indistinguishable from the old aristocracy. The inhibitions on economic enterprise that this ideal still enforced even for those in the City – resulting in the high value placed on amateurism, for instance – were counterbalanced by the great political power they wielded. Through its integration into the elite, the City could call upon government much more effectively than could industry to favor and support its interests. Further, the City did not depend upon the prosperity of the domestic economy. It was increasingly bound up more with foreign economies than with its own, and could flourish with them while British industry languished. The City, in short, offered a way (more difficult in industry) to be a gentleman and still get rich. Given all these advantages, it is not surprising that finance prospered while industry struggled.

In industry, attainment of gentlemanly status was more difficult, and normally required a greater degree of detachment from one's economic role. Gentrified industrialists became psychological, if not actual, rentiers, and their business behavior mirrored this evolution. Industry after industry exhibited the pattern of gentrification accompanied by changes in strategy and structure that hampered future growth. In shipping, the years between 1875 and 1914 saw a decline in internal competition through amalgamations and market-sharing arrangements. At the same time the character of management changed. The two areas of change, as S. G. Sturmey pointed out, were interrelated:

> The possibility of shipowners associating with their rivals depended upon the replacement of the older type of owners by people with skills in negotiating and a smaller personal pride in achievements of the ships of the lines bearing their names. A result of the reduction of competition was that shipowners became more remote from ships and the smell of the salt than were their predecessors. Coincident with these changes, shipowners became more socially important figures, the purchasers of land and the recipients of titles. It would be an exaggeration to say that in fifty years shipowners had changed from bearded salts to courtiers, but the change had differed from this only in degree.

This new structure and outlook of the shipping industry proved less and less competitive in world markets in the new century; the tonnage of ships registered in the United Kingdom declined from over 45 percent of the world total in 1900 to about 16 percent of that total in 1960, and became substantially lower thereafter.[69] This decline had many causes, some of them purely external. Yet its steepness suggests that internal structure and outlook also played their role.

In steel, D. L. Burn noted the prevalence in many firms, during the years in which they were being surpassed by German and American rivals, of "the habit of using up resources extravagantly for social and political purposes," so as to establish and keep up the new social status of the owners.[70] In the new industry of petroleum, a classic entrepreneur made a rapid transition to gentleman in just this fashion. Marcus Samuel (1853-1927), a Jew born in the East End of London, created in the late nineteenth century one of the world's leading oil companies, Shell. His enterprise made it possible for him to stake a claim on the social elite; in 1895 Samuel bought a great country estate, and in 1902 became lord mayor of London. Samuel began to devote more and more of his attention to the estate and to his largely ceremonial public duties. The result was the loss of control of Shell to a Dutch rival, Henry Deterding. When Deterding, who controlled Royal Dutch, had first proposed a merger, he had been willing to take a minority position. Samuel, too busy with his dual ceremonial roles of lord mayor and Kentish country gentleman, had put off any action. A few years later, his position undermined by Shell's loss of impetus, Samuel was forced to agree to a merger with 60:40 Dutch control.[71] The two men made an instructive contrast. For Samuel, his biographer observed, "The making of money was a very minor consideration: it was only a means to an end. His aim *was* exalted: it was through public service that he and his family could win acceptance; and more than this, he enjoyed public service for its own sake." Deterding, on the other hand, "was utterly single-minded" in his management of Royal Dutch, seeking maximum profits; Samuel had other interests, many of which had priority over Shell. What were the early goals of which Samuel dreamed? "Eton and Oxford for his sons; affluence for his more remote descendants, a country house for his family; horses, gardens, angling, watching cricket in comfort, the devotion of subordinates and servants, the respect of acquaintances, the chance to be charitable on a large scale and to give generous hospitality." Not surprisingly, then, as his biographer concluded, in business Samuel remained an "amateur," whereas Deterding was a "professional."[72]

Samuel's career pattern was repeated over and over again: The vigorous, unpolished outsider achieves a business (or professional) triumph, trades his winnings for a knighthood (or if he were important enough, like Samuel, a peerage) and a country estate, and soon becomes absorbed in the rituals of his new position, while his business touch slips away (as if, having achieved its end, it is hardly needed any longer).

Sometimes successful industrialists left business altogether; other times they stayed in business, but viewed it ever more as a social duty rather than an economic opportunity. This pattern is particularly evident in the history of family firms, which were slow in Britain to give way to more impersonal forms of organization.[73] P. Sargent Florence observed in 1953 that for the hereditary manager "the pecuniary incentive to large-scale expansion . . . may be weak, since the family are [sic] already well-established. The transpecuniary objects are often stability and a conventional standard of life with plenty of leisure and long weekends devoted to sport and other gentlemanly pursuits, rather than making one's way farther up the ladder."[74] This sort of industrialist tended to take a relaxed, "social" attitude toward his role. Sir Tatton Brinton was not untypically reluctant in the sixties to be too concerned about profits or expansion: "We are here [he confided reflectively to a journalist] to make carpets as pleasantly as possible, and to make a profit without sacrificing the provision of a good civilized life for the work-people. Human beings are first on my list. I've always been well off and I don't want to make a million quid." Even when, as was more and more the case, families lost control of their companies, the ideal of the benevolent "lord of the manor" was slow to give way. When Sir William Carr successfully defended the News of the World organization he chaired (his family then owned less than a third of the voting shares) against a takeover bid from the Pergamon Press in 1968, he appealed to this ideal. Pergamon's offer was worth a good deal more than the current market price, but "many shareholders," Sir William told the meeting, "have held shares since before the beginning of the twentieth century, and they are not complaining. The News of the World employs 8,000 people and *looks after* 20,000 or more people in the families of workers ... What is cash, money, when you have had so much other out of life as well." If his alternative plan went through, he observed, he would "have the privilege of remaining as chairman of this company – a position held by my father and grandfather."[75] Such vignettes could populate a gallery of British industry. Such attitudes limited economic performance, even in firms that had been "modernized" organizationally. Derek Channon, against his own preference for structural explanation, found in the early seventies that even when British companies adopted the American multidivisional form of organization, its "full potential" was rarely realized. Channon could explain this gap only by a "lack of desire" on the part of top management.[76]

Cultural norms resisted the challenge of dynamic entrepreneurs. Although some enthusiasts held up men like Arnold Weinstock – whom Anthony Sampson in 1971 called "a symbol for ruthless rationalization" – as a model, no rush to emulate him followed. Weinstock rose from obscurity in the sixties to become managing director of the stagnating General Electric Company and then to turn it, by the seventies, into the ninth-largest and most efficiently run company in Britain. The response to his highly publicized rise in many boardrooms, as well as elsewhere, is indicated by the widely reported remark that "what Britain needs is to use the Weinstocks to build a world in which they will be out of place."[77]

The dominant model of higher management was still the gentleman's club. The pattern was set at the top, by the prestigious Institute of Directors, which inhabited three mansions in Belgrave Square. The institute, which in 1971 numbered 43,000 members, including about 200 members of both Houses of Parliament, defended "free enterprise" in a traditionally genteel fashion, keeping aloof from the more mundane role of management. Its director-general once explained that "directors are a kind of aristocracy: they should be men of parts, and they should have interests outside their business ... you could say we were a gigantic Old Boy network."[78]

As histories of British firms are written and as their findings become known, this model stands out more and more. D. C. Coleman found the club ideal, like that of the family, running through the history of Samuel Courtauld's company. He cited the private observations in 1952 of Sir John Hanbury-Williams, Courtauld's successor as chairman (and a public school graduate and diplomat's son):

> For a long time there has been no fundamental change in the Board ... The executive Directors have directed and managed, and on the

whole they have been successful. There has been a Gentleman's Club atmosphere in the Board Room, and I believe it is true to say that over the years this has spread to all the departments of our business. It is, in fact, part of the goodwill of the company which we must safeguard.[79]

This atmosphere nourished cautious policies. Under Samuel Courtauld and Hanbury-Williams, the rapid Edwardian growth of the company was more or less consciously replaced by consolidation verging on stagnation. As Courtauld told the shareholders in 1930, the firm had "always stood for conciliation, agreement, and ordered growth."[80]

Even innovative companies often maintained features of the club idea. W. J. Reader discovered such a pattern embedded in the structure of the dynamic forerunner of ICI (Imperial Chemical Industries). By the Edwardian era, the corporate life of the management of Brunner, Mond had come to center on what was called the Winnington Hall Club, which had a narrowly restricted membership:

> Technical men of graduate standing – meaning, for practical purposes, chemists – could perhaps take [election] for granted: no one else could, least of all engineers and commercial men . . .
> The whole structure rested on class distinction. University men and professional men (amongst whom engineers were by no means automatically included) were gentlemen: the rest were not, unless they achieved the status by consent of those already holding it.

The club and its atmosphere helped Brunner, Mond to recruit the scientists that it was among the first British firms to seek by assimilating their work into the established upper-class patterns of behavior. The social structure of Brunner, Mond's management, Reader concluded, "reproduced the split in the English middle classes between 'the professions' and 'trade'." The club continued after the creation of the giant combine of ICI in 1926, and indeed flourished as never before in the thirties. "The Winnington world" then, Reader described, "was the world of a gentleman's club, with a background of affluence, expensive schools and the ancient universities in the afterglow of their Edwardian glory, and with the hard cutting edge of professional efficiency always present but never indelicately exposed.[81] Was this cutting edge, however, remaining hard in such surroundings? From its creation, ICI completely dominated the chemical industry in Britain. But like most other British companies, it did not compare favorably with its chief rivals, IG Farben in Germany and DuPont in America, in financial enterprise, marketing zeal and skill, and even its particular pride, research.[82] With its virtual monopoly of the British market, government encouragement, and the worldwide expansion of the industry, ICI grew in the wake of its international rivals through its half century of life, while the "Winnington ethos" lived on.

Marketing remained the corporation's Achilles' heel. Graham Turner noted in 1969 that

> while ICI men, not unnaturally, look upon themselves as something of an elite, they do not necessarily regard themselves as being an elite of business. "We think of ourselves as being a university with a purpose," said one of ICI's divisional chairmen. "We are very similar," said another senior executive, "to the Administrative Class of the Civil Service."

The chairman of ICI, Peter Menzies, admitted difficulty in getting his young scientists interested in "things which they may consider vulgar, like selling plastic zip fasteners."[83]

The gentlemanly ideal left its mark even on the British segment of the thoroughly international oil world. The legacy of Marcus Samuel, "never sure whether he was concerned simply with profit or with public service," was perpetuated in what Anthony Sampson has called "the ambivalence of the British oil industry."[84] In the seventies the binational colossus of Royal Dutch/Shell still had a distinctive managerial atmosphere. Sampson was struck by this when he visited the firm's head offices in London after talking to the top managers of the American oil giants, led by Exxon: "Shell men like to cultivate almost the opposite style to Exxon's: while the men in Sixth Avenue prefer not to talk about diplomacy, Shell men prefer not to talk about anything as squalid as profits." "We've never been greedy," Shell's finance coordinator told Graham Turner, and recalled that when he went about after the war saying that the prime aim of the business was profit, he was told to "tone it down a bit." Shell's history shows that of course a firm need not talk about profits to make them, or about growth to expand, but it does reveal a style and self-image characteristic of British industrialists, who have always rejected the role of "capitalist." Sampson observed how British Shell executives, mostly graduates of Oxford and Cambridge, "were inclined to talk about oil not as a profitable fluid but as part of a public duty: as one rebel complained to me: 'I wish they'd stop talking about it as if it was a bloody faith. Anyone would think it was a church'."[85]

A church, or perhaps more exactly, a department of state; as the state grew, and as the modern archetype of the gentleman came to be found in the bureaucracy, industrialists increasingly molded their behavior upon the pattern of the civil servant. In this process, the initiative did not necessarily lie with the men of industry. J. P. Nettl observed in 1965 that English businessmen had rejected the rugged individual entrepreneur as an image but had been unable to find a substitute model. Consequently, Whitehall pressured business leaders to conform to its own ideal type – that of the public servant.[86] This was most obvious in the nationalized industries,[87] but it was really a general phenomenon. Throughout big business and industry, a consensus of outlook and behavior emerged that was based on the cultural dominance of Whitehall. The normal attitude of large firms and their agents – like the Federation of British Industries – became one of acquiescence toward government: "British industry nationalizes itself," complained a professor at the London Business School in the late sixties.[88] With acquiescence came imitation: Not only the outlook but also the very procedures and modes of operation of the civil service were adopted by big business; procedures that had been developed to administer the existing society and economy, not to create new wealth. When such acculturated businessmen were called upon to play entrepreneur, the outcome tended to either "schizophrenia" or a "charade," in Nettle's terms, with nominal and actual norms failing to match.

The natural habitat of the gentleman-industrialist, of the industrialist as imitation civil servant, was a conservative one, where pervasive regulation and control (from government, and from within) substituted for innovation, where the overriding aims were the maintenance of the status quo, the ensuring of equity, the securing of stability, and the preservation of psychological space for nonbusiness activities. It was an environment in which lip service was paid to competition, enterprise, innovation, invention, and salesmanship, while the disruptive and time-consuming consequences of these were feared.[89]

This conservative managerial culture braked growth. Although other countries transformed their economic life, change came more slowly in Britain. Concern for security and stability lessened innovation and competition. The *Engineer* characteristically warned in a 1901 leader that "a hasty acceptance of apparent improvements is to be deprecated," and sixty-five years later a leading American management consultant could still note that "so many of the people who run companies are skilled maintainers of the status quo."[90]

What change there was was often rearguard action, primarily defensive in intent.[91] Conservatism meant both a gradual running down of the great industries of the first industrial revolution, and a failure to wholeheartedly develop new industries.[92] Even industrialists who criticized others for this wound up doing it themselves. "I have a suspicion," confessed Ebenezer Parkes, MP, a prominent Staffordshire ironmaker in 1903, "that perhaps we have not sufficient pluck in this country . . . in scrapping old and effete plant." But he had himself just started a new works whose power unit was an old beam engine reassembled on a new site.[93]

Most important, conservatism meant a failure to work out new and more efficient structures of organization.[94] The characteristic change that British firms made under pressure of international competition was amalgamation – but not, like many of the similar moves in America, as a springboard to new possibilities of growth. British amalgams were often seen as solutions in themselves. Starting with the mergers of the eighteen-nineties, many British amalgamations were "desperate and half-hearted alliances apparently motivated more by a desire to preserve the status quo than to tackle markets more aggressively."[95] Not untypical was the merger of the two tube-making firms of A. J. Stewart and Menzies and Lloyd and Lloyd in 1902, with minimal internal change, expressly for the purpose of "the extinction of competition."[96] Such restrictive moves were not viewed askance by public opinion, government, or the courts, as they were in the United States; if anything, quite the contrary. Business and government colluded to stifle competition. The restrictionist trend was ratified by the decision of the House of Lords in 1937 in *Thorne v. The Motor Trade Association*, in which the court found it perfectly legitimate for an association of wholesalers and retailers to blacklist price-cutters and refuse to supply them. Many, perhaps most, judges came to share Lord Chancellor Haldane's view that competition could frequently be quite undesirable, because it "may, if it is not controlled, drive manufacturers out of business, or lower wages and so cause labour disturbance."[97] British businessmen were thus encouraged by judges to multiply restrictive practices yet further. "A group of producers today," wrote a contemporary historian in 1937,

> could exterminate all competitors with a programme of vicious price-cutting, rigid tying contracts, exclusive dealing agreements, resale price maintenance, deferred rebates and commercial boycotts; they could then proceed to exploit the public through price manipulation and restriction of output; and all the while not only would they be well within their legal rights, but they could successfully defend their policies in the Courts on consideration of public welfare.[98]

This behavior was not just a matter of putting narrow self-interest ahead of the national interest. Most big businessmen (and their organizations, like the Federation of British Industries) saw restrictive practices as humane guarantees of regular employment at higher wages for working people; the alternatives were either control or anarchy. Roy Lewis and Rosemary Stewart described such industrialists in the thirties: "They feared the 'self-regulating and automatic quality of laissez-faire' as much as the small businessmen of fifty years before had made it their light."[99] Despite the dedication to efficiency often avowed by proponents of the "rationalization" movement of the interwar years, security far preceded efficiency as an aim. Schemes to control output and prices, and arrangements to share markets, overshadowed halfhearted efforts to improve operating efficiency.[100]

Restrictive practices – collusive tendering, market sharing, and the like – which had flourished in the thirties as protective measures against depression, long outlived the depression. In the boom years of the fifties, industrialists were reluctant to abandon such insurance. "With all these gentlemen's agreements still operating," remarked the director of a large engineering company, "there was no great incentive to efficiency on the factory floor."[101] Although government, its concern turning from protecting to expanding production, began to disapprove of such practices, its actions were hesitant. The first piece of legislation, the Monopolies and Restrictive Practices Act of 1948, did not assume that competition was necessarily good, but only that barriers to competition *might* be against the public interest, and ought to be looked into; the commission established by the act carried out some investigations, but these had little practical consequence. Most Labour and Conservative politicians were of two minds about competition and its restriction; both parties (as we have seen) feared the specter of an economic free-for-all. However, opinion was slowly shifting. In 1956 a stronger incentive to competition, the Restrictive Practices Court, was created. The act bringing it into being moved the burden of proof from government to the industries involved; for the first time restrictive practices were assumed to be harmful unless they could be shown to be beneficial. Over the next decade the court began to strike down price-fixing agreements. With the Wilson and Heath governments of 1964-74, the movement of opinion away from restrictionism seemed finally to have triumphed: The 1965 Monopolies and Mergers Act gave government sweeping powers to delay and even prevent any significant proposed merger, and Heath took office as an avowed economic liberal whose proudest domestic accomplishment had been seeing through the abolition of resale price maintenance. Yet the triumph of the gospel of competition was superficial and short-lived, for these very governments instituted a powerful countertrend. Although only a handful of mergers was actually referred to the monopolies commission, the Labour government became more and more involved in promoting and even subsidizing concentration in industry under the rationale of creating national industrial units large enough to stand up to giant foreign firms. The Conservative government of 1970-4, after initial rhetorical flourishes about competition and free enterprise, soon came round to the same policy. Throughout British industry in the seventies arrangements and reorganizations that lessened market pressures continued to flourish.[102]

These arrangements and reorganizations were accompanied by a rhetoric of "modernization," but in fact they amounted to restrictive practices, designed primarily to protect the status quo.[103] Much government support reduced in practice to rescuing "lame ducks," that is, preventing through subsidies large, politically significant firms from falling into the bankruptcy that was looming before them. Similarly, the wave of mergers carried out privately could show little clear evidence of benefit to the economy as a whole. Through the twentieth century, perhaps even increasingly, the first desire of British industrialists has been stability. R. E. Pahl and J. T. Winkler perceived this (although they saw it as a fairly recent development) at "that temple of Victorian enterprise, the Albert Hall," during an annual Institute of Directors conference in the early seventies:

> Edward Heath preached his Selsdon philosophy of expansion and growth through competition. He was tepidly received. Vic Feather offered the prospect of a deal for labour peace. He was cheered. The assembled business leaders knew what they wanted: order.[104]

This capitalist yearning for security was echoed in the trade unions, which had evolved, in these special British circumstances, a similarly conservative and defensive outlook. Thus in the course of the twentieth century, as the historian S. G. Checkland explained to Japanese business historians,

> when in Britain a business *ethos* based on unaggressive continuity met a labour outlook that placed great insistence upon security, and could back this with a solidarity based on ideology, the inevitable result was an unwillingness to remake the British industrial structure or its locational pattern. The two sides joined in a forlorn attempt to maintain industry substantially as it had been formed generations earlier.[105]

Over the past century, then, high among the internal checks upon British economic growth has been a pattern of industrial behavior suspicious of change, reluctant to innovate, energetic only in maintaining the status quo. This pattern of behavior traces back in large measure to the cultural absorption of the middle classes into a quasi-aristocratic elite, which nurtured both the rustic and nostalgic myth of an "English way of life" and the transfer of interest and energies away from the creation of wealth.

PART IV

Industrialism and English values

8

An overview and an assessment

It is a very difficult country to move, Mr. Hyndman, a very difficult country indeed, and one in which there is more disappointment to be looked for than success.
    —Disraeli to H. M. Hyndman (1881)

Now we ask ourselves more and more if the so-called progress we see going on about us at breakneck speed is what we really want. This is the age of the international companies – the commercial dinosaurs that stride from continent to continent. It is the age of supertankers, superstores, supersonic flight. The only thing which for many is not super is life itself.
    —*Folkestone Herald* (31 July 1971)

The cultural domestication of the industrial revolution

At the time of the Great Exhibition of 1851, Britain was the home of the industrial revolution, a symbol of material progress to the world. It was also the home of an apparently triumphant bourgeoisie. Observers like Carlyle and Marx agreed in pointing to the industrialist as the new aristocrat, a figure that was ushering in a radically new order and a new culture. Yet they were misled. From the time of their assertions, social and psychological currents in Britain began to flow in a different direction.

By the nineteen-seventies, falling levels of capital investment raised the specter of outright "de-industrialization" – a decline in industrial production outpacing any corresponding growth in the "production" of services.[1] Whether or not such a specter had substance, it is true that this period of recognized economic crisis in Britain was preceded by a century of psychological and intellectual de-industrialization. The emerging culture of industrialism, which in the mid-Victorian years had appeared, for good or ill, to be the wave of the future, irresistibly washing over and sweeping away the features of an older Britain, was itself transformed. The thrust of new values borne along by the revolution in industry was contained in the later nineteenth century; the social and intellectual revolution implicit in industrialism was muted, perhaps even aborted. Instead, a compromise was effected, accommodating new groups, new interests, and new needs within a social and cultural matrix that preserved the forms and even many of the values of tradition. Potentially disruptive forces of change were harnessed and channeled into supporting a new social order, a synthesis of old and new. This containment of the cultural revolution of industrialism lies at the heart of both the achievements and the failures of modern British history.

The new society created by the later Victorians rested on a domestication of the wilder traits of earlier British behavior; the riotous populace, the aggressive and acquisitive capitalists, and the hedonistic aristocrats of the Georgian world became endangered, if not extinct, species of Englishmen. Their descendants were more restrained, more civilized, and also more conservative, in that they now had an established and secure place in the social order, or, in the case of the aristocracy, had come to terms with social change and recemented their place in the status quo. By Victoria's death, British society had weathered the storms of change, but at the cost of surrendering a capacity for innovation and assertion that was perhaps the other face of the unruliness and harshness of that earlier Britain.

In particular, the later nineteenth century saw the consolidation of a national elite that, by virtue of its power and prestige, played a central role both in Britain's modern achievements and its failures. It administered the most extensive empire in human history with reasonable effectiveness and humanity, and it maintained a remarkable degree of political and social stability at home while presiding over a redistribution of power and an expansion of equality and security. It also presided over the steady and continued erosion of the nation's economic position in the world. The standards of value of this new elite of civil servants, professionals, financiers, and landed proprietors, inculcated by a common education in public schools and ancient universities and reflected in the literary culture it patronized, permeated by their prestige much of British society beyond the elite itself. These standards did little to support, and much to discourage, economic dynamism. They threw earlier enthusiasms for technology into disrepute, emphasized the social evils brought by the industrial revolution, directed attention to issues of the "quality of life" in preference to the quantitative concerns of production and expansion, and disparaged the restlessness and acquisitiveness of industrial capitalism. Hand in hand with this disparagement went the growth of an alternative set of social values, embodied in a new vision of the nation.

The dominant collective self-image in English culture became less and less that of the world's workshop. Instead, this image was challenged by the counterimage of an ancient, little-disturbed "green and pleasant land." "Our England is a garden," averred the greatest poet of Imperialism; another Imperialist, a poet laureate, celebrated England at the height of Imperial fervor for its "haunts of ancient peace"; and an anti-Imperialist socialist has inspired his readers with the aim of making England once again, as it had been before the industrial revolution, the "fair green garden of Northern Europe." The past, and the countryside – seen as inseparable – were invested with an almost irresistible aura. These standards and images supported a very attractive way of life, geared to maintenance of a status quo rather than innovation, comfort rather than attainment, the civilized enjoyment, rather than the creation, of wealth.

British political opinion bore the imprint of the aristocracy long after the demise of the aristocracy's power. The politicians, civil servants, churchmen, professional men, and publicists who did so much to shape modern British political opinion and policy moved in a climate of opinion uncongenial to the world of industry. Most of them showed a striking fondness for gentry tastes and standards, making such tastes an essential part of the modern British style of government. Political calls for economic growth went against the grain of the values and style of life actually believed in by most politicians and civil servants, as well as by the rest of the elite.

Industrialists themselves were far from immune to this antiindustrial culture; like others, they breathed it in ever more deeply the higher they rose in social position. The new British elite was open to industrialists, if they adapted to its standards. With few exceptions, they were ready to do so, although such adaptation required a degree of disavowal of their own former selves and their very function in society. By modeling themselves – in varying proportions – upon civil servants, professional men, and men of landed leisure, industrialists found acceptance at the upper reaches of British society. Thus, the famed "Establishment" and its consensus was created. Social integration and stability were ensured, but at a price – the waning of the industrial spirit.

Postindustrialism or de-industrialism?
The peculiar pattern of British social and cultural history has involved both benefits and costs. Which, however, has predominated? Has this pattern been on balance a fortune or a misfortune for Britain? And what signposts to the future – if any – does this cultural history set out?

Many, within and without Britain, have praised the cultural path thus taken. Even the business historian D. C. Coleman was at pains to point out in his argument for the importance of the gentlemanly ideal that he was not *criticizing* its sway:

> If, by some unlikely magic [Victorian and Edwardian businessmen] had turned themselves into single-minded, constantly profit-maximizing

> entrepreneurs, what sort of world might have resulted? If it is true
> that one of the costs of Public Schools producing "first-class admini-
> strators" was some lag in industrial advance, how can we know that
> the price was not worth paying?[2]

Others, on both Left and Right, have thought the gain certainly more
than worth the price. The *Times* spoke for many of them in 1971 when
it reflected on the lack of enthusiasm for "wealth, as such," and found
it good. "The secret hope of Britain," it concluded,

> is indeed that the monetary obsession has penetrated our society less
> deeply than it has others. There are probably still more people in
> Britain who will give total effort for reasons of idealism than for
> reasons of gain.[3]

A peculiar English gift for the "quality" rather than the "quantity" of
life was claimed as early as 1907, by the cosmopolitan novelist Ford
Madox Ford. "The especial province of the English nation," he reflected, "is the evolution of a standard of manners . . . The province of
the English is to solve the problem of how men may live together."[4]
Around the same time, foreign visitors (particularly Americans)
began to note the pleasantness and relaxed quality of English life.
Arthur Shadwell, an Edwardian "efficiency expert," reported: "An
American gentleman said to me one day: 'We are a tearing, driving,
scheming lot here. The Englishman leads a tranquil, happy life, and I
for one envy him'."[5] The direct descendant of this nameless American was the *New York Time*'s London correspondent during the later
sixties and early seventies, Anthony Lewis, who observed in a farewell
"love letter": "There is a larger reality than the pound and inflation
and the GNP. It is life, and the British are good at that."[6] Some have
gone even further in their admiration, and see the British as pioneer-
ing new forms of "postindustrial society." John Kenneth Galbraith,
interviewed on the BBC, told his hosts that

> your real problem is that you were the first of the great industrialized
> nations, and so things happen here first. You are living out the
> concern for some more leisurely relationship with industrial life that
> the other people have been discussing for 50 years or more.[7]

To Bernard Nossiter, London correspondent for the *Washington Post*
during the 1970s, "Britons . . . appear[ed] to be the first citizens of the
post-industrial age who are choosing leisure over goods on a large
scale," and he heartily approved of their choice.[8]

However, others have sounded a more somber note, portraying
rustic-gentlemanly values as sliding imperceptibly into decadence.
Donald Horne expressed it with the vehemence of an expatriate:

> Kindness, tolerance and love of order become snobbery, woolliness
> and love of the past. Effortless ease becomes the ease of not making

any effort to do anything. Gentlemanly intuitive wisdom becomes the inability to make up one's mind. Doing the decent thing comes to mean that there should be no sharp clash of attitudes, no disagreeable new beliefs, that might disturb someone. The sense of fairness becomes the belief that competition is unfair: it might benefit some new person, but it might also harm some old person.[9]

This point of view was expressed succinctly by Lord Nuffield in 1959, when he called Britain a "nation in semi-retirement."[10] Others have shared Nuffield's perception of a failure of national energies, adaptability, or will. One of the most eloquent and earliest was C. P. Snow, who in the same year, 1959, delivered this warning to his fellow members of the British governing class:

> More often than I like, I am saddened by a historical myth. Whether the myth is good history or not, doesn't matter; it is pressing enough for me. I can't help thinking of the Venetian Republic in their last half-century. Like us, they had once been fabulously lucky. They had become rich, as we did, by accident. They had acquired immense political skill, just as we have. A good many of them were tough-minded, realistic, patriotic men. They knew, just as clearly as we know, that the current of history had begun to flow against them. Many of them gave their minds to working out ways to keep going. It would have meant breaking the pattern into which they had crystallised. They were fond of the pattern, just as we are fond of ours. They never found the will to break it.[11]

Nearly two decades later, Snow's Venetian analogy seemed more relevant than ever to the Marxist Tom Nairn. "The House of Lords," he complained in 1977,

> is a better gauge of British futures than IBM. Underneath the ceaseless speechifying about new starts, the dominant dream is of a Venetian twilight: a golden-grey steady state where staid arts and moderate politics join to preserve the tenor of things English. The true impulse is not really to "catch up" with the greater, evolving world outside, but to hold one's own somehow, anyhow, and defend the tribe's customs and weathered monuments.[12]

Sixteenth-century Venice, of course, had nothing equivalent to North Sea oil; but similar windfalls to other nations, when unreinforced by a favorable social environment, have had little lasting effect. The classic historical example is seventeenth-century Spain. The historian J. H. Elliot laid responsibility for that nation's decline at the feet of its ruling class, which

> lacked the breadth of vision and the strength of character to break with a past that could no longer serve as a reliable guide to the future... At a time when the face of Europe was altering more rapidly than ever before, the country that had once been its leading power proved to be lacking the essential ingredient for survival – the willingness to change.[13]

The vision was given literary form when one of Britain's best contemporary writers, known previously as a novelist of personal relations, was impelled by the crisis of the seventies to explore the condition of the national spirit. Margaret Drabble had become increasingly concerned by what seemed to her to be negative and retreatist social values,[14] and in her novel *The Ice Age* portrayed an English elite in a state of psychic and moral exhaustion. Returning to the moralist tradition of the early Victorians, Drabble sought within her dark canvas for sources of renewal, and was unafraid to court ridicule by calling upon John Milton and his vision of "a noble and puissant Nation, rousing herself like a strong man after sleep." *The Ice Age* summed up one view of the "condition of England."

It has also been argued that the pleasant vision of English "post-industrialism" is a mirage; that the quality of life cannot be readily opposed to the quantity or even their constituents easily separated.[15] Recent studies of public opinion, moreover, suggest that, as Rudolf Klein has regretfully put it, "altruism appears to be largely a function of economic prosperity."[16] A no-growth society does not seem likely to be a more humane, more tolerant, or even more comfortable society. One recalls Edward Heath's 1973 warning:

> The alternative to expansion is not, as some occasionally seem to suppose, an England of quiet market towns linked only by trains puffing slowly and peacefully through green meadows. The alternative is slums, dangerous roads, old factories, cramped schools, stunted lives.[17]

"Modernization": un-English?

To mention Edward Heath is to raise the question of whether this national culture can be – or is being – changed. The gentlemanly consensus of "domesticated progress" began to come under strain in the early 1960s, as the continental economic surge sowed anxiety about national decline in the minds of British observers. These anxieties brought the issue of modernization into the political arena. Beginning in 1964, this new issue played an important role, at least rhetorically, in every general election. The general election of 1979, in particular, was fought around the question of national economic decline. In a historic exchange, whose outlines were first perceptible in 1970, the Labour party stood for English tradition, the status quo, and "safety first," whereas the Conservatives – their leader especially – gave the calls for sweeping change. "I am a reformer," Margaret Thatcher announced, "and I am offering change."[18] The Conservative victory gave Britain a leader well known for her resolve to reverse the pattern of the past century. Thatcher indeed seeks, as her opponents charged, to "turn the clock back" – to restore nineteenth-century economic dynamism by reintroducing the disciplines and incentives of the market.

If the argument of this book is valid, the outcome of Thatcher's crusade may turn on how successful methods like lowering marginal tax rates and restricting the money supply will be in altering cultural attitudes formed over many years.[19] The least tractable obstacle to British economic "redevelopment" may well be the continuing resistance of cultural values and attitudes. A recent survey of British attitudes toward money and work commissioned by *New Society* revealed a nation "remarkably unambitious in a material sense":

> Very few sincerely want to be rich. Most people in Britain neither want nor expect a great deal of money. Even if they could get it, the vast majority do not seem prepared to work harder for it: most of our respondents thought we should work only as much as we need to live a pleasant life ... It seems clear that the British today prefer economic *stability* to rapid economic growth.[20]

Indeed, the 1970s saw in Britain (as elsewhere) a *reaction* against the calls of the 1960s for modernization and growth. Edward Heath, after painfully imposing the gospel of efficiency upon the Conservatives, failed even more painfully to impose it upon the nation. The acute Labor Minister Richard Crossman commented on Heath's difficulties with "the traditional Right" in the sixties: "The policy he is putting across seems to me to be attractive only to young and thrusting businessmen" – no prescription for successful politics.[21] "Technophobia," as two journalists put it in 1967, persisted in the grass roots of the Tory party.

> What[ever] aspirations the present leadership may have [they warned] ... the party traditionalists take little account of doctrines of business efficiency, and largely loathe the Americans who invented most of the concepts. How lonely the evangelistic Mr. Marples looks in the Tory Party when he tries to convince the ranks of the devoted that their concern is with technology and business efficiency, and how curious has been his fate! What applause there was for Mr. Angus Maude's "for Tories simply to talk like technocrats will get them nowhere"![22]

Nonetheless, Heath pushed on, seeking to break the psychological resistance, within and outside the party, to modernization. He described Britain in December 1969 as "a Luddite's paradise ... a society dedicated to the prevention of progress and the preservation of the status quo." He seized the surprise Conservative victory in 1970 as a mandate for the transformation of Britain, announcing to the first party conference after the election that "we were returned to office to change the course of history of this nation – nothing less." More and more Heath saw the root problem facing him as psychological: the shortsighted tendency of his countrymen to "prefer comfort to progress."[23] Yet it was by no means clear how this tendency could be changed by government. Heath was soon labeled a "radical" and a "divisive" figure,[24] and most of his initial program was abandoned, gutted, or proven ineffective even before his government was swept away in the wake of the 1973-4 confrontation with the miners.

After a taste of Heath's crusade, in February 1974 the public found more appealing the Labour campaign, which, despite the party program's pledges of nationalization and redistribution, was remarkably conservative in spirit. The party leadership had moved from promising in 1964 to reshape Britain in the "white heat of a new technological revolution" to pledging a decade later an end to "divisiveness," a taming of the "ruthless, pushing society," and "a quiet life."[25]

In office, Harold Wilson, and especially his emollient successor, James Callaghan, followed the tone set by the general election, seeking above all to promote social harmony and stability, and cushioning the social fabric and the economic status quo from the stresses of change. The modernizing rhetoric of the 1960s, evoking Joseph Chamberlain and Lloyd George, was gently laid to rest, and the spirit of Stanley Baldwin hovered over Downing Street. Both Wilson and Callaghan, in contrast to Heath, acquired farms and were often photographed there, appearing in Baldwinesque fashion as men of the country. For both men these farms (neither was a serious agricultural enterprise) maintained a link to what Callaghan's wife called "the peasant in us."[26]

Many intellectuals and publicists took the two Conservative electoral defeats in 1974 as a repudiation of "growthmania." Christopher Price, a Labour MP, was one of a number who argued that "Labour is now the natural party to rein back" from such misguided zeal. The "ancestral virtues" of the party, which had provided a "moral authority" during the Attlee-Cripps era of austerity, could now again, Price argued, do good service.[27] In the sixties, he later reflected, whatever party, "The message was the same: 'Out with the old, on with the new.' New towns, new tower blocks, new supersonic planes, new motorways. And if a few greenhouse windows were broken to let Concorde fly, if good houses were torn down for roads and redevelopment, too bad. 'You couldn't make omelettes...' Now it is all suddenly different." Novelty had soured, and "bigness" – which, Price recalled, "some Socialists had been preaching against for a century" – had become unfashionable. Price set out a "non-economic" agenda for what he called a socialist political program. Its aim was to protect the existing "social and environmental fabric of Britain" – its "pleasant, fraternal, convivial" character, and its countryside. "All this," he conceded, "may sound negative." Well and good. "Labour has always been used to start things. I suspect its role in the future will be more concerned with stopping them."[28]

After 1974, educated opinion seemed more disillusioned than ever with "progress." Ramsay Macdonald's biographer, David Marquand, found Macdonald's antimaterialism freshly relevant: "Ten or fifteen years ago," he remarked in 1977, "Macdonald's warning that the quality of life might be sacrificed in the pursuit of material prosperity, and that socialists might lose sight of their non-material objectives in the struggle for votes, could be dismissed as a piece of sentimental obscurantism. It cannot be dismissed so easily today."[29]

A new cultural phenomenon came of age in the 1970s: explicit and organized opposition to the results of technical and material advance. This was of course part of a development embracing the entire industrialized world, where antigrowth and antitechnology movements had taken root among left-wing university students and had become a force to be reckoned with in public life. In Britain, this general movement took on a more popular and nationalistic form. The ranks of English critics of progress extended far beyond the universities or the Left; these critics tended to see their mission as inseparable from English patriotism – to save traditional English life from unwelcome change. The great variety of new or resurgent causes taken up in the late sixties and early seventies, from environmentalism to historical preservation to the Campaign for Real Ale, constituted a nonpartisan "movement to protect English culture."[30] As Marquand argued (all the more powerfully for being a well-known critic of the Left): "The issue of the future is small against big, community against *anomie*, peace-of-mind against rate-of-growth, grass roots against tower blocks, William Morris against both Sidney Webb and Henry Ford."[31]

Perhaps the chief literary embodiment of this spirit of resistance was the immensely popular poet laureate John Betjeman, who was more widely read than any previous laureate. Betjeman extended the pastoral nostalgia of his predecessors, John Masefield and Alfred Austin, to suburbia, now an integral part of Old England. His writing disparaged the new and evoked the security of old, familiar things. The public responded with enthusiasm to his Tory "longing for the simplicity of irremovable landmarks."[32] This longing moved the Left as well as the Right: The *New Statesman* in 1973 hailed Betjeman's denunciation of urban redevelopment. "At last," it anounced in its front-page leader,

> a Poet Laureate has expressed the nation's feelings. This week Sir John Betjeman observed that destroying the surroundings in which people live – and which they like, and are accustomed to – amounts to straightforward robbery. It is stealing the people's property, said Sir

John; exactly the same as being burgled. In some ways, maybe worse. You can buy substitutes for the contents of a house. A familiar narrow street, with its obscure chapel, tree and corner shop, is irreplaceable.[33]

Similarly, the socialist playwright and critic Dennis Potter wrote with approval in the Sunday *Times* (London) that "Betjeman is the surviving proof that it is all right, after all, to be an Englishman. He stands at the wrought-iron gates, ready to hold back the flood."[34]

The identification of "English" with "holding back the flood" of change had been made familiar by that widely read man of the Left, J. B. Priestley, who had by the 1970s become a popular authority on the national character. He reveled in attacking the modernizers, arguing in 1970 that they failed to understand that, as he had implied as early as 1949, the modern world was "alien to the English temperament." It was natural and good that the English did not take readily to its characteristic activities. "We are instinctively opposed," he announced, "to high-pressure industry and salesmanship, wanting something better than a huge material rat race." The nation's future, Priestley urged three years later, hung upon resisting "change for change's sake."[35]

At the end of the day, it may be that Margaret Thatcher will find her most fundamental challenge not in holding down the money supply or inhibiting government spending, or even in fighting the shop stewards, but in changing this frame of mind. English history in the eighties may turn less on traditional political struggles than on a cultural contest between the two faces of the middle class.

Appendix: British retardation – the limits of economic explanation

Economic explanations of British retardation begin with the classical factors of supply – capital, labor, and natural resources. Yet these by themselves explain little. Late-Victorian and Edwardian Britain boasted capital resources unprecedented in world history, resources clearly adequate to support continued rapid growth. Charles Kindleberger concluded after a careful study of the period from 1851 to 1950 that "by any reasonable test the supply of British capital was sufficient." To explain why domestic investment was not greater, he felt it necessary to discover why it was not more attractive.[1] The size and competency of Britain's labor force posed no obvious obstacle to growth. There was neither a shortage of labor nor such a surplus as to discourage industrial investment.[2] Supplies of the chief industrial resources – coal, iron, and other minerals – were more than adequate to maintain vigorous expansion.[3] It was, as Kindleberger concluded, the *use* made of resources, of labor, and of capital that was crucial.

The other side of the classical economic equation – demand – offers equally insufficient illumination. Overseas demand was not slackening. Quite the contrary, the economic development of the world, broken only by the Great Depression of the nineteen-thirties, was providing ever-growing opportunities to British industry, which were on the whole not taken. The loss of the empire has been popularly seen as a fundamental cause of economic difficulties. In this view, Britain's Victorian economic preeminence had been supported by its worldwide possessions and power. "Trade follows the flag," as the nineteenth-century slogan went. Yet students of the question over the past several decades have agreed that the empire was not, on balance, a crucial economic asset.[4]

If material conditions were not wanting, was there then a social or psychological obstacle to continued economic leadership? Was at least one important part of the emerging problem a *human* one?[5] Two otherwise quite different schools of thought have converged in denying this.

The first of these have been Marxists. E. J. Hobsbawm, the most distinguished of British Marxist historians, insisted in 1968 that, understood rightly, British economic retardation involved no "irrationalities." The "fault" lay not with the temperament, attitudes, or abilities of businessmen or workers, but with the self-defeating nature of the capitalist *system*. How, specifically, was this system self-defeating? It depended for its dynamism on one unreliable motor – private profit:

> In a capitalist economy (at all events in its nineteenth-century versions) businessmen will be dynamic only in so far as this is rational by the criterion of the individual firm, which is to maximize its gains, minimize its losses, or possibly merely to maintain what it regards as a satisfactory long-term rate of profit. But since the rationality of the individual firm is inadequate, this may not work to the best advantage of the economy of the whole, or even of the individual firm.[6]

Given this mechanism of change, as Hobsbawm saw it, Britain's early start as an industrial power ultimately proved its undoing. Pioneer industrialization naturally created a particular pattern of both production and markets that would not remain the one best fitted to sustain economic growth. Yet to change to a new pattern involved both the scrapping of old investments still capable of yielding good profits, and the venturing of new investments of even greater initial cost. "So long as satisfactory profits were to be made in the old way, and so long as the decision to modernize had to emerge from the sum-total of decisions by individual firms, the incentive to do so would be weak."[7] Britain thus – almost inevitably (to Hobsbawm), given its capitalism – stuck with the status quo while the rest of the advanced world developed.

Much of this line of reasoning is plausible, and indeed does not preclude the importance of social and psychological factors. Yet Hobsbawm's insistence on the inherent weakness of capitalist economic organization bordered on dogma. To base an explanation of British economic performance upon the general nature of capitalism makes it very difficult to account for the very real differences in national experiences. If British retardation stemmed from the universal inherent flaws of capitalism, they are strange universals that are so easy to locate in Britain and so hard to find elsewhere. It seems much more likely that we are dealing with a phenomenon at least in part shaped by factors peculiar to late-nineteenth- and early-twentieth-century British society.

Ironically, an even stronger tendency to dogmatism and universalizing abstractions is evident in the work of a new school of non-Marxist and indeed often anti-Marxist economic historians who also deny the need for noneconomic explanations. Addressing the problem of British performance up to 1900, a group of econometricians have concluded that there really *was* no problem.[8] Business and industry did about as well as they possibly could have. "There is, indeed, little left," Donald N. McCloskey summed up, "of the dismal picture of British failure painted by historians." In its place McCloskey unveiled a portrait of an economy "not stagnating but growing as rapidly as permitted by the growth of its resources and the effective exploitation of the available technology."[9] Applying the new model-building techniques of econometric analysis, McCloskey and his colleagues discovered eminently rational behavior everywhere they looked. Like Hobsbawm, McCloskey (from a very different ideological standpoint) saw businessmen, investors, workers, and consumers as tightly fixed within an economic system that operated according to immutable laws. If the pace of economic development in Britain slowed, or if Britain's relative position fell sharply, this was explained by the prevailing market situation. Nobody was to "blame"; profit was being maximized. In the analyses of these "Cliometricians" (after Clio, the Muse of History), social institutions, values, and sentiments played no role. Whereas Marxists often failed to appreciate the power of social and cultural context, Cliometricians were virtually indifferent to – almost contemptuous of – any evidence merely "qualitative."

Does the method of the Cliometricians fit this subject? Many economic historians doubt it. Sidney Pollard observed that *Essays on a Mature Economy*, the product of a conference of "new economic historians" devoted to this issue, tended to prove "that the econometric method works well and beyond cavil only where it is used to answer an econometric question" – which the general performance of a national economy is not. Two drawbacks in the use of econometric methods here stand out. First, in such an enterprise, Pollard warned, "It is the definitions that will determine the conclusions." It is perilously easy to assume, for instance, "that competition will force entrepreneurs to take the optimal decisions open to them, and then to arrive, after lengthy argument and calculation, at the conclusion that [one has] (on these premises) proved that entrepreneurs did take the optimal decisions." Second, it is all too easy to rely on inappropriate data, or data so weak that they could not carry the conclusions built upon them. Pollard found McCloskey's particular contribution to this controversy, a "proof" that British productivity in steel and coal before World War I was ("given the differences in factor endowment and prices") as great as, indeed greater than in the United States, to be riddled with this type of error.[10] Other historians, as versed in econometric techniques as McCloskey and his colleagues, have begun to question their findings as highly "sensitive to debatable assumptions and tentative estimates."[11]

The determination to explain all economic phenomena with a self-contained model of purely economic factors pushes much of social life to a dimly lit periphery. It excludes much of what is most interesting to a general historian. Behavior not conforming to the assumption of "rational," profit-, and wage-maximizing action is attributed to a catchall category such as "imperfections in the market." When this obscure category is opened to the light, it turns out to be a pathway back to the social world enveloping economics. "Market imperfections" often resolve into social and political structures or patterns of behavior that, although not "rational" in the strict economic sense, are nonetheless real. Efficient allocations of resources, for example, may be impeded by a variety of such imperfections (as one British sociologist has pointed out): "Skilled labour is unwilling to migrate, governments legislate against unfamiliar activities, communities demand protection against threatening disruptions of their environment, management cannot assimilate new forms of organization, businessmen foresee only the kinds of demand and technical developments already allowed for in their experience."[12]

The question of the causes of British economic decline remains beyond the sole grasp of the economists. "The problems [involved]," Peter Mathias has concluded, "cannot be explained just in simple terms of economic hypotheses such as wage rates, shifting terms of trade or deteriorating natural resources."[13] Similarly, as an economist, Michael Fores, reminded an audience of businessmen and civil servants, "The variables acting on growth are many, and not concerned only with quantities of economic resources and with industrial techniques."[14] But the need for extra-economic explanation should not be taken as an admission of ignorance. John Saville, a social and economic historian, has reminded business historians that

> Historical analysis involves different levels of precision and imprecision, and once we become more aware than is common at present of the considerable margins of error in many of our statistical series – which are often so effortlessly moulded into unnatural shapes without any indication being given of what the dimensions of error are likely to be – we shall perhaps be less worried about the admittedly more difficult problems of evaluating cultural, social or ideological factors.[15]

Notes

Preface
1. "Capitalism and the Cultural Historian," in *From Parnassus: Essays in Honor of Jacques Barzun*, ed. Dora B. Weiner and William R. Keylor (New York, 1976), 223.
2. See J. A. V. Chapple, *Documentary and Imaginative Literature, 1880-1920* (London, 1970), Raymond Williams, *The Country and the City* (London, 1973), and Noel Annan, "The Possessed," *New York Review of Books 23*, no. 1 (5 February 1976), 22. See also Mark Girouard, *Sweetness and Light: The "Queen Anne" Movement, 1860-1900* (Oxford, 1977); Walter Arnstein, "The Survival of the Victorian Aristocracy," in *The Rich, the Well Born, and the Powerful*, ed. F. C. Jaher (New York, 1973), 203-57; T. F. Lindsay and Michael Harrington, *The Conservative Party, 1918-1970* (New York, 1974), and Tom Nairn, *The Left Against Europe?* (Harmondsworth, 1973). William B. Gwyn surveys a variety of cultural explanations for British economic retardation in "Perceptions of British Decline," in a forthcoming collection of essays on Britain's economic state, edited by himself.
3. *The Long Revolution* (London, 1961), 47.
4. Frank Field ("Literature, Society and Twentieth Century Historians," *History 64* [1979], 55) has recently observed and deplored this aversion. Major British historians of premodern times, like Christopher Hill and Keith Thomas, have been more open-minded, with a consequent gain of vitality to their field.

1. The Janus face of modern English culture
1. "Obsolescence – and Dr. Arnold," Sunday *Telegraph*, 26 January 1975.
2. "Europe: Some Are More Equal," *Listener 96* (14 October 1976), 460.
3. *Industry and Empire: An Economic History of Britain since 1750* (London, 1968), 157.
4. The shortcomings of exclusively economic explanations of British retardation are discussed in the Appendix.
5. See two "classics," W. Arthur Lewis, *The Theory of Economic Growth* (London, 1955), ch. 2; and W. W. Rostow, *The Process of Economic Growth* (New York, 1960), chs. 1-2.
6. See David C. McClelland, *The Achieving Society* (New York, 1961), and David C. McClelland and David G. Winter, *Motivating Economic Achievement* (New York, 1969); Everett E. Hagen, *On the Theory of Social Change: How Economic Growth Begins* (Homewood, Ill., 1962); Alex Inkeles and David Smith, *Becoming Modern* (Cambridge, Mass., 1974).

7. *Asian Drama: An Inquiry into the Poverty of Nations* (New York, 1968).

8. See, in addition to Myrdal, Ronald Segal, *The Anguish of India* (Harmondsworth, 1965), and V. W. Naipaul, *India: A Wounded Civilization* (New York, 1977).

9. See, for example, Norman Macrae, "The Risen Sun" [survey], *Economist*, 27 May 1967 and 3 June 1967, and Brian Beedham, "No One Quite Like Them" [survey], *Economist*, 31 March 1973; see also Cyril Black et al., *The Modernization of Japan and Russia: A Comparative Study* (London, 1976). "It is surprising," Derek Aldcroft noted in reviewing this book (*History 62* [1977], 92), "how frequently economists and economic historians obsessed with the growth records of countries take [social and political] matters for granted." Ronald Dore, in his book *British Factory – Japanese Factory* (London, 1973), has shown how Japanese enterprises using similar technology, and often even similar patterns of production as their Western counterparts, can provide quite different social situations.

10. Recent studies have stressed the importance of managerial attitudes and policies for workplace behavior. See Peter Stearns, *Paths to Authority: The Middle Class and the Industrial Labor Force in France, 1820-1848* (Champaign, Ill., 1979) and Michael B. Miller, *The Bon Marché: Bourgeois Culture and the Department Store, 1869-1920* (Princeton, 1980).

11. Lincoln Allison, "The English Cultural Movement," *New Society 43* (16 February 1978), 358.

12. See Leo Marx, *The Machine in the Garden* (New York, 1964), and its important connection as well as extension in Thomas Bender, *Towards an Urban Vision: Ideas and Institutions in Nineteenth Century America* (Lexington, Ky., 1975). See also the perceptive essay by Howard P. Segal, "Leo Marx's 'Middle Landscape': a Critique, a Revision, and an Appreciation," *Reviews in American History 5* (1977), 137-49.

13. See Allan Nevins and Frank Ernest Hill, *Ford: Expansion and Challenge, 1915-1933* (New York, 1957), 500-6, and Keith Smart, *The Legend of Henry Ford* (New York, 1948), 261-5.

14. See Talcott Parsons, "Democracy and Social Structure in Pre-Nazi Germany," in his *Essays in Sociological Theory* (New York, 1954), 104-23; Ralf Dahrendorf, *Society and Democracy in Germany* (New York, 1967); Fritz Stern, *The Politics of Cultural Despair* (Berkeley and Los Angeles, 1961): George Mosse, *The Crisis of German Ideology* (New York, 1964). Such stable nations as the United States and France were not unaffected by such tensions. On America, see, in addition to Leo Marx, T. L. Hartshorne, *The Distorted Image* (Cleveland, 1968). On France, see Stanley Hoffman et al., *In Search of France* (Cambridge, Mass., 1963).

15. A stimulating essay on the subject is Stanley Rothman, "Modernity and Tradition in Britain," in *Studies in British Politics*, ed. Richard Rose (London, 1966), 6. Peter Berger's concept of "contamination" between cognitive systems in contact is suggestive of what happened, to some degree, to modern values in the embrace of English tradition. See his *The Sacred Canopy* (New York, 1967), part II.

16. "Is Beckerman among the Sociologists?" *New Statesman* (18 April 1975), 501.

17. "Origins of the Present Crisis," *New Left Review*, no. 23 (January-February, 1964), 31.

18. Contribution to symposium, "Who's Left, What's Right?" *Encounter*, March 1977, 29.

19. This was first noted and examined by Thorstein Veblen in his *Imperial Germany and the Industrial Revolution* (New York, 1915).
20. Martin Kitchin, *The Political Economy of Germany, 1815-1914* (Montreal, 1978), 126-7, offers some informed generalizations, and Fritz Stern, *Gold and Iron: Bismarck, Bleichröder and the Building of the German Empire* (New York, 1977), is a brilliant case study.
21. In David Spring, ed., *European Landed Elites in the Nineteenth Century* (Baltimore, Md., 1977), 51-2.
22. See Helmut Böhme, "Big-Business Pressure Groups and Bismarck's Turn to Protectionism, 1873-79," *Historical Journal 10* (1967), 218-36.
23. Fritz Stern ("Capitalism and the Cultural Historian," in *From Parnassus*, 219) observes free enterprise giving way to "a new kind of cartelized capitalism, at times in collusion with the government." Kitchin (*Political Economy of Germany*, 127-8) describes the "industrial feudalism" of Krupp and other big industrialists. Charles Medalen, "State Monopoly Capitalism in Germany: The Hibernia Affair," *Past and Present*, no. 78 (February, 1978), 82-112, is interesting on the Prussian approach to industry.
24. *The Break-up of Britain* (London, 1977), 32. Similar limits were also, in Nairn's argument, thus imposed upon working-class social and political development. The most notable criticism of Anderson's initial interpretation, that by E. P. Thompson in 1965, is (to this reader) unfair and unconvincing. See E. P. Thompson, "The Peculiarities of the English," *The Socialist Register, 1965* (New York, 1965), 311-62, and Anderson's reply, "Socialism and Pseudo-Empiricism," *New Left Review*, 35 (January-February, 1966), 2-42.
25. *The Swordbearers* (London, 1963), 181.

2. Victorian society: accommodation and absorption
1. C. P. Snow, *The Masters* (New York, 1951), 349.
2. Quoted in George Lichtheim, *Marxism* (New York, 1961), 136.
3. See W. L. Guttsman, *The British Political Elite* (London, 1963); Walter Arnstein, "The Survival of the Victorian Aristocracy," in *The Rich, the Well Born, and the Powerful*, ed. F. C. Jaher (New York, 1973), 203-57, and F. M. L. Thompson, "Britain," in *European Landed Elites in the Nineteenth Century*, ed. David Spring (Baltimore, Md., 1977), 22-44.
4. *Economist*, 29 June 1850 and 16 July 1879; quoted in F. M. L. Thompson, "Britain," 29.
5. *The Origins of Modern English Society, 1780-1880* (London, 1969), 435. Richard Helmstadter has described the parallel absorption of Nonconformity in *The Conscience of the Victorian State*, ed. Peter Marsh (Syracuse, N.Y., 1979), 162-4.
6. "Economic Functions of English Landowners in the 17th and 18th Centuries," in *Explorations in Enterprise*, ed. H. G. J. Aitken (Cambridge, Mass., 1965), 339. This is not to say that there were not many individual cases of development-minded aristocrats, and even peers very interested in industrial enterprise. See *Land and Industry: The Landed Estate and the Industrial Revolution*, ed. J. T. Ward and R. G. Wilson (Newton Abbot, Devon, 1971), and Michael W. McCahill, "Peers, Patronage, and the Industrial Revolution 1760-1800," *Journal of British Studies 16*, no. 1 (Fall, 1976), 84-107. Ward and Wilson, in particular, stress the keen interest of the landed proprietors in new sources of income, and their importance in the industrial revolution. Yet one can accept the eco-

nomic vitality of the landed elite and still argue for their long-run inhibiting effect on the national economy: If the landed families had consistently held themselves aloof from the new economic currents, they would have been swept aside. Instead, they were economically aggressive enough to preserve their predominance without abandoning their distinctive set of values and style of life, to which the new businessmen and industrialists came to aspire.

7. The appeal of the gentlemanly ideal was well-nigh irresistible. Even the most well-known ideologist of industrial capitalism, Samuel Smiles, sought to appropriate it. In the final chapter of *Self-Help* (entitled "The True Gentleman"), he took the gentleman as his standard, seeking to strip him only of his outward, class-bound associations. Gentility, for Smiles, was the ultimate crown to be worn by those who had helped themselves.

8. Cited by Alan Brien, Sunday *Times* (London), 1 August 1971.

9. See W. G. Rimmer, *Marshalls of Leeds* (Cambridge, 1960), 276-303. Mark Girouard (*The Victorian Country House* [Oxford, 1971]) has shown how this social fusion shaped mid- and late-nineteenth-century country house architecture. William Thomas (*The Philosophic Radicals* [Oxford, 1979], 449) has noted how "the rage for titles and pedigrees, for heraldic pomp and castellated architecture" overtook even some radical politicians: "One of the most sustained attempts to create a medieval setting which would reinforce his social pretensions was the rebuilding, or rather smothering in gothic additions, of Bayons Manor, by Charles Tennyson, radical M.P. for Southwark."

10. Thompson, "Britain," 30.

11. *Social Leaders and Public Persons: A Study of County Government in Cheshire since 1888* (Oxford, 1963), 36.

12. Quoted in John Morley, *Life of Richard Cobden* (London, 1881), *II*, 481-2. This attitude became more entrenched with time. Friedrich Engels (who in 1850 had announced the triumph of the bourgeoisie) observed in 1892, with a mixture of bewilderment and contempt, that "the English bourgeoisie are, up to the present day, so deeply penetrated by a sense of their inferiority that they keep up at their expense and that of the nation, an ornamental caste of drones to represent the nation worthily at all state functions; and they considered themselves highly honoured, whenever one of themselves is found worthy of admission into this selected and privileged body, manufactured, after all, by themselves" (*Socialism, Utopian and Scientific* [New York, 1935], 26).

13. See Brian Heeney, *A Different Kind of Gentleman: Parish Clergy as Professional Men in Early and Mid-Victorian England* (Hamden, Conn., 1976).

14. W. J. Reader, *Professional Men* (New York, 1966), 211 and passim.

15. *England: Her People, Polity and Pursuits* (London, 1885), 355-6.

16. *Origins of Modern English Society*, 256.

17. For an American contrast, see Burton Bledstein, *The Culture of Professionalism* (New York, 1976).

18. Magali Sarfatti Larson, *The Rise of Professionalism: A Sociological Analysis* (Berkeley, 1977), concludes (103) that "the English case shows with clarity that the internal characteristics of professionalization and of the professional model are subordinate to broader social and economic structures." Using Philip Elliot's distinction (in *The Sociology of the Professions* [London, 1972]) between "status professionalism" and "occupational professionalism," we can see that the transition from the first to the second form was less complete in Britain than, for example, in

America. The most valuable discussion of the English nineteenth-century professional outlook is in Reader, *Professional Men*; see also Sheldon Rothblatt, *The Revolution of the Dons* (London, 1968), 90-2; G. Kitson Clark, *The Making of Victorian England* (Cambridge, Mass., 1962), 258-74; W. L. Burn, *The Age of Equipoise* (London, 1964), 253-67.

19. W. D. Rubinstein, "Wealth, Elites and Class Structure in Britain," *Past and Present*, no. 76 (August, 1977), 122n.

20. *Schools and Universities on the Continent* [1868], ed. R. H. Super (Ann Arbor, Mich., 1964), 308-9.

21. For a detailed substantiation of this claim, see J. R. de S. Honey, *Tom Brown's Universe: The Development of the Victorian Public School* (London, 1977), ch. 4.

22. *Parl. Papers 1864 20, Report of H. M. Commissioners appointed to inquire into the Revenues and management of certain Colleges and Schools and the Studies pursued and instruction given therein* [hereafter called *Public Schools Commission*] *1*, 56. As the novelist and translator Rex Warner, himself a schoolmaster, observed in a brief popular account, the Clarendon report "is evidence of the complete acceptance of the public school system as the best possible means of education for those who were to be leaders of the country in peace or war." (Rex Warner, *English Public Schools* [London, 1945], 30).

23. Quoted in T. W. Bamford, *The Rise of the Public Schools* (London, 1967), 15.

24. See J. H. Plumb, "The New World of Childhood in the Eighteenth Century," *Past and Present*, no. 67 (May, 1975), 64-95, and Bamford, *Rise of the Public Schools*, 87, 97.

25. Bamford, *Rise of the Public Schools*, 88.

26. Quoted in Martin J. Wiener, *Between Two Worlds: The Political Thought of Graham Wallas* (Oxford, 1971), 6.

27. *Public Schools Commission* 2, 42. J. R. de S. Honey concluded (*Tom Brown's Universe*, 128), "The position of the classics, public schools and in English education in general, was if anything more powerful at the end of the nineteenth century then it had been at the beginning."

28. *Parl. Papers 1868 28, Report of the Schools Inquiry Commission 1*, 17-18.

29. See Bamford, *Rise of the Public Schools*, 105.

30. *Education and School* (1864), quoted in Reader, *Professional Men*, 108.

31. F. W. Farrar, "Public School Education," *Fortnightly Review 3* (new series) (March, 1868), 239-40.

32. Thomas Hughes, *Tom Brown's School Days* [1857] (New York, 1968), 46, 276-7. The dean of Lincoln, addressing Wellington College on its fiftieth anniversary, typically described the school as a place where the young might "learn to put honour before gain, duty before pleasure, the public good before private advantage" (*Wellington College Year Book*, 1909, quoted in David Ward, "The Public Schools and Industry in Britain After 1870," *Journal of Contemporary History* 2, no. 3 [July, 1967], 49).

33. Hughes, *Tom Brown*, 54.

34. Quoted in Ward, "Public Schools and Industry," 38.

35. *Schools Inquiry Commission 1*, 18. See E. C. Mack, *Public Schools and British Opinion, 1780-1860* (New York, 1938), 391.

36. See, for example, Rupert Wilkinson and T. J. H. Bishop, *Winchester and the Public School Elite* (London, 1967), passim.

37. Sir John Otter, *Nathaniel Woodard: A Memoir of His Life* (London, 1925), 240. Woodard, a High Church clergyman, was the son of a country gentleman of modest means. See Honey's account of Woodard's and

others' efforts to provide public schools for a wider section of the middle classes (*Tom Brown's Universe*, ch. 2).

38. See Honey, ibid., 286.
39. See Bamford, *Rise of the Public Schools*, 16. When cities threatened to encroach, as at Eton and Harrow, expensive defensive measures were taken: Both schools, in effect, sealed off their buildings with a green belt. Harrow's land purchases between 1885 and 1898 were described at the time as a necessary preservative of the invaluable "beauty and dignity" of the school's "rural" setting, upon which "the romantic affection which gathers round an ancient public school" would soon erode (C. Colbeck, quoted in E. W. Henson and G. T. Warner, *Harrow School* [London, 1898], 155).
40. See W. H. G. Armytage, *Four Hundred Years of English Education* (London, 1970), 232.
41. Foreign imitations of the public schools, developing in different societies, moved in different directions. Wilkinson and Bishop, for example, found that comparing their subject, Winchester, with the most fashionable boarding schools in the eastern United States brought out all the more clearly "how often the public schoolboy's outlook on careers resisted the pull of private money-making": "Although the founders of Groton and St. Paul's tried sincerely to emulate the public school way, it has been estimated that the major American boarding schools have sent less than one percent of their boys into government since 1900" – a vastly lower proportion than that at Winchester (Wilkinson and Bishop, *Winchester and the Public School Elite*, 72).
42. Bernard Darwin, *The English Public School* (London, 1929), 28.
43. Roy Lewis and Angus Maude, *The English Middle Classes* (London, 1949), 22, 232.
44. See Brian Simon, "Introduction," in *The Victorian Public School*, ed. Brian Simon and Ian Bradley (London, 1975), 16-17.
45. Chuter Ede, in Parliament, 4 February 1943; quoted in Bamford, *Rise of the Public Schools*, 260.
46. One effect was, in Bamford's view, to delay "lower-class (elementary school) aspirations...for a generation and more. With those aspirations went any hope of a massive development of technical and scientific education that the scientists and industrialists had been urging for half a century" (*Rise of the Public Schools*, 261).
47. *Parl. Papers 1868 15, Report of the Select Committee on Scientific Instruction*, 402. In that very year a proposal that the Cambridge colleges should contribute to the establishment of a temporary professorship of experimental physics and a laboratory (that eventually became, with outside money, the Cavendish Laboratory) was foundering before fierce opposition. "A Prussian is a Prussian," said Dr. Phelps, the master of Sidney Sussex, "and an Englishman is an Englishman, and God forbid it should be otherwise" (quoted in Armytage, *Four Hundred Years*, 167).
48. See Michael Sanderson, *The Universities and British Industry, 1850-1970* (London, 1972), 48-50; and Rothblatt, *Revolution of the Dons*, 86-7.
49. Elliot (*The Sociology of the Professions*, 52) has summarized this development in Britain: "The ideology of liberal education, public service and gentlemanly professionalism was elaborated in opposition to the growth of industrialism and commercialism. This is one reason why it drew so heavily on the older tradition of gentlemanly leisure and the established professions. It incorporated such values as personal service, a dislike of competition, advertising and profit, a belief in the principle

of payment in order to work rather than working for pay and in the superiority of the motive of service."

50. Thomas Hughes, *Tom Brown at Oxford* [1861] (London, 1869), 100-1, 305, 395. See Rothblatt, *Revolution of the Dons*, 244-6, 256-7, 267-73; Sanderson, *The Universities and British Industry*, 51-2.
51. *Revolution of the Dons*, 256-7.
52. Ibid., 273.
53. Oliver Macdonagh, *Early Victorian Government* (London, 1977), 212. Macdonagh noted an "irony" about the creation of the new civil service: "that the radical ideals of open competition and selection of the fittest by examination contests should have been interlinked with the reactionary ideal of education as an experience and an exercise rather than the acquisition of particular skills or knowledge, or being graded according to intellectual attainment." Newman's *Idea of a University*, published almost contemporaneously with the Northcote-Trevelyan report, proved as influential as the latter in shaping the character of the new governing class. The result of the battle launched by Trevelyan and the other education and administrative reformers was, à la 1832, "to enlarge and rebuild, not to destroy or even weaken the exclusive elite" (Macdonagh, *Early Victorian Government*, 212-13).
54. See the statistics on recruitment and later occupations of Oxford and Cambridge undergraduates in Sanderson, *The Universities and British Industry*, 37, 53-4, and Rothblatt, *Revolution of the Dons*, 272-3.
55. See Chapter 7.
56. See David Landes, *The Unbound Prometheus* (Cambridge, 1969), 343-8, and Peter Mathias, *The First Industrial Nation* (London, 1969), 423-4.

3. A counterrevolution of values

1. *Victorian People* (Chicago, 1955), 16.
2. *Economist*, 4 January 1851.
3. *Henry Mayhew's 1851* (London, 1851), 160.
4. *Lives of the Engineers* [1861-2] (London, 1904), I, xxiii.
5. Quoted in David Thomson, *England in the Nineteenth Century* (Harmondsworth, 1950), 32.
6. Quoted in Nikolaus Pevsner, *Some Architectural Writers of the Nineteenth Century* (Oxford, 1972), 115, 133, 154. This is not to dismiss great differences within the Gothic revival – for example, the difference between the Gothic of Pugin and that of Ruskin. Pevsner is an excellent guide on this subject.
7. The best account of this reaction remains Raymond Williams, *Culture and Society, 1780-1950* (London, 1958).
8. *Sir Thomas More: or, Colloquies on the Progress and Prospects of Society*, 2, quoted in Williams, *Culture and Society* (New York, 1959), 25.
9. "Southey's Colloquies on Society," *Edinburgh Review 50* (1829-30), 528-65.
10. *Victorian Engineering* [1970] (Harmondsworth, 1974), 162-3.
11. Nikolaus Pevsner perceived this mid-Victorian shift in art. See *The Englishness of English Art* (London, 1956), 188-9.
12. *Victorians and the Machine* (Cambridge, Mass., 1968), 91.
13. *Sweetness and Light: The "Queen Anne" Movement, 1860-1900* (Oxford, 1977), 3.
14. See Noel Annan, *Leslie Stephen: His Thought and Character in Relation to His Age* (London, 1951); Melvin Richter, *The Politics of Conscience: T. H. Green and His Age* (Cambridge, Mass., 1964); and Martin J. Wiener,

Between Two Worlds: The Political Thought of Graham Wallas (Oxford, 1971). Noel Annan has explored this from the angle of family relationships in "The Intellectual Aristocracy," in *Studies in Social History*, ed. J. H. Plumb (London, 1955), 243-87.

15. *Doctor Thorne* [1858] (London, 1934), 11-12.
16. *The Way We Live Now* [1875] (New York, 1974), 383.
17. *The Victorian Age in Literature* (New York, 1903), 37.
18. Letter to Gustave D'Eichthal, 8 October 1929, in *Collected Works* (London, 1962), *12*, 35.
19. "The Negro Question," *Fraser's Magazine 41* (January, 1850), 27.
20. *Principles of Political Economy* [1848] (New York, 1961), 748-51.
21. *Letters*, ed. Madeline House, Graham Story, and Kathleen Tillotson (Oxford, 1974), *3*, 481.
22. Letter to Charles Eliot Norton, 19 June 1870, in *Works of John Ruskin*, ed. E. T. Cook and Alexander Wedderburn (London, 1905), *37*, 7.
23. This interpretation was begun by G. B. Shaw in several prefaces to new editions of Dickens's novels (his 1912 introduction to *Hard Times* is reprinted in *The Dickens Critics*, ed. G. H. Ford and Lavriat Lane, Jr. [New York, 1961], 125-35). A more recent example is Grahame Smith, *Dickens, Money, and Society* (Berkeley and Los Angeles, 1968).
24. The most succinct exposition of this view is Michael Goldberg's "From Bentham to Carlyle: Dickens' Political Development," *Journal of the History of Ideas 33* (1972), 61-76.
25. *Dombey and Son* (Harmondsworth, 1970), 50, 354.
26. Quoted in Angus Wilson, *The World of Charles Dickens* (London, 1970), 229.
27. *Little Dorrit* (New York, 1911), *1*, 195.
28. Robin Gilmour, "Dickens and the Self-Help Idea," in *The Victorians and Social Protest*, ed. J. Butt and I. F. Clarke (Newton Abbot, 1973), 99.
29. *Our Mutual Friend* (London, 1865), *1*, 15.
30. *The World of Charles Dickens*, 291.
31. *Culture and Anarchy and Friendship's Garland* (New York, 1886), 243. See also Arnold's essay, "My Countrymen" (1866), in the same volume, 317-57.
32. Ibid., 264. By contrast, see Arnold's benign remarks on the public schools, quoted in W. F. Connell, *The Educational Thought and Influence of Matthew Arnold* (London, 1950), 244-5.
33. *Mixed Essays*, 379. Lionel Trilling understood this when he entitled the first of two chapters on Arnold's social thought "The Failure of the Middle Class." Trilling, *Matthew Arnold* [1939] (New York, 1955), 203.
34. *Culture and Anarchy and Friendship's Garland*, 178, 343, 344, 340, 16.
35. Henry Sidgwick, "The Prophet of Culture," *Macmillan's Magazine 16* (August, 1867), 271-80.
36. *Culture and Anarchy and Friendship's Garland*, 16.
37. "The Two Paths," in *Works*, *16*, 348-9. Gillian Naylor (*The Arts and Crafts Movement* [Cambridge, Mass., 1971], 23) has drawn an illuminating contrast between the "American" outlook toward nature, exemplified by Ralph Waldo Emerson, and Ruskin's "English" stance. In 1847, Emerson spoke in Manchester, full of praise for the industry, thoroughness, and skill of English mechanics. A decade later, Ruskin spoke to a similar audience in Manchester, but admonished rather than praised them. "Emerson [Naylor observed], whose reverence for nature was as profound as that of Ruskin, saw within it organic principles that could be emulated by both art and industry, and in so doing he was blazing the trail that led to Sullivan, Frank Lloyd Wright and Buckminster Fuller.

Ruskin, too, urged his followers to turn to nature for both intellectual and emotional stimulus, but for them the field and the factory could have nothing in common, and the lessons they learned from nature bore little relationship to the world of industry."

The Arts and Crafts Movement in England followed in Ruskin's steps. C. R. Ashbee, the movement's leading figure, described (in *Craftmanship in Competitive Industry* [London, 1908], 11) the prevalent view within the movement that "the proper place for the Arts and Crafts is in the country . . . away from the complex, artificial and often destructive influences of machinery and the great town." This was not mere talk; the Guild of Handicraft, the chief Arts and Crafts body, moved in 1902 from London to Chipping Campden. Ruskin's successors, following his path away from the machine, ended in a cul-de-sac. The guild's move defied economic sense and went against the trend of related movements in Scandinavia, Germany, and America, but the emotional appeal of the historic rustic setting won out. The guild declined in its remote locale, and dissolved in 1914, a victim of following its beliefs to their logical conclusion.

Design leadership passed to others – America, Germany, France, Scandinavia – more hospitable to industry. Even when a fusion was deliberately sought, Ruskinite prejudices doomed it: The unsuccessful history of the National Association for the Advancement of Art and Its Application to Industry, founded in 1888 with some fanfare and support from Establishment cultural figures, was a case in point. The association lasted a mere three years, and accomplished nothing beyond holding three congresses, in which "art" was richly represented but "industry" hardly at all. These congresses were dominated by figures from the art world. Some aristocratic patrons and politicians were drawn in, but no significant number of manufacturers, the very people to whom the founders of the association were supposedly reaching out. In truth, little sustained effort was made to link up with them: The sole evidence for such an effort was a letter in the *Times* (London) before the first congress calling for manufacturers to come forward. The conception of the association was essentially de haut en bas: to elevate the standards of benighted industrialists by exposing them to the best thinking of artists and designers. Its leaders consequently waited for their "students" to apply, and waited, not very surprisingly, in vain. A scholar who studied William Martin Conway, the moving force behind the association, could find "no evidence of his having ventured into the precincts of a single factory" (Peter Stansky, "Art, Industry, and the Aspirations of William Martin Conway," *Victorian Studies 19*, no. 4 [June, 1976], 484).

38. *Works, 17,* 38-40, 105, 264, 281, 388; *16,* 344.
39. *Works, 34,* 314-15; *17,* 112.
40. *Works, 5,* 382.
41. *Works, 17,* 56.
42. *Victorian Essays* (London, 1962), 125.
43. E. T. Cook, *Life of John Ruskin* (London, 1911), 2, 542.
44. See Humphrey House, *The Dickens World* (London, 1941), 9-10.

4. The "English way of life"?

1. Donald Horne, *God is an Englishman* (Sydney, Australia, 1969), 22-3.
2. Asa Briggs (*Victorian Cities* [London, 1963], 355-61) has noted how in the later nineteenth century the social and cultural importance of the

northern industrial cities began to recede. A fervent and not untypical literary disparagement of the "northern way of life" is made by George Gissing in his *Private Papers of Henry Ryecroft* ([1903] New York, 1961), 163: "The vigorous race on the other side of the Trent only found its opportunity when the age of machinery began; its civilization, long delayed, differs in obvious respects from that of older England . . . The rude man of the north is . . . just emerged from barbarism, and under any circumstances would show less smooth a front [than the man of the south]. By great misfortune, he has fallen under the harshest lordship the modern world has known – that of scientific industrialism, and all his vigorous qualities are subdued to a scheme of life based upon the harsh, the ugly, the sordid."

3. *God is an Englishman*, 38.
4. "The English Dream," *Spectator 206* (1 March 1961), 334. For another description of the same cultural form, see John Holloway, "The Myth of England," *Listener 81* (15 May 1969), 670-3.
5. "Transatlantic Letter to England," *Encounter*, January 1976, 7.
6. *Lives of the Engineers 2*, 30.
7. *Public Schools Year Book*, 1889, quoted by Sheldon Rothblatt, *The Revolution of the Dons* (London, 1968), 51.
8. Anthony Sampson, *Anatomy of Britain* (New York, 1962), 638.
9. *Victorian Cities*, 381, 391-2. Briggs observed that the author of a series of articles in the *Athenaeum* on places about to be visited by the British Association made almost no mention of the nineteenth century. He most enjoyed writing about Exeter, Norwich, or York, but when he came to Bradford he concentrated on the Civil War of the seventeenth century and about Birmingham said little of anything after Dr. Priestley. "Fortunately for him the British Association did not hold a meeting in Crewe" (*Victorian Cities*, 392).
10. G. W. Kitchin, *Winchester* (London, 1890), 217-18.
11. Quoted in Briggs, *Victorian Cities*, 381.
12. *The Story of Our English Towns* (London, 1897), 34. Ditchfield's antiquarian titles ran to several dozen.
13. William Watson, preface to Alfred Austin, *English Lyrics* (London, 1896), xiv.
14. *Haunts of Ancient Peace* [1902] (London, 1908), 18-19.
15. *Old Country Life* (London, 1890), 235.
16. "How I Became a Socialist" (1894), in *William Morris: Selected Writings and Designs*, ed. Asa Briggs (Harmondsworth, 1962), 36; "First Lines from the Prologue to *The Earthly Paradise*," in Briggs, quoted *William Morris*, 68.
17. "Early England" (1886), in *The Unpublished Lectures of William Morris*, ed. Eugene Le Mire (Detroit, Mich., 1969), 158; "Art and the Beauty of the Earth" (1881), in *Collected Works* (London, 1910-15), 22, 172.
18. *Industry and Empire: An Economic History of Britain since 1750* (London, 1968), 142.
19. *Our English Villages: Their Story and Their Antiquities* (London, 1889), 4.
20. The political theorist Giovanni Botero was typical, declaring in 1588 that "although the country do abound in plenty of all good things, yet there is not a city in it [London excepted] that deserves to be called great" (G. Botero, *The Reason of State and the Greatness of Cities*, ed. P. J. and D. P. Waley [London, 1956], 235).
21. The most recent account of the growth of London's role as an aristocratic social center is in Mark Girouard, *Life in the English Country House*

(New Haven, Conn., 1978), 5-9. See also Penelope Corfield's account of Norwich as a provincial center of gentry life in *Crisis and Order in English Towns*, ed. Peter Clark and Paul Slack (London, 1972), 287-94. On the rise of an urban mercantile elite culture in the eighteenth century (whose growth was to be aborted in the nineteenth century by gentrification), see Nicholas Rogers, "Money, Land and Lineage: The Big Bourgeoisie of Hanoverian London," *Social History 4* (1979), 437-54.

22. F. M. L. Thompson has described the decline of the landed interest in *English Landed Society in the Nineteenth Century* (London, 1963), chs. 10-12.

23. *The Country and the City* (London, 1973), 248. Several very interesting essays on this subject are to be found in *Victorian Writers and the City*, ed. Jean-Paul Hulin and Pierre Coustillas (Lille, France, 1979), which appeared too late for me to use here.

24. See David Cannadine, "From 'Feudal' Lords to Figureheads: Urban Landownership and Aristocratic Influence in Nineteenth-Century Towns," in *Urban History Yearbook, 1978*, (Leicester, England) 23-35.

25. This integration has been discussed from a variety of angles: See Christopher Hill, *Reformation to Industrial Revolution: British Economy and Society, 1530-1780* (London, 1967); Barrington Moore, *Social Origins of Dictatorship and Democracy* (Boston, Mass., 1966), 3-39; Williams, *The Country and the City*. Girouard (*Life in the English Country House*, 7-10) touches on the seventeenth- and eighteenth-century cultural "urbanization" of the English countryside.

26. This subject has of course a vast literature; particularly relevant are Kenneth Barkin, "A Case Study in Comparative History: Populism in Germany and America," in *The State of American History*, ed. Herbert J. Bass (Chicago, 1970), 373-404; Gordon Wright, *Rural Revolution in France: The Peasantry in the Twentieth Century* (Stanford, Calif., 1964); and Suzanne Berger, *Peasants Against Politics: Rural Organization in Brittany, 1911-1967* (Cambridge, Mass., 1972).

27. See two masterful recent studies: Eugen Weber, *Peasants into Frenchmen: The Modernization of Rural France, 1870-1914* (Stanford, Calif., 1976); Jerome Blum, *The End of the Old Order in Rural Europe* (Princeton, N.J., 1978).

28. This was apparent even in "practical" efforts for agricultural reform. These revolved in the later nineteenth and early twentieth centuries around schemes for the creation of smallholdings, despite the lack of grass-roots demand in England (such as certainly existed in Ireland) for such land redistribution. J. R. Fisher ("Public Opinion and Agriculture, 1875-1900," Ph.D. diss., University of Hull, 1972) concluded that the economic case for smallholdings was weak, and that the policy was advocated and supported for social rather than economic reasons. The land, in various ways for various advocates, held out the hope of regenerating English society. "The pathetic delusion," as the sociologist O. R. McGregor has called it (introduction to Lord Ernle, *English Farming Past and Present*, 6th ed. [London, 1961], cxxxvii), "that some sort of land settlement scheme contained the secret cure for the ills of industrial society had great survival value." Such survival owed much to the nature of its appeal: Harold Perkin had noted ("Land Reform and Class Conflict in Victorian Britain," in *The Victorians and Social Protest*, ed. J. Butt and T. F. Clarke [Newton Abbot, Devon, 1973], 177-217) that the land reform issue drew its greatest support from the new professional classes, for whom it was less an economic issue than a moral (and

cultural, we might add) one. The issue drew on the early-nineteenth-century tradition of antilandlordism, but this source of feeling was gradually fading. A newer source lay in the rising wave of nostalgia and distaste for urban industrial society. In continental Europe and the United States, large numbers of politically organized rural smallholders ensured the issue a permanent place in politics and in the perennial jockeying between economic interests. In England the issue remained in the realm of symbol and myth.

29. Christopher Hussey, *The Fairy Land of England* (London, 1924), 65.
30. Ford Madox Ford [Hueffer], *The Heart of the Country* (London, 1906), 58.
31. See Glen Cavaliero, *The Rural Tradition in the English Novel, 1900-1939* (Totowa, N.J., 1977): "The country . . . was interpreted through the eyes of the town" (9).
32. Quoted on concluding page of Alfred Austin, *The Garden That I Love*, 2nd series [1894] (London, 1907). Perceptive contemporaries had noted this trend early on: See Leslie Stephen, "Country Books," *Cornhill* 42 (1880), 662.
33. *The Country* (London, 1913), 17; see also 36-9. Jerome Bump has re-iterated that "most of the individuals in the 'rural' tradition [of writing] actually lived in the city at various times or imported the trappings of industrial technology into the country; more importantly, they all wrote for city readers" (*Victorian Studies* 20 [Autumn, 1976], 97).
34. *My England* (London, 1938), 62.
35. See Malcolm Bradbury, *The Social Context of Modern English Literature* (Oxford, 1971), 46.
36. W. J. Keith, *Richard Jefferies* (Toronto, 1965), locates the appearance of "an appreciation of the English countryside . . . as a popular taste" around 1880, as did J. A. V. Chapple in his survey of the period from 1880 to 1920. Robert Hamilton, writing on W. H. Hudson, placed it at the end of the century, as did E. D. Mackerness in his introduction to the journals of George Sturt. Elizabeth Haddow, in "The Novel of English Country Life, 1900-1930," a useful University of London Master's thesis (1957), cited the 1890s as the crucial decade. Cavaliero, in *The Rural Tradition in the English Novel* (London, 1977), took Hardy as his departure point. Leslie Stephen was noting this increased interest in 1880. Precise dating of such intangible cultural phenomena is rarely possible, but general agreement clearly locates this change in the late-Victorian years. Other evidence: *Country Life* magazine was started in the 1890s by a romantic and country-loving businessman, and quickly became a great success. In 1904, the urban, Liberal *Manchester Guardian* began a column entitled "Country Diary."
37. *John Davidson: A Selection of His Poems*, ed. Maurice Lindsay (London, 1961), 7.
38. One very explicit example is P. H. Ditchfield's *The Old English Country Squire* (London, 1912), vii.
39. William Watson, preface to Austin, *English Lyrics*, xv. See also S. Baring-Gould, *An Old English Home and Its Dependencies* (London, 1898).
40. Girouard, *Life in the English Country House*, 303. On the literary preoccupation with the country house, see Richard Gill, *Happy Rural Seat* (New Haven, Conn., 1972).
41. *The Heart of the Country*, 164; *England: A Nation*, ed. Lucien Oldershaw (London, 1904), 99; "Appeal to the Squires," *New Witness* 2 (9 October 1913), 721; see George Sturt, *Change in the Village* (London, 1912).

42. Henry Nash Smith, *Virgin Land* (Cambridge, Mass., 1950); Morton and Lucia White, *The Intellectual vs. the City* (Cambridge, Mass., 1962); Leo Marx, *The Machine in the Garden* (New York, 1964); Roderick Nash, *Wilderness and the American Mind* (New Haven, Conn., 1967); Donald Fleming, "Roots of the New Conservation Movement," *Perspectives in American History 6* (1972), 7-91.

43. *Victorian Cities,* 80.

44. See, for example, the discussion by Walter Berns, "Thinking about the City," *Commentary 56,* no. 4 (October, 1973), 75.

45. "Haymaking," in *Collected Poems* (London, 1920), 58.

46. *The Heart of the Country,* 50.

47. J. Bruce Glasier, *William Morris and the Early Days of the Socialist Movement* (London, 1921), 152.

48. *New Statesman 88* (27 September 1974), 428.

49. Quoted in L. Lerner and J. Holmstrom, *Thomas Hardy and His Readers* (New York, 1968), 15.

50. Randall Williams, *The Wessex Novels of Thomas Hardy* (London, 1924), 4.

51. Quoted in Edmund Blunden, *Thomas Hardy* (London, 1941), 39; J. M. Barrie, "Thomas Hardy," *Contemporary Review 56* (1889), 57-66.

52. "The Novels of Thomas Hardy," *Quarterly Review 199* (1904), 500-1.

53. W. J. Keith, "Thomas Hardy and the Literary Pilgrims," *Nineteenth Century Fiction 24,* 1 (June, 1969), 80-92; Blunden, *Hardy* (London, 1941), 115-17; Lerner and Holmstrom, *Hardy and His Readers,* 22, 56, 163-4; Merryn Williams, *Thomas Hardy and Rural England* (London, 1972), xi-xiii; G. S. Cox, "The Hardy Industry," in *The Genius of Thomas Hardy,* ed. Margaret Drabble (London, 1976), 170-81.

54. Interview in *Black and White,* 27 August 1892, quoted in Lerner and Holmstrom, *Hardy and His Readers,* 94.

55. F. E. Hardy, *The Early Life of Thomas Hardy* (London, 1928), 25-6. See also Hardy's preface to the 1895 edition of *Far From the Madding Crowd,* in *Thomas Hardy's Personal Writings,* ed. Harold Orel (Lawrence, Kans., 1966), 10-11.

56. See Roy Morrel, *Thomas Hardy: The Will and the Way* (London, 1965), Irving Howe, *Thomas Hardy* (New York, 1967), and, from a different angle, Williams, *The Country and the City,* ch. 18.

57. Hardy, *Early Life,* 270. See also ch. 51 of Hardy's *Tess of the D'Urbervilles.*

58. *An Old English Home* (London, 1898), 204.

59. Augustus Ralli, *Critiques* (London, 1927), 43-4.

60. Williams, *The Country and the City,* 192-3. I have drawn, in the text that follows, on Williams's discussion of Jefferies.

61. *The Longest Journey* [1907] (London, 1947), 146.

62. W. J. Keith, *The Rural Tradition* (Toronto, 1974), 132.

63. Samuel J. Looker and Clifton Porteous, *Richard Jefferies: Man of the Fields* (London, 1965), 233.

64. *Hodge and His Masters* [1880] (London, 1890), 276-7.

65. Ibid., 132-4, 167-8, 373, 375, 382.

66. Quoted in Looker and Porteous, *Jefferies,* 237.

67. In one typical collection of about 300 patriotic poems (*The Call of the Homeland,* ed. R. P. Scott and K. T. Wallas [London, 1907]), not one poem mentions in any way the technical advance of the nineteenth century as a matter of national pride. When industry was (rarely) noted, it was as in the poem by Lord Hanmer entitled "England," which begins: "Arise up, England, from the smoky cloud that covers thee, the din of whirling wheels."

68. *Lyrical Poems* (London, 1891), 148.
69. *Haunts of Ancient Peace*, 18-19, 168.
70. "Why England is Conservative," *English Lyrics*, 116. C. K. Stead, in *The New Poetic* (London, 1964), sees these lines as typical of 1890s and Edwardian poetry.
71. See Hobsbawm, *Industry and Empire*, 120-6; Bernard Porter, *The Lion's Share* (London, 1975), chs. 3 and 4.
72. See J. A. Froude, *Oceana* (London, 1886), 8-11, 17, 386-8.
73. Letter to H. Rider Haggard, 22 December 1902, *Rudyard Kipling to Rider Haggard: The Record of a Friendship*, ed. Morton Cohen (Cranbury, N.J., 1965), 50.
74. Letter to C. E. Norton, 30 November 1902, quoted in C. E. Carrington, *The Life of Rudyard Kipling* (New York, 1956), 286.
75. R. Thurston Hopkins, *Rudyard Kipling's World* (London, 1925), 11, 266. Hopkins also wrote *The Kipling Country* (London, 1924) and *Thomas Hardy's Dorset* (London, 1922).
76. On this side of Kipling, see Roger Lancelyn Green, "The Countryman," in *Rudyard Kipling: The Man, The Work and His World*, ed. John Gross (London, 1972), 125.
77. Rudyard Kipling, *Something of Myself* (New York, 1937), 182.
78. *The Later Life and Letters of Sir Henry Newbolt*, ed. Margaret Newbolt (London, 1942), 34.
79. *Private Papers of Henry Ryecroft*, 69, 106, 214-15, 220.
80. John Holloway, "The Myth of England," *Listener 81* (15 May 1969), 672.
81. "Farmers in Arms," *New York Review of Books 12*, no. 12 (19 June 1969), 37.
82. *Collected Works*, ed. May Morris (London, 1911-14), *16*, 3.
83. James Bryce, *Impressions of South Africa* (London, 1897), 571.
84. *In Peril of Change* (London, 1905), 7, 16, 34.
85. G. K. Chesterton, *Autobiography* (New York, 1936), 108-15.
86. *England: A Nation*, 38.
87. Ibid., 96, 99.
88. Brougham Villiers [Frederick J. Shaw], *England and the New Era* (London, 1920), 231-2. For his political ideas, see idem, *The Opportunity of Liberalism* (London, 1904).
89. Quoted in Anthony Lister, "George Sturt: A Study of His Development as a Writer and His Conception of Village Life," Master's thesis, University of Manchester, 1961, 183.
90. *The Bettesworth Book* (1902), quoted in Lister, "George Sturt," 72-3.
91. *Howards End* [1910] (New York, 1962), 29, 323, 331, 268-9.
92. *Letters of D. H. Lawrence*, ed. Aldous Huxley (New York, 1932), 277, 287.
93. Samuel Hynes, *Edwardian Occasions* (New York, 1972), 186.
94. Robert H. Ross, *The Georgian Revolt: Rise and Fall of a Poetic Ideal* (Carbondale, Ill., 1965), 12.
95. Quoted in *Collected Poems of Rupert Brooke* [1918], ed. Edward Marsh (London, 22nd impression, 1936), C (Memoir by Marsh).
96. Hugh Dalton's recollection of Brooke's remark to him, quoted in Timothy Rogers, *Rupert Brooke: A Reappraisal and Selection* (London, 1971), 25.
97. Rupert Brooke, "The Old Vicarage, Grantchester," in *Collected Poems*, ed. Marsh, 94.
98. *Poetry and the Modern World* (Chicago, 1940), 41-2. This interpretation is, admittedly, not entirely fair to Brooke and some of his fellow poets, who

saw themselves as rebels against the stilted, conventional verse of an older generation. To a degree, the Georgian image was created by Edward Marsh's "packaging" and a receptive public, although the raw material was there, and amenable to such shaping. On this subject, see Christopher Hassell, *Rupert Brooke* (London, 1964); C. K. Stead, *The New Poetic* (London, 1964); Ross, *Georgian Revolt*; and Rogers, *Rupert Brooke*. Like Hardy and Morris, the Georgians were more complex than was their image in the public mind.

99. E. C. Pulbrook, *The English Countryside* (London, 1915), 2.

100. *The Old Country: A Book of Love and Praise of England*, ed. Ernest Rhys (London, 1917), V, 161. (Lucas's poem was originally written for a gramophone record.)

101. "England of My Heart" [1914], in Rhys, *The Old Country*, 204.

102. *Georgian Poetry, 1913-1915*, ed. Edward Marsh (London, 1915), 115-16.

103. W. F. Law and I. Law, *The Book of the Beresford-Hopes* (London, 1925), 161.

104. Igor Webb, "The Bradford Wool Exchange: Industrial Capitalism and the Popularity of Gothic," *Victorian Studies 20*, 1 (Autumn, 1976), 45-68.

105. Paul Thompson, *William Butterfield* (London, 1971), 374.

106. *Sweetness and Light: The "Queen Anne" Movement, 1860-1900* (Oxford, 1977), 5. *Sweetness and Light* is a crucial work on this subject, as is another of Girouard's works, *The Victorian Country House* (Oxford, 1971), and Andrew Saint, *Richard Norman Shaw* (New Haven, Conn., 1976). See also Robert Furneaux Jordan, *Victorian Architecture* (Harmondsworth, 1966), 180-91, 226-35, and Robert Macleod, *Style and Society: Architectural Ideology in Britain, 1835-1914* (London, 1971), 52-3.

107. Girouard, *Sweetness and Light*, 13.

108. *The Letters of William Morris to His Family and Friends*, ed. Philip Henderson (London, 1950), 265; quoted in Paul Thompson, *The Work of William Morris* (London, 1967), 55.

109. "English Feeling," *Listener 98* (8 December 1977), 751.

110. *The Victorian Country House*, 42, 46.

111. Paul Thompson, *The Edwardians* (London, 1975), 39.

112. See "C. P. A. Voysey," in Nikolaus Pevsner, *Studies in Art, Architecture and Design* (London, 1968), II, 140-51.

113. Quoted in *Sweetness and Light*, 15.

114. Walter Creese, *The Search for Environment* (New Haven, Conn., 1966), 169-71.

115. Alan A. Jackson, *Semi-Detached London* (London, 1973), 136-8; *Leslie Bailey's BBC Scrapbooks, Volume 2: 1918-1939* (London, 1968), 51. Nostalgia affected even pub design: From the nineties, most pubs, particularly in the new suburbs, were no longer designed as flamboyant urban gin palaces but as rustic Old English inns (Robert Thorne, "Cut Glass to Half Timber: The Development of the Pub, 1880-1930," Ph.D. diss. Leicester University, 1976).

116. Quoted in Thompson, *Work of William Morris*, 57-8. Similarly, William Butterfield, one of the most active – and later, one of the most condemned – of restorers, became increasingly sensitive to the dangers of unnecessary alterations. In 1861, while rebuilding the chapel tower at Winchester College, he wrote that he intended "on principle [to] reuse as much of the old work as possible in the reconstruction" (Thompson, *Butterfield*, 416).

117. *Athenaeum*, 10 March 1877, quoted in *Morris*, ed. Briggs, 81-2.

118. SPAB report and general meeting, 1889. An article against restoration in the *Globe* of March 14, 1889, was quoted with the observation that "such an article would not have appeared a few years ago." In 1886 the new secretary, Thackeray Turner, had informed the annual meeting that the piecemeal destruction of Lincoln's Inn, against which the society had protested without much hope, had been halted upon an unexpectedly enthusiastic response to that protest by the inhabitants (SPAB report and general meeting, 1886, 34).

119. SPAB report and general meeting, 1920, 41. For a typical observation on the change in public opinion, see Percy Wyndham, SPAB report and general meeting, 1904, 74.

120. J. W. Mackail, *Life of William Morris* (London, 1899) *1*, 354.

121. *Works, 8,* 233-4; *36,* 239.

122. SPAB report, 1879, 42.

123. "English Architecture Thirty Years Hence" (1884), in Nickolaus Pevsner, *Some Architectural Writers of the Nineteeth Century* (Oxford, 1972), 309. Another contemporary architectural critic of the "nostalgia" of the SPAB was H. H. Statham; see his address, "What Are the Proper Limits of Conservatism in regard to Ancient Buildings?" in *Transactions of the National Association for the Promotion of Social Science, 1882* (London, 615-26).

124. *Style and Society,* 52-3.

125. SPAB report and general meeting, 1885.

126. SPAB report, 1878, 36.

127. Quoted in Thompson, *Work of William Morris,* 56, and in Pevsner, *Some Architectural Writers,* 289n.

128. W. R. Lethaby, *Philip Webb and His Work* (London, 1935), 136.

129. See, for some instances of opposition to Sir John Lubbock's National Monuments Preservation Bill in the 1870s and 1880s, Wayland Kennet, *Preservation* (London, 1972), 23-30.

130. *Vanishing England* (London, 1910), 4.

131. SPAB report and general meeting, 1890, 8.

132. SPAB report and general meeting, 1878, 24.

133. *Vanishing England,* 398, 28.

134. SPAB report and general meeting, 1880, 7; SPAB report and general meeting, 1890, 8-9.

135. SPAB report and general meeting, 1882, 24.

136. SPAB report and general meeting, 1898, 66-7.

137. *William Morris to Whistler* (London, 1911), 77, 76.

138. "Mrs. Miniver," in *Two Cheers for Democracy* (London, 1951), 306-7.

139. See, for what are two of many examples, Henry Williamson, "Recipe for Country Life," *Listener 14* (24 December 1935), 1165, and William O'Neill, "Living in the Country" *Time and Tide 17* (4 January 1936), 18-19.

140. Quoted in Edith Moore, *E. Nesbit* [1933] (London, 1967), 114.

141. *Cartoon History of Architecture* (London, 1975), 130-1.

142. *So Long to Learn* (London, 1952), 117-18, 165-6; see also John Masefield, *St. George and the Dragon* (London, 1918), 7-11.

143. *The English Middle Classes* (London, 1949), 180. C. E. M. Joad similarly remarked at the end of the war: "There have never been so many books on 'Beautiful Britain' or so large a sale for them" (*The Untutored Townsman's Invasion of the Country* [London, 1946], 221). "Country life" began to be listed separately in the *Subject Index to Periodicals* in 1926.

144. *The Heart of England* (London, 1935), 39.

145. Haddow, "The Novel of English Country Life, 1900-1930," 327, 112.

146. *Leslie Bailey's BBC Scrapbooks, Volume 2*, 113-23, gives a variety of evidence of this trend. The *Listener* reprinted many such talks, and listed others.

147. "The Country Listens" (leader), *Listener 1* (3 April 1929), 424. During the thirties, the *Listener* carried a section called "Out of Doors," but no section on urban life or problems.

148. "Eyes Upon England," *Listener 17* (7 April 1937), 638. This was a comment on a series of twelve talks broadcast on the Empire Programme entitled "This is England." This series, heavily weighted with rural subjects, sought to inform listeners in the empire of typical English life.

149. Cited in H. D. Wilcock, *Britain and Her People* (London, 1951), 140-1.

150. Frederick Cowle, *This is England* (London, 1946), 147; see, for similar remarks, Thomas Burke, *The English and Their Country* (London, 1943), 28; J. B. Priestley, in *The Beauty of Britain: A Pictorial Survey* (London, 1935).

151. *Exploring English Character* (London, 1955), 43.

152. Some examples are: Edmund Blunden et al., *The Legacy of England* (London, 1935); W. J. Blyton, *English Cavalcade* (London, 1937); Frederick Cowles, *Not Far From the Smoke* (London, 1935); Dorothy Hartley, *Here's England* (London, 1934).

153. *The National Character* (London, 1934), 67, 23.

154. *Ordeal in England* (London, 1937), 273.

155. *From Surtees to Sassoon* (London, 1931), 209, 197, 204. See also his *English Fabric* (London, 1935), a search for national continuity in the rural England of Wessex. Parts of *English Fabric* appeared in the *Times* (London) and *Spectator*.

156. *My England* (London, 1938), 47, 45-6.

157. *The Fairy Land of England*, 5.

158. "The Abinger Pageant" (1934), in *Abinger Harvest* [1936] (New York, 1964), 363. The second pageant was written and performed in 1938: See E. M. Forster, *England's Pleasant Land* (London, 1940).

159. *Illustrated London News* [hereafter called *ILN*] *188* (13 June 1936), 1077; *190* (13 February 1937), 273.

160. *I Saw Two Englands* (London, 1942), 288-9.

161. *England is a Village* (London, 1941), 250, ix. A work that makes a similar equation of the national essence and the village is Francis Brett Young's *Portrait of a Village* (London, 1937).

162. For some examples, see J. B. Priestley, *Out of the People* (London, 1941), 21, 25; Arthur Bryant's "Notebook," in *ILN 198* (31 May 1941), 694; H. J. Massingham, *Chiltern Country* (London, 1940), 70, and Massingham, *Remembrance* (London, 1942), 127.

163. *England is a Village*, ix.

164. *ILN 198* (15 March 1941), 334.

165. *My Cambridge*, ed. Ronald Hayman (London, 1977), 123.

166. Assessing the impact of the still-running program, Sir William Haley, former director general of the BBC, has observed that "whatever practical success *The Archers* had in rural England was far exceeded by its urban appeal" ("Far from the Madding Crowd," *Times Literary Supplement*, 20 January 1978). Mary Evans views the program much as I do in "Down on Old Comfort Farm," *New Society*, 4 October 1979.

167. *The New Anatomy of Britain* (London, 1971), 555.

168. *Akenfield* (London, 1969), 15-16.

169. *England* (London, 1971), 39 (Introduction by Angus Wilson, photographs by Edwin Smith).
170. Anthony Thwaite, "Country Matters," *New Statesman* 77 (27 June 1969), 914-15.
171. "Suspect Sages," *New York Review of Books 19*, no. 4 (21 September 1972), 12.
172. "The Village Life," *New Society 29* (26 September 1974), 790.
173. *Daily Telegraph Magazine*, 1 March 1974, 15.
174. "An Austen-ized Village," *Atlantic*, July 1977, 80. A former urban radical now happily living in an ancient village described his transformation in the *New Statesman*: Peter Buckman, "Town and Country," *New Statesman 86* (23 November 1973), 772.
175. *The Living Village* (London, 1968), 18-19, 244, 199.
176. "An Austen-ized Village," 81.
177. Priestley's play is reminiscent of the Kipling story "An Habitation Enforced," in which an American couple is captured by the spell of rural England; despite opposed political stances, writers such as Priestley and Kipling were joined by a remarkably similar vision of England. Again and again, a rural national image was associated with a relaxed harmony with nature, the secret of the easy-going English way of life. Mary Webb's best-selling rustic novel of the twenties, *Precious Bane*, lauded by Prime Minister Baldwin, was structured around a contrast between two chief characters – Prudence, in harmony with nature, and Gideon, who, obsessed by the desire for achievement and wealth, works compulsively to master nature and "cannot rest"; Gideon's way brings destruction.
178. The *Guardian*, 26 November 1972, 9. At the same time, the journalist Francis Hope, observing the nation's mind turning inward with economic decline, accurately predicted that "the next decade will see an enormous increase in cultural and social nationalism. Growth stocks are: the English countryside, the preservation of British architecture (cheaper than tearing it down), the National Trust, the Georgian Group, remote cottages, porridge, tweed," and so on ("Funny Foreigners, Poor Us," *New Statesman 86* [19 October 1973], 557).

5. The wrong path?

1. *Lives of the Engineers*, *1*, xvii.
2. Introduction to Dickens, *Hard Times* (London, 1912).
3. "Wages and the Natural Law," in *Lectures on the Industrial Revolution of the Eighteenth Century in England* [1884] (London, 1923), 190.
4. "Are Radicals Socialists?" in ibid., 237.
5. *Lectures*, 64, 73, 205-6.
6. "William Cobbett," *Nineteenth Century 19* (1886), 255-6.
7. See Milner's "Reminiscence" (1894), in Toynbee, *Lectures*, ix-xxx, and A. M. Gollin, *Proconsul in Politics* (New York, 1964), 14-15.
8. C. R. L. Fletcher and Rudyard Kipling, *A History of England* (London, 1911), 204-6, 235. For other Tory examples, see Samuel Hynes, *The Edwardian Turn of Mind* (Princeton, N.J., 1968), 24-6.
9. Frank Swinnerton, *The Georgian Literary Scene* (London, 1935), 95.
10. *A Short History of England* (New York, 1917), chs. 11, 14, 16, and 17.
11. *What's Wrong with the World* (London, 1910), 91, 94.
12. "Appeal to the Squires," *New Witness 2* (1913-14), 722. See the similar view of English history of the land reform propagandist, Montague Fordham: *Mother Earth* (London, 1908), 119-20, and *The Rebuilding of Rural England* (London, 1924), 6-22.

13. See publishing information in R. M. Hartwell's introduction to the 1966 edition of the Hammonds' *Rise of Modern Industry*. *The Village Labourer* and *The Town Labourer* were reprinted in paperback in Britain in 1966.
14. Quoted by R. H. Tawney, "J. L. Hammond," *Proceedings of the British Academy 46* (1960), 293.
15. Preface to second edition of *The Town Labourer* (London, 1928), vi.
16. *Town Labourer*, 1-2, 31; *The Skilled Labourer* [1919] (New York, 1970), 6; *Rise of Modern Industry* (New York, 1926), 232, 217.
17. Peter Clarke, *Liberals and Social Democrats* (Cambridge, 1978), 243. Clarke (243-52) gives an illuminating account of the Hammonds' work in the context of its time.
18. *Town Labourer*, v, 327; *Rise of Modern Industry*, 232. See also *Town Labourer*, 16, and *Skilled Labourer*, 6.
19. *Rise of Modern Industry*, 212, 232, 244, 240, 250. See the similar work of the Hammonds' chief colleague in writing the history of that period, Gilbert Slater, principal of Ruskin College, Oxford. Slater's text, *The Making of Modern England*, painted a bleak picture of the state of England in the years after 1815, which he portrayed as the culmination of a century and more of "gross materialism" and an inhumane scramble for wealth. Slater's reserved attitude toward the industrial revolution contrasted strikingly with the enthusiasm of his later American editor, who saw it as "more than anything else, responsible for the greatness of England)" (*The Making of Modern England* [1912] (New York, 1916), 1-59, and, in that volume, James T. Shotwell, "Prefatory Note," vi). The Hammond tradition has been carried on in recent years by an active body of socialist historians; the most notable individual being E. P. Thompson and the purest collective expression the *History Workshop Journal*. Brian Harrison (*New Statesman 98* [26 October 1979], 635) described the first seven issues of the journal: "The emphasis is entirely upon the sufferings industrialization brought to the workers as producers rather than on the benefits it brought them as consumers; and those sufferings are described with all too little comparative reference to the conditions prevailing in earlier centuries."
20. *The English Middle Classes* (London, 1949), 80, 84: "By the 'forties the bill had grown very long; two wars, the wreck of the League, sabotage of the one Socialist state, unemployment, depressed areas, a desolated countryside and a heritage of ugly towns, the stunting of art and culture, the awful revelations of the Hammonds, the unsolved problems of the Empire."
21. *ILN 197* (28 December 1940), 844.
22. Henry Winkler, "George Macaulay Trevelyan," in *Some Twentieth Century Historians*, ed. S. William Halperin (Chicago, 1961), 54.
23. In *Churchill Revised*, ed. A. J. P. Taylor (New York, 1969), 168. Trevelyan's chief concerns are sympathetically examined in Joseph M. Hernon, Jr., "The Last Whig Historian and Consensus History: George Macaulay Trevelyan 1876-1962," *American Historical Review 81*, no. 1 (February 1976), 66-97.
24. *English Social History* (London, 1942), 527-8, 554, 578; *Youth Hostels Association Handbook*, 4th ed., 1931, remarks by Trevelyan.
25. Quoted in Hernon, "The Last Whig Historian," 83, 89.
26. "Land and People," in *The Character of England*, ed. Ernest Barker (London, 1947), 26-8. Such disavowal of industrialism eventually reached the level of cliché. A popular book on industrial archeology, published in 1975, offers one instance out of many: The jacket describes the

machines dealt with inside the volume as "the heartless iron monsters whose speed and efficiency eroded the gentler, more picturesque life of pre-industrial Britain and put in its place a society riven with inequalities and divisions which lie at the back of our political life to this day" (jacket for Anthony Burton, *Remains of a Revolution* [London, 1975]). Such an image must have been deeply engrained on the jacket writer's mind, for Burton's text says nothing like this. This vision was lodged in the back of the minds of policymakers as well as the public. In that same year, for instance, John Pinder, director of the Political and Economic Planning Institute, traced the nation's economic difficulties to the social strains consequent upon the fact that "we industrialized brutally." "Brutally," one wants to ask, compared to the United States? To Soviet Russia? (Pinder quoted in *Newsweek*, 27 October 1975, 89).

27. "Falling Backward Down an Escalator," *New Statesman 80* (25 December 1970), 860.
28. *Dissertations and Discussions* (Boston, 1868), 2, 65.
29. *Letters*, ed. G. W. E. Russell (London, 1895), *1*, 287; *Five Uncollected Essays of Matthew Arnold*, ed. Kenneth Allott (Liverpool, 1953), 6.
30. One example is in a letter of 1867, quoted in J. L. Garvin, *Life of Joseph Chamberlain* (London, 1932) *1*, 91.
31. *News from Nowhere* [1890], James Redmond (London, 1970), 84. See the similar identification of America with "the cult of size and heedless development" by G. K. Chesterton a half century later, in *ILN 188* (11 April 1936), 616.
32. Letter, 18 May 1886, quoted in B. J. Hendrick, *Life of Andrew Carnegie* (London, 1933), 240-1. Another Americanophile of the next generation, W. T. Stead, concluded his largely appreciative tract entitled *The Americanization of the World* ([London, 1902], 164) with a similar admission that its materialistic ethos was after all rather unappealing.
33. Quoted in E. M. Forster, *Goldworthy Lowes Dickinson* [1934] (London, 1973), 107.
34. "Does England Dislike America?" *The Forum* (New York) *80* (July-December, 1928), 692-8. Another example of this sort of criticism was O. N. Pisgah [pseud.], "Impressions of America," *The Forum 77* (January-June, 1927), 586-94. See George H. Knoles, *The Jazz Age Revisited: British Criticism of American Civilization during the 1920s* (Stanford, Calif., 1955), and, for a broader perspective, *America through British Eyes*, ed. Allan Nevins (New York, 1948), and Richard L. Rapson, "The British Traveller in America, 1860-1935," Ph.D. diss. Columbia University, 1966.
35. See the section titled "Education and the image of industry" in Chapter 7 for illustrations and consequences of this.
36. *Economics and Policy: A Historical Study* (London, 1969), 32.
37. See Winch, *Economics and Policy*, 35.
38. Quoted in *Memorials of Alfred Marshall* [1925], ed. A. C. Pigou (New York, 1956), 71, 376, 37.
39. *Principles of Economics* [1890] (London, 1920), 85, 751-2.
40. See his *Work and Wealth – A Human Valuation* (London, 1914).
41. *Confessions of an Economic Heretic* (London, 1938), 39-40.
42. Quoted in Donald Read, *Edwardian England, 1901-1915* (London, 1972), 130. Hobson's dissatisfaction with the industrial spirit was also reflected in his nostalgia for the rural society of earlier times. In 1908 (in a preface to Montague Fordham's *Mother Earth*), he warned that "while this persistent migration from the country to the town has doubtless been attended by an increase of national wealth and of certain sorts of

comforts and luxury, the price paid in health, character and the more enduring sources of happiness has been incalculably great."

43. Roy Harrod, *The Life of John Maynard Keynes* (London, 1951), 333.
44. *Essays in Persuasion* [1932] (New York, 1963), 297-311, 369-73.
45. In *The General Theory of Employment, Interest and Money* (London, 1936), quoted in Walter Eltis, "The Failure of the Keynesian Conventional Wisdom," in *Lloyds Bank Review*, no. 122 (October, 1976), 14.
46. Ibid., 16.
47. "How Good was Keynes' Cambridge?" *Encounter*, August, 1976, 91. For support, see the admission of the Cambridge economist Robin Marris (note 29 to Chapter 7).
48. On Tawney, see chapter 6.
49. *The Economic Consequences of Progress* (London, 1934), 201, 209-10. Glenday, it must be noted, did not represent orthodox economic opinion. The *Economist 119* (November, 1934, Book Supplement, 5-6, attacked his "philosophy of economic negation," and reviewer for the *Economic Journal 45* ([September, 1935], 534-44) complained that his reliance upon personal assumptions and prejudices yielded a "reactionary" outlook.
50. D. M. Bensusan-Butt, *On Economic Growth* (Oxford, 1960), 213.
51. *Roots of Economic Growth* (Calcutta, 1961), 7.
52. "A Survey of Welfare Economics, 1939-59," *Economic Journal 70* (June, 1960), 256.
53. Bensusan-Butt, *On Economic Growth*, 214.
54. *Growth: The Price We Pay* (London, 1969), 154-5.

Introduction to Part III
1. *The Unfinished Revolution* [1960] (New York, 1964), 140. In this way he accounted for the failure of Marxism to plant roots in Britain. Much the same argument has been used to explain the inability of extreme right-wing movements to make headway. See also David Coates, *The Labour Party and the Struggle for Socialism* (Cambridge, 1975), 139 and passim.
2. *Ramsay Macdonald's Political Writings*, ed. Bernard Barker (New York, 1972), 44 (introduction).

6. Images and politics
1. *Victorian England: Portrait of an Age* [1936] (London, 1960), 85.
2. *English History, 1918-1945* (Oxford, 1965), 172.
3. T. F. Lindsay and Michael Harrington, *The Conservative Party, 1918-1970* (New York, 1974), 4.
4. Harvey Glickman, "The Toryness of British Conservatism," *Journal of British Studies 1*, no. 1 (November, 1961), 136.
5. Lindsay and Harrington, *The Conservative Party*, 10. This anticapitalist and even antiindustrial "country gentleman" strain in British Conservatism has frequently drawn praise from radicals and socialists. See, for example, Herbert Read, *The Innocent Eye* [1940] (New York, 1947), 136.
6. *Competition and the Corporate Society: British Conservatives, the State and Industry, 1945-1964* (London, 1972), 66. See also L. P. Carpenter, "Corporatism in Britain 1930-1946," *Journal of Contemporary History II* (1976), 3-25.
7. Richard Shannon, *The Crisis of Imperialism, 1865-1915* (London, 1974), 358. Tom Nairn (*The Break-Up of Britain* [London, 1977], 46) has also seen this episode as a neglected turning point in modern British history, "a forsaken ruling class strategy which prefigured a very different state-form in the 20th century."

8. Quoted in Peter Fraser, *Joseph Chamberlain* (London, 1966), 226.
9. Quoted in Kenneth Young, *Balfour* (London, 1963), 126.
10. Keith Middlemas and John Barnes, *Baldwin* (London, 1969), 8-12, 19.
11. *On England* (London, 1926), 6; see Stanley Baldwin, *This Torch of Freedom* (London, 1935), 125.
12. A. W. Baldwin, *My Father* (London, 1956), 69.
13. Wickham Steed, *The Real Stanley Baldwin* (London, 1930), 147.
14. The *Times, Lord Baldwin: A Memoir* (London, 1937), 21.
15. "Our National Character" (1933), in *This Torch of Freedom*, 14; "The Love of Country Things" (1931), ibid., 120.
16. *On England*, 6-7. Ruralism did not *have* to be tranquilizing; Baldwin's rival, Lloyd George, was attached to an ideal of rural life, and filled his speeches with rural imagery. Yet his countryside was, like himself, dynamic and forceful, a wellspring of energy. As the *Times* (London) had observed: "When Lloyd George spoke of mountains and torrents, Baldwin spoke of meadows and streams." It was Baldwin's version that by their time had become orthodox, condemning Lloyd George's to the category of "the fictitious sublimity of Ossian" (The *Times, Baldwin: A Memoir*, 21).
17. *Memoirs of a Conservative: J. C. C. Davidson's Memoirs and Papers, 1910-37*, ed. Robert Rhodes James (London, 1969), 105.
18. *This Torch of Freedom*, 126.
19. *The Impact of Labour, 1920-1924* (Cambridge, 1971), 427.
20. *The Road to 1945: British Politics in the Second World War* (London, 1975), 27.
21. *Churchill: A Study in Failure* (London, 1970), 190.
22. "Peace in Industry II," in *On England*, 42.
23. *An Interpreter of England* (London, 1939), 63-4, 74.
24. Worshipful Company of Stationers, *Happenings of Interest at Stationers' Hall* (London, 1927), 11-12.
25. From a 1930 speech quoted in The *Times, Baldwin: A Memoir*, 20.
26. Foreword to Sidney Rogerson, *The Old Enchantment* (London, 1938), xii-xiii.
27. *Viscount Halifax* (New York, 1941), 130-1.
28. Foreword to Rogerson, *The Old Enchantment*, xiii.
29. *The Impact of Hitler: British Politics and British Policy, 1933-1940* (Cambridge, 1975), 271-2.
30. Begbie's book went through several editions, including a popularly priced one in 1925; quotations are from pp. 37-8; see particularly the chapters on Baldwin and Halifax.
31. *Whither England?* (London, 1932), 139-40. The book has an admiring preface by the minister of agriculture, Walter Elliot.
32. Cowling, *Impact of Hitler*, 52.
33. "Cultivating Our Own Home Garden," *Listener 6* (23 December 1931), 1090-1, and *Democracy on Trial* (London, 1931), 154. See also L. S. Amery, *The Forward View* (London 1935), for another Tory call for policies of rural revival coupled with economic reorganization in the interests of stability.
34. *Democracy on Trial*, 18, 24-7; *Government in Transition* (London, 1934), 41; "The Case for Group Settlement," *Listener 13* (20 February 1935), 339.
35. W. S. Morrison, MP, "Economics," in *Conservatism and the Future*, ed. Lord Eustace Percy (London, 1935), 59.
36. *Democracy on Trial*, 27.

37. *Churchill Revised*, ed. A. J. P. Taylor (New York, 1969), 155.
38. Quoted in Ebenezer Howard, *Garden Cities of Tomorrow* (London, 1902), 42.
39. Quoted in Paul Johnson, *The Offshore Islanders* (New York, 1972), 367n., and Keith Robbins, *Sir Edward Grey* (London, 1971), 372.
40. Quoted in Robert Rhodes James, *The British Revolution* (London, 1976), 265.
41. *England After War* (London, 1922), 143.
42. "An Overseas Englishman," in *England* (London, 1922), 8-9; Rawdon Hoare, *This Our Country* (London, 1935), throughout; Sir R. G. Stapledon, *The Land Now and To-morrow* (London, 1935), 231; S. L. Bensusan, *The Town vs. the Countryside* (London, 1923), 6 (foreword by Lord Bledisoe). For Edwardian forerunners, see W. M. Flinders Petrie, *Janus in Modern Life* (London, 1907), and Elliot E. Mills, *The Decline and Fall of the British Empire* (Oxford, 1905).
43. Quoted by Michael Wharton, "A Few Lost Causes," in *The Baldwin Age*, ed. John Raymond (London, 1960), 88.
44. *Freedom and Reality* (London, 1969), 338; see Douglas Schoen, *Enoch Powell and the Powellites* (London, 1977), 11.
45. *Freedom and Reality*, 339. Tom Nairn has interesting observations on Powell's English nationalism in *The Break-Up of Britian*, ch. 6.
46. Lindsay and Harrington, *The Conservative Party*, 52.
47. Ibid
48. Ibid., 85.
49. See Cowling, *Impact of Hitler*, 52.
50. Quoted in Lindsay and Harrington, *The Conservative Party*, 115.
51. Ibid., 118.
52. Quoted in Peter Self and Herbert J. Storing, *The State and the Farmer* (London, 1962), 197.
53. Quoted in *The Conservative Tradition*, ed. R. J. White (London, 1950), 203-5.
54. Stephen Blank, *Industry and Government in Britain: The Federation of British Industries in Politics, 1945-65* (Lexington, Mass., 1973), 125.
55. S. E. Finer et al., *Backbench Opinion in the House of Commons* (New York, 1961), 83-5.
56. For one example of many, see Lord Butler's remarks reported in *New Statesman 91* (20 February 1976), 225.
57. Quoted in Addison, *The Road to 1945*, 232-3.
58. *The Pendulum of Politics* (London, 1946), 161, 166.
59. *The Case for Conservativism* (Harmondsworth, 1947), 51-2.
60. Quoted in Samuel Beer, *British Politics in the Collectivist Age* (New York, 1967), 271.
61. Conservative and Unionist Central Office, *The Right Road for Britain* (London, 1949), 65.
62. *The Baldwin Age*, ed. John Raymond (London, 1960), 10.
63. Quoted in Adam Fox, *Dean Inge* (London, 1960), 202.
64. *All Saint's Sermons* (London, 1907), 51.
65. *Lay Thoughts of a Dean* (London, 1926), 195; *Outspoken Essays* (London, 1919), 23, 24; *The Fall of the Idols* (London, 1940), 140.
66. *Outspoken Essays*, 23, and *The Fall of the Idols*, 155; *England* (London, 1926), xi.
67. *The Fall of the Idols*, 150. Inge pointed to the generally accepted "ugliness and ruthlessness" of early Victorian society as witness to "the blunder of sacrificing the higher values to the increase of wealth and population."
68. *Our Present Discontents* (London, 1938), 205.

69. Ibid.
70. *The Fall of the Idols*, 11.
71. "Whither Britain III," *Listener 11* (24 January 1934), 142.
72. *ILN 192* (12 March 1938), 422.
73. *ILN 204* (29 April 1944), 474.
74. *ILN 189* (21 November 1936), 900.
75. *ILN 205* (12 August 1944), 170.
76. *The Idea of a Christian Society* (London, 1939), 61-2.
77. "Richard Henry Tawney, 1880-1962," *Proceedings of the British Academy 48* (London, 1962), 461.
78. *The Acquisitive Society* [1920] (New York, 1948), 184.
79. Ibid., 45-6. Tawney was one of the most important influences on the younger generation of historians. One can understand the intemperate outburst of G. R. Elton, in a letter to the *Times Literary Supplement*, that Tawney's *Religion and the Rise of Capitalism* ("one of the books which everyone [in universities] read," recalled the economic historian W. H. B. Court [*Scarcity and Choice in History* (London, 1970), 187]) "has some claims to being one of the most harmful books written in the years between the wars. At least one generation, and that a crucial one, was given grounds for believing that everything that contributed to the greatness and success of their country derived from sinful selfishness and money-grubbing wickedness" (*Times Literary Supplement 76* [11 February 1977] 156).
80. *Religion and the Rise of Capitalism* [1926] (New York, 1946), 19.
81. E. R. Norman, *Church and Society in England, 1770-1970: An Historical Study* (Oxford, 1976), 228, 305, 317.
82. In pointing out the unfortunate role of the Reformation in setting economic appetites loose, for example, Tawney was only the most important among many Anglicans developing this theme. Archdeacon William Cunningham of Ely had in 1913 given a lecture at the London School of Economics titled "Calvinism and Capital," in which he attacked Political Economy, claimed that all "the human activities with which Economics deals lie within the sphere of Christianity," and pointed out that it was the Reformation that had "rejected the authority by which Christian morals had been enforced at active centers of economic life" (*Christianity and Economic Science* [London, 1914], 1, 58). See also *Competition: A Study in Human Motive*, a symposium published in London in 1917 by a clerical group led by William Temple.
83. In COPEC's discussions on its report on leisure, the games and pastimes recommended to the working classes reflected a romanticized passion for folk culture. E. R. Norman (*Church and Society*, 296-7) summed up: "The working classes, who not unreasonably wanted leisure in order to play football or to drink in the pub, were seen by Miss Dashwood as given instead to the performance of medieval Mystery plays; by Miss Shepherd, as introduced to "community music"; by the Revd. A. B. Bateman, as attaining to "the joy of creation, the sphere of art and handicrafts"; by Lord Aberdeen, as well as by almost everybody else, as enjoying folk-dancing; by Miss Cropper, as devotees of drama. When it came to the cinema, the new and popular entertainment, there was a call for censorship."
84. For a sympathetic account of Noel's strange career, see Reg Groves, *Conrad Noel and the Thaxted Movement* (London, 1967). See also Norman, *Church and Society*, 247-9 and passim, and John Oliver, *The Church and*

Social Order: Social Thought in the Church of England, 1918-1939 (London, 1968), 20 and passim. On both leagues, see Norman, Oliver, and Maurice B. Reckitt, *As It Happened* (London, 1941).

85. *Christendom* (quarterly journal of the Christendom Group), September, 1931, 210.
86. Oliver, *Church and Social Order*, 132-3.
87. Maurice B. Reckitt and J. V. Langmead Casserley, *The Vocation of England* (London, 1941). This book summed up the views of the summer 1940 meeting of the Church Union School of Sociology, an offshoot of the Christendom Group.
88. *Malvern, 1941: The Life of the Church and Order of Society* (London, 1941), 3, 9, 12. See Angus Calder's evaluation of Malvern in *The People's War* (London, 1969), 483-7.
89. A recent example was the controversial appointment in 1977 of the Right Reverend Hugh Montefiore as bishop of Birmingham, the engineering capital of Britain. The new bishop, noted the *Guardian*, "believes that fewer cars would make the country a better place" (*Manchester Guardian Weekly*, 23 October 1977).
90. "Farmers in Arms," *New York Review of Books 12*, no. 12 (19 June 1969), 36-7.
91. In addition to the discussion below, see Martin J. Wiener, "The Changing Image of William Cobbett," *Journal of British Studies 13*, no. 2 (May, 1974), 135-54.
92. *The Untutored Townsman's Invasion of the Country* (London, 1946), 215.
93. "The Intellectual Left," in *The Left*, ed. Gerald Kaufman (London, 1966), 113.
94. Hugh Gaitskell, "At Oxford in the Twenties," in *Essays in Labour History*, ed. Asa Briggs and John Saville (London, 1960), 12; Edith, marchioness of Londonderry, *Retrospect* (London, 1938), 225 and passim; Harold Laski, *The Dangers of Being a Gentleman, and Other Essays* (London, 1939), 29; H. N. Brailsford's essay in *The English Spirit*, ed. Anthony Weymouth (London, 1940); Richard Hoggart, *Speaking to Each Other II: About Literature* (London, 1970), 170. Brailsford's ideal radical was an "aristocrat," like Shelley, Byron, and his friend, Wilfred Blunt: "If their birth in a long line of squires meant anything, it meant that England lived in them as she lived in the oaks of their estates ... My memory went back to a house built in the depths of an oak forest. These was more in that house and round it of the enduring changeless England than I have ever met elsewhere ... It had stood there untouched and unchanged since Charles II was restored to his throne. No touch of modernity spoiled the wainscoted walls ... The old man to whom this changeless fragment of England belonged came of a long line of squires, a family so conservative that it had refused to change its religion at the reformation. Through many centuries they had never given the smallest sign of originality or even of unconventionality, until like a changeling from another world Wilfred Blunt appeared." To Brailsford, he was the perfect combination of a fierce anti-imperialist and a true representative of the "old English character" (*The English Spirit*, 51-2, 54).
95. *News from Nowhere* [1890], ed. James Redmond (London, 1970), 146. Wilfred Scawen Blunt's "Satan Absolved" is an intriguing turn-of-the-century poem that bridges Romanticism and science fiction. Blunt was a friend and admirer of Morris, a writer, traveler, and publicist, and a country gentleman. This long poem is a violent denunciation of indus-

try for raping the earth, "destroying happiness in the name of progress" ("Satan Absolved: A Victorian Mystery" [1899], in *Poetical Works of Wilfred Scawen Blunt* [London, 1914], 2, 254-91).

96. Quoted in J. Bruce Glasier, *William Morris and the Early Days of the Socialist Movement* (London, 1921), 81-2.

97. *Merrie England* (London, 1894), 21, 35; see also G. D. H. Cole, *A History of Socialist Thought 3*, part 1 (London, 1956), 166.

98. Quoted in Willard Wolfe, *From Radicalism to Socialism* (New Haven, Conn., 1975), 212. In Fabian discussion that year Webb argued again that the "keynote" of socialism was "extreme social asceticism."

99. *Beatrice Webb's Diaries, 1912-1924*, ed. Margaret Cole (London, 1952), 50. See also Gertrude Himmelfarb, "Process, Purpose and Ego," *Times Literary Supplement*, 75 (25 June 1976), 789-90.

100. "Past and Future," in *The Heart of the Empire*, ed. C. F. G. Masterman (London, 1901), 407.

101. See W. T. Stead's survey of labour MPs in the *Review of Reviews*, June, 1906.

102. Letter from Macdonald to Oswald Garrison Villard, 4 June 1923, quoted in *Times Literary Supplement*, 76 (4 March 1977), 231.

103. Mary Agnes Hamilton, *Remembering My Good Friends* (London, 1934), 128; Margaret Cole, *Growing Up into Revolution* (London, 1949), 138; Macdonald, *At Home and Abroad* (London, 1936), 80-1, 94, 104 (Most of the essays on England and Scotland in this volume were written before the National government.). See also Macdonald's earlier collection of addresses and essays, *Wanderings and Excursions* (London, 1924).

104. Quoted in David Marquand, *Ramsay Macdonald* (London, 1977), 459-60. The compatibility of this side of Macdonald's socialism with Tory anti-materialism can be seen in his complaints to Lady Londonderry about vulgar plutocrats and "the system in which money has made all things possible" (Edith, marchioness of Londonderry, *Retrospect* [London, 1938], 225).

105. *Ramsay Macdonald*, 403.

106. Quoted in Ross Terrill, *R. H. Tawney and His Times* (Cambridge, Mass., 1973), 71.

107. 'The Last Item on the Agenda," *Countryman I* (April, 1927), 33-4.

108. See Lansbury's 1923 letter to Buxton, quoted in Mosa Anderson, *Noel Buxton: A Life* (London, 1952), 120; George Lansbury, *My England* (London, 1934), 93.

109. *The Economic Advisory Council, 1930-1939* (Cambridge, 1977), 159-60.

110. *Report of Proceedings at the 60th Annual Trades Union Congress* (London, 1928), 66.

111. Alan Bullock, *Ernest Bevin I* (London, 1960), 358, 360.

112. *Midnight on the Desert* (London, 1937), 236.

113. *English Journey* (London, 1934), 400, 404, 405. See also Priestley's *Rain Upon Godshill* (London, 1939), 36, and his *Out of the People* (London, 1941), 52.

114. J. B. Priestley and Jacquetta Hawkes, *Journey Down a Rainbow* (London, 1955), 51-2.

115. *The Edwardians* (London, 1970), 108.

116. *As It Happened* (New York, 1954), 174.

117. 1942 speech, quoted in Paul Addison, *The Road to 1945*, 205.

118. Quoted in Colin Cooke, *The Life of Richard Stafford Cripps* (London, 1957), 361.

119. *The Future of Socialism* (London, 1956), 517.
120. Michael Foot, *Aneurin Bevan* (London, 1963), *I*, 193-4. Rodo's remark is from his book, *The Motives of Proteus* (1929), from which Bevan would often "recite favourite passages" (Foot, *Aneurin Bevan*, 192). Foot himself has been characterized as a "conservative rebel" (*Spectator*, 15 July 1972).
121. *In Place of Fear* [1952] (New York, 1964), 66.
122. To T. F. Lindsay and Michael Harrington (*The Conservative Party*, 202-3), this episode highlighted a hostility to mass affluence among large sections of the "Establishment"; see also Donald Horne, *God is an Englishman* (Sydney, Australia, 1969), 88-9, on the "contempt for the economic" underlying these reactions. Ironically, Macmillan himself was no simple admirer of material progress. In his memoirs (*At the End of the Day, 1961-1963* [London, 1973], 521-2) he lamented how "the invention of the internal combustion engine had destroyed our quiet...All this repose and quiet [of the horse-drawn England of his childhood] has been drowned by a ceaseless roar on earth and in the sky."

7. The gentrification of the industrialist

1. W. D. Rubinstein, "Wealth, Elites and the Class Structure of Modern Britain," *Past and Present*, no. 76 (August. 1977), 99-126, and "The Victorian Middle Classes: Wealth, Occupation and Geography," *Economic History Review*, series 2, *30* (1977), 602-23; see also J. P. Cornford, "The Parliamentary Foundations of the Hotel Cecil," in *Ideas and Institutions of Victorian Britain*, ed. Robert Robson (London, 1967), 284-5.
2. As testified to by the late Labour minister, Anthony Crosland: "In terms of personal wealth and profit [British manufacturing industry] came a very poor second-best [in the nineteen-sixties] to the worlds of property and finance; and its influence and prestige (relative, for example, to that of the mercantile tradition of the City) are less than in any other advanced Western country" (Crosland, *Socialism Now* [London, 1974], 33).
3. "The Victorian Middle Classes," 623.
4. "Institutional Response to Economic Growth: Capital Markets in Britain to 1914," in *Management Strategy and Business Development: An Historical and Comparative Study*, ed. Leslie Hannah (London, 1976), 151-83.
5. Ibid, 159.
6. This aloofness continued through the twentieth century. Leaders of the Federation of British Industries from the thirties on hoped to develop closer relations between industry and the financial community, but the financiers of the City refused to form an association corresponding to the FBI, or to participate in joint activities with the federation. "As late as 1966," Stephen Blank observed, "four years after the formation of the National Economic Development Council provided industry with a new and far more authoritative platform from which to deal with government, industrial members were reported as being 'jealous of the enormous deference paid by successive administrations to the banks, and representatives of the City'" (*Industry and Government in Britain* [Lexington, Mass., 1973], 197; Blank quotes David Hayworth, whose comments appeared in the *Observer*.).
7. *The New Anatomy of Britain* (New York, 1962), 597. The American economic historian, Thomas C. Cochran, similarly concluded that "the pervasive values, interests and attitudes of a society and the business

structure resulting therefrom constitute causal forces that shape the nature of both executive action and the markets in which companies operate" ("The Business Revolution," *American Historical Review* 79 (1974), 1465-6); see his *Two Hundred Years of American Business* (New York, 1977).

8. *What Has Happened to Economic History?* (Cambridge, 1972), 10.

9. Neil McKendrick, introduction to R. J. Overy, *William Morris, Viscount Nuffield* (London, 1976), vii-viii, and Roy Lewis and Rosemary Stewart, *The Managers* [1958] (New York, 1961), 29; see also G. H. Copeman, *Leaders of British Industry* (London, 1955).

10. Kenneth Young, *Balfour* (London, 1963), xviii and xx; see Chapter 6.

11. Quoted in Margery Pesham, *Lugard I: The Years of Adventure* (London, 1956), 35.

12. "Million Dollar Yeggs," *New York Review of Books* 22, no. 4 (20 March 1975), 21. The ambassador was a product of Eton and Balliol.

13. Quoted in Cowling, *The Impact of Hitler* (Cambridge, 1975), 413. As one of C. P. Snow's fictional characters put it, speaking for most, "I'm still convinced that successful business is devastatingly uninteresting" (*Strangers and Brothers* [London, 1951], 93).

14. "The Possessed," *New York Review of Books* 23, no. 1 (5 February 1976), 22. See C. P. Snow's well-known remarks on this in *The Two Cultures and the Scientific Revolution* (New York, 1959), esp. 26; see also Graham Hough, "Crisis in Literary Education," in *Crisis in the Humanities*, ed. J. H. Plumb (Harmondsworth, 1964), 96. Patrick Parrinder has brought out the consciousness of many Edwardian novelists of a "widening gap between the goals of the capitalist economy and those of intellectual and artistic life." ("Historical Imagination and Political Reality: A Study in Edwardian Attitudes," *Clio 4* (1975), 5-25)

15. In Overy, *William Morris*, xxxix.

16. *Times Literary Supplement* 68, 617 (5 June 1969); quoted in Graham Turner, *Business in Britain* (London, 1969), 439; *New Society 28* (18 April 1974), 122. Typical of the kind of attitude the directors had in mind were the reviews by Ian Taylor in *New Society* that year of Richard Lynn's collection of case studies, *The Entrepreneur*. Taylor was contemptuously amazed that such "parasitism" could be presented as some kind of model, and took the "startlingly amoral collection" as a sign of the degeneration of the discipline of psychology (*New Society 28* (6 June 1974), 588-9).

17. Quoted in Michael Sanderson, *The Universities and British Industry, 1850-1970* (London, 1972), 37.

18. Sanderson concluded (ibid., 391) that "the increasing involvement of the universities with industry is perhaps the most important single development in the history of British universities over the last hundred years." Yet this involvement was far more characteristic, as he demonstrates, of the civic universities of the North and the Midlands than of the much more prestigious older universities of Oxford and Cambridge, or even of London and the post-World War II universities. Moreover, the increasing involvement of universities and industry was a universal trend throughout the world. The real question is a relative one: Was this development more thorough or less thorough in Britain than elsewhere? Though the question has not been settled, the evidence suggests the latter.

19. *Technology and the Academics* (London, 1958), 51; see also W. J. Reader, *Professional Men* (New York, 1966), 70-1, 112-14, 131-45.

20. Quoted in Sanderson, *The Universities and British Industry*, 308.
21. Quoted in Overy, *William Morris*, xi.
22. Ashby, *Technology and the Academics*, 66.
23. On the persistence of an antiindustrial bias in British higher education, and for comparisons of the education of managers in Britain and managers in other industrial nations, see Derek F. Channon, *Strategy and Structure of British Enterprise* (Boston, Mass., 1973); Anthony Bambridge, "Why Britain Can't Manage," *Observer*, 30 November 1975; Michael Crick, "Glittering Prizes," *New Statesman* 92 (5 November 1976), 631; Richard Lynn, "The Universities and the Business Community," *Twentieth Century* 179 (1971-2), 40-3; David Granick, *Managerial Comparisons of Four Developed Countries* (Cambridge, Mass., 1972); Chitoshi Yanaga, *Big Business in Japanese Politics* (New Haven, 1968); and Koya Azumi, *Higher Education and Business Recruitment in Japan* (New York, 1969).
24. Sampson, *The New Anatomy of Britain*, 165-7; Michael Beloff, *The Plateglass Universities* (London, 1968), 28; Peter Wilby, "The Outdated University Tradition," *New Statesman* 91 (21 May 1976) 669-70; and Sanderson, *The Universities and British Industry*, 368-72.
25. *Warwick University Ltd.*, ed. E. P. Thompson (Harmondsworth, 1970), quoted in Sampson, *New Anatomy*, 184; see also Sanderson, *The Universities and British Industry*, 371.
26. Quoted in Sampson, *New Anatomy*, 170; see the *Economist*'s complaint (25 February 1978, 75): "The great central technical institutes...were transformed into what are now admitted to be second-rate universities"; Sanderson, *The Universities and British Industry*, 372-6, has a more optimistic view.
27. "Our Obsolete Attitudes," *Encounter*, November, 1977, 14-15. This helps explain why, as the economists Robert Bacon and Walter Eltis observed (*Britain's Economic Problem: Too Few Producers* [London, 1976], 24), "successive governments have allowed large number of workers to move out of industry and into various service occupations, where they still consume and invest industrial products and produce none themselves; their needs have, therefore, been met at the expense of the balance of payments, the export surplus of manufacturers, and investment in industry itself."
28. Peter Wilby, "Engineering for Survival," *New Statesman* 92 (3 December 1976), 782; "Snobbery and the Engineer" (letter), *New Statesman* 92 (10 December 1976), 840; Alastair Mant, *The Rise and Fall of the British Manager* (London, 1977), 6-7.
29. *The Student in the Age of Anxiety* (London, 1963), 36; the *Times* (London), 3 August 1970; quoted by Bambridge, in *Observer*, 30 November 1975; Lewis and Stewart, *The Managers*, 65; *The Ice Age* (London, 1977), 16. "The typical British manager in the 1960s and 1970s," summed up the economist Robin Marris ("Is Britain an Awful Warning to America?" *New Republic*, 17 September 1977, 28), "has been a self-made person inadequately prepared for the commercial and technological conditions of the modern world." He acknowledged a certain responsibility on his part and on the part of his profession: "I cannot remember a single ex-pupil from my 25 years at Cambridge who has gone into industry."
30. Ian Glover and Peter Lawrence, "Engineering the Miracle," *New Society* 37 (30 September 1976), 711.
31. "Not so very long ago," John Talbott has reflected ("The Old Ecole Tie," *New York Review of Books* [25 October 1979], 43), "the servants of the state administered economic policies designed to protect the little

man – the peasants, shopkeepers, and artisans, who were the backbone
of the Third Republic. Toward businessmen they maintained an attitude of suspicion and disdain; they exalted the virtues of solidarity and
stability over competition and profit; they insisted the state had interests
distinct from those of private enterprise. Now those trained in the state's
service shuttle back and forth between ministerial cabinets and corporate boardrooms. The large industrial enterprises, the nationalized
industries, and the public administration are all the preserve of the
grands corps." See also John Ardagh, *The New France* (Harmondsworth,
1973), 36-45, and Theodore Zeldin's comments in passing in his review
of Eugen Weber, *Peasant into Frenchmen*, in *New York Review of Books* (24
November 1977), 45. Zeldin himself provides evidence (in *France, 1848-
1945* [Oxford, 1973], I, 87-101) of a gradual, partial, but noticeable
shift between the mid-nineteenth century and the early twentieth century in the attitudes of French middle-class guides to careers toward a
less cautious and critical view of money making and material production
(although, true to his general approach, Zeldin plays down change in
favor of continuity).

32. For the traditional place of the businessman in Japan, see Charles
Sheldon, *The Rise of the Merchant Class in Tolugawa Japan* (Locust Valley,
N.Y., 1958), ch. 2, and for the twentieth-century transformation, see
Chitoshi Yanaga, *Big Business in Japanese Politics*, 20-3, 29-35; Koya
Azumi, *Higher Education and Business Recruitment in Japan*, 26; and
Ronald Dore, *British Factory – Japanese Factory* (Berkeley and Los
Angeles, 1973), 46-8.

33. See Granick, *Managerial Comparisons*, 178, 370, and his earlier, more
popular *The European Executive* (Garden City, N.Y., 1962) esp. chs. 7 and
18. Differing social images of industry leap out in Peter Lawrence's
suggestive comparison of executive advertisements in Britain and
Switzerland ("Executive headhunting," *New Society 44* [25 May 1978],
416-17). Lawrence concludes: "How can we explain the difference in
Swiss executive adverts? Specific on content, qualifications, requirements, and technical knowledge; vague, relatively speaking, about the
standing of the company, status, considerations, and material rewards.
Does any theory fit all or even most of these facts? . . . If industry is 'at
home' in a country, in the broadest cultural sense, then it can be more
easily described with reference to its own operations and requirements.
It doesn't have to be 'located' in terms of a rewards and status map.
Companies can be seen as places where things get made, and later sold,
rather than as machines for having careers in. If as part of this being at
home in a certain country, people will want to work in manufacturing
companies, then less emphasis is needed on material rewards, or on
underlining the success and prestige of particular companies seeking to
attract executive talent . . . In a gentle way, the comparison suggests that,
in Britain, working in industry needs some kind of rationalisation. The
rewards and sacrifices must balance. When placed side by side the
British adverts are an exercise in persuasion, the Swiss ones more an
exchange of information." This argument is continued in Michael Fores
and Peter Lawrence, "Industrial Phobia," *New Society 46* (5 October
1978), 28-9.

34. W. G. Rimmer, *Marshalls of Leeds* (Cambridge, 1960), concluded (298):
"In the last analysis Marshall and Co. declined owing to social barriers
which could not be surmounted."

35. Quoted in Ronald S. Edwards and Harry Townsend, *Business Enterprise* (London, 1958), 566-67.
36. Introduction to Overy, *Morris*, xxxii-xxxiii.
37. *Lombard Street: A Description of the Money Market* (London, 1873), 11.
38. Contribution to symposium, "Who's Left, What's Right?" *Encounter*, March, 1977, 29.
39. Reader, *Professional Men*, 212-13.
40. Copeman, *Leaders of British Industry*, 101.
41. *British Industrialists: Steel and Hosiery, 1850-1950* (Cambridge, 1959), 33-5, 38, 115.
42. D. C. Coleman, "Gentleman and Players," *Economic History Review*, series 2, *26* (1973), 109.
43. In many trades there developed a mystique of practical experience: What was needed, as one manufacturer in the tinplate trade put it, was "practical men who were in sympathy with their rolls and everything else. They could do a lot with their machinery if they were in sympathy with it" (W. E. Minchinton, "The Tinplate Maker and Technical Change," *Explorations in Entrepreneurial History* 7 [1954-5], 7; see also Stephen F. Cotgrove, *Technical Education and Social Change* [London, 1958], 23-8). These manufacturers and their men had themselves done without technical education. Why change what had worked for so long? In their veneration of the practices of their predecessors, they departed crucially from the outlook of these predecessors, who had themselves readily broken with precedent, and made use of available advances in science and technology. The "practical tradition" in English industrial history was raised to the level of myth, turning past circumstances into an ideal, and in the process, distorting that past as well. To the Samuelson Commission in 1884, the great china firm, Wedgwood, confessed no use for a chemist, or indeed for any research, on the grounds that it would take time and be " a great nuisance." This was "a curious observation," Sanderson has pointed out, "from a firm whose founder had used Joseph Priestley for his chemical work" (*Universities and British Industry*, 17; the earlier importance of applied science can be seen in A. E. Musson and Eric Robinson, *Science and Technology in the Industrial Revolution* [Manchester, 1969]).
44. See the full argument of D. C. Coleman, "Gentlemen and Players," and the corroborating observations of Channon, *Strategy and Structure of British Enterprise*, 221.
45. *England's Crisis* (London, 1931), 17. As an American manager based in London observed to Stephen Toulmin, "The British are the only managers I know who make a habit of boasting to you about how *little* work they do . . . Lots of British managers just want to get back to their place in the Cotswolds, to their daughters with their pony clubs, and all the rest" (Stephen Toulmin, "You Norman, Me Saxon," *Encounter*, September, 1978, 92).
46. "The Comforts of Stagnation," in Arthur Koestler, ed., *Suicide of a Nation?* (London, 1963), 62.
47. *The Managers*, 191. See a suggestive essay that makes some of the same points about the nineteenth-century business elite of Boston: F. C. Jaher, "The Boston Brahmins in the Age of Industrial Capitalism," in *The Age of Industrialism in America*, ed. F. C. Jaher (New York, 1968), 188-262.
48. *ILN 189* (29 August 1936), 340.

49. *Rise and Fall of the British Manager*, 100-2.
50. "The Danger of Being a Gentleman" (1932), in *The Danger of Being a Gentleman and Other Essays* (London, 1939), 23. As an executive of a domestic appliance manufacturing firm complained to a business researcher around 1960: "There was a time when we sold to the better middle-classes . . . These days we have a new orientation. We practically sell to anyone who has the money to buy . . . Do you know what they buy? A stupid TV set. Here we spent thousands of pounds on medical research to show how important it is for the health of people to buy refrigerators. But do they take advantage of it?" (Quoted in Tibor Barna, *Investment and Growth Policies in British Industrial Firms* [Cambridge, 1962], 55n).
51. Peter Wilby, "Engineering for Survival," and Ian Glover and Peter Lawrence, "Engineering the Miracle"; also see Dore, *British Factory – Japanese Factory*, 46-8, and Yanaga, *Big Business*, 20-3. Yet, the predominance of accountants in high places in British industry has not been associated with the development of sophisticated methods of operations control. In this area, as in most other matters of organization, British firms have been reluctant to innovate (See Alfred Chandler in *Management Strategy*, ed. Hannah, 26).
52. *Rise and Fall of the British Manager*, 56.
53. "Why Britain Can't Manage," *Observer*, 30 November 1975.
54. *New Anatomy of Britain*, 579. See also Turner, *Business in Britain*, 301-2.
55. *Listener 60* (July-December 1958), 552.
56. D. C. Coleman, *Courtaulds: An Economic and Social History, II* (Oxford, 1969), 218.
57. Turner, *Business in Britain*, 217, 433.
58. For example, a BBC series of documentaries on Japan in early 1974 focused heavily on such evils.
59. Turner, *Business in Britain*, 432.
60. Ibid., 14-15.
61. *Leader*, 19 May 1911; see L. Urwick and E. F. L. Brech, *The Making of Scientific Management II: Management in British Industry* (London, 1946), ch. 7.
62. O. Sheldon, *Philosophy of Management* (London, 1923), quoted in John Child, *British Management Thought* (London, 1969), 73. Child emphasized the "historical continuity" of British management thought from the Edwardian era to the fifties and even the sixties (123).
63. Quoted in ibid., 121.
64. *Ideals and Industry* (London, 1949), 26. This tradition of Dickensian benevolence was attacked by some of the most successful (and self-made) British industrialists, like W. H. Lever and William Morris, who saw themselves as swimming against the current. "There could be no worse friend to labour," Lever (described as "Mr. Smiles' Disciple" by Charles Wilson) warned in 1909, "than the benevolent, philanthropic employer who carries his business on in a loose, lax manner, showing 'kindness' to his employees; because, as certain as that man exists, because of his looseness and laxness, and because of his so-called kindness, benevolence, and lack of business principles, sooner or later he will be compelled to close." (Quoted in Charles Wilson, *The History of Unilever I* [London, 1954], 143.)
65. *The English Tradition: The Heritage of the Venturers* (London, 1934).
66. *Reflections on Britain and the United States* (London, 1959), 35-9.

67. Quoted in Turner, *Business in Britain*, 444.
68. In *The Character of England*, ed. Ernest Barker (London, 1948), 207.
69. *British Shipping and World Competition* (London, 1962), 395-6, 1.
70. *The Economic History of Steelmaking, 1867-1939* (Cambridge, 1940), 301; see also pp. 296-305 on declining enterprise in the industry. Another example of increasing concentration on prestigious public duties rather than on business was Archibald Kenrick and Sons Ltd.: See Roy Church, "Family and Failure: Archibald Kenrick and Sons Ltd, 1900-1950," in *Essays in British Business History*, ed. Barry Supple (Oxford, 1977), 113-14.
71. Robert Henriques, *Marcus Samuel* (London, 1960), ch. 8.
72. Ibid., 87, 333. It is instructive to compare Samuel's career with that of Gerson Bleichröder, one of the leading Jewish capitalists of Bismarck's Germany. Despite his political services to Bismarck, Bleichröder's social acceptance was much more problematical, although his economic energies (perhaps partly for that very reason) never flagged (see Fritz Stern, *Gold and Iron: Bismarck, Bleichröder and the Building of the German Empire* [New York, 1977]).
73. Channon, *Strategy and Structure of British Enterprise*, 75-7.
74. *The Logic of British and American Industry* (London, 1953), 303. The classic argument for the retarding effects of family control of firms is David Landes's, on France: See his "French Business and the Business Man: A Social and Cultural Analysis," in *Modern France*, ed. E. M. Earle (Princeton, N.J., 1951), 334-53. Landes's view has since been challenged, most interestingly in Michael B. Miller, *The Bon Marché: Bourgeois Culture and the Department Store, 1869-1920* (Princeton, N.J., 1980). See *Essays in British Business History*, ed. Supple, for examples of successful and unsuccessful family firms.
75. Turner, *Business in Britain*, 221-2 (Turner's emphasis).
76. *The Strategy and Structure of British Enterprise*, 242. Outsiders, less prone to such sentiments, had disproportionate success in modern British business. Even before the First World War, much of the output of the rapidly growing new industries was produced by American firms operating in Britain. Two of the four largest electrical machinery producers, for example, British Westinghouse and British Thomson-Houston, were American-owned, whilst a third, Siemens, was German-owned. Indeed, the remaining one, GEC, although under nominal British ownership, was controlled and managed by an immigrant from Germany (I. C. R. Byatt, "Electrical Products," in *The Development of British Industry and Foreign Competition, 1875-1914*, ed. D. H. Aldcroft [London, 1968], 238-73). By the end of the 1950s, the most efficient firms in Britain were predominantly enterprises that had been started by immigrants as early as 1940, were controlled by minorities (Quakers or Jews, chiefly), or were branches of international corporations (Tibor Barna, *Investment and Growth Policies*, 57). American firms operating in Britain in the fifties and sixties consistently earned a higher rate of return on capital than their British competitors. Their success in fact was roughly proportional to the degree of U.S. control. The American firms were on the whole more capital intensive, paid more attention to marketing, looked for higher academic and technical qualifications from managers, and planned more professionally. Underlying these differences was a difference in attitude – a "greater will to be efficient" among U.S. subsidiaries (John H. Dunning, *American Investment in British Manufacturing*

Industry [London, 1958], 316; and Dunning, "U.S. Subsidiaries in Britain and their U.K. Competitors," *Business Ratios*, no. 1 [Autumn, 1966], 5-18). By the close of the seventies, a similar comparison could be made with German and Japanese subsidiaries in Britain.

77. Sampson, *New Anatomy of Britain*, 607; Turner, *Business in Britain*, 308-25; *Economist*, 21 May 1977, 83; Donald Horne, *God is an Englishman* (Sydney, Australia, 1969), 205.

78. Quoted in Sampson, *New Anatomy of Britain*, 609.

79. "Gentlemen and Players," 100-1, 109.

80. *Courtaulds, II*, 217. This outlook prevailed until new leadership (of a chemical engineer) in the sixties brought a radical shakeup, the end of much of the gentleman's club spirit, and the opening of a new era of expansion. See Arthur Knight, *Private Enterprise and Public Intervention: The Courtaulds Experience* (London, 1974). Knight was deputy chairman of Courtaulds.

81. *Imperial Chemical Industries: A History, I. The Forerunners, 1870-1926* (Oxford, 1970), 218, and *Imperial Chemical Industries: A History, II. The First Quarter-Century, 1926-1952* (Oxford, 1975), 70, 72. See also *I*, 91-2, on the origins of the club in the beautifully symbolic, if accidental, preservation of a Tudor manor house within one of the largest chemical plants in the world.

82. Ibid., *I*, 319; *II*, 34-7, 77, 80, 135.

83. *Business in Britain*, 141, 139-59. Yet at ICI, as at Courtaulds, this atmosphere showed signs of dissipating from the sixties on, as new leadership brought a shakeup in structure and attitudes and a new surge of growth.

84. *The Seven Sisters: The Great Oil Companies and the World They Made* (New York, 1975), 44.

85. Ibid., 11, 198, Turner, *Business in Britain*, 111.

86. "Consensus or Elite Domination: The Case of Business," *Political Studies 13* (1965), 22-24. This brilliant essay has yet to be superseded.

87. Turner, *Business in Britain*, 171-201.

88. Nettl, "Consensus or Elite Domination," 22-9; see Blank, *Industry and Government*, 70, on the civil service ideal in industry; professor quoted in Turner, *Business in Britain*, 99.

89. See the argument for viewing twentieth-century British government along these lines in Keith Middlemas, *Politics in Industrial Society: The Experience of the British System since 1911* (London, 1979).

90. 19 April 1901, quoted in A. L. Levine, *Industrial Retardation in Britain, 1880-1914* (New York, 1967), 59; quoted in Turner, *Business in Britain*, 432. On the general conservatism of British management, see Richard E. Caves et al., *Britain's Economic Prospects* (London, 1968), 305.

91. Turner, *Business in Britain*, 432. D. C. Coleman ("Gentlemen and Players," 114) remarked on the prevalence of "an attitude to business relations which emphasized careful strategical moves and the making of deals and agreements which lessened the intensity of competition."

92. Charles Kindleberger, *Economic Growth in France and Britain, 1851-1950* (Cambridge, Mass., 1964), 133. Despite his criticisms of "entrepreneurial" explanations of economic history, P. L. Payne (*British Entrepreneurship in the Nineteenth Century* [London, 1974], 38) agreed that "there is no gainsaying the belated recognition of the growth and profit-potential of motor cars, some branches of chemicals, electrical engineering and the like."

93. Burn, *Economic History of Steelmaking*, 296.

94. Alfred Chandler and his students have pointed to a variety of ways in which British firms in the twentieth century have lagged in organizational development. See Channon, *Strategy and Structure of British Enterprise*, and *Management Strategy and Business Development*, ed. Hannah. Chandler's key works are: *Strategy and Structure: Chapters in the History of the Industrial Enterprise* (Cambridge, Mass., 1962), and *The Visible Hand: The Managerial Revolution in American Business* (Cambridge, Mass., 1977). The influence of Chandler's approach on British scholars is evident in *Essays in British Business History*, ed. Supple.

95. Peter Mathias, "Conflicts of Function in the Rise of Big Business: The British Experience," in *Evolution of International Management Structures*, ed. Harold F. Williamson (Newark, Del., 1975), 41-3.

96. Turner, *Business in Britain*, 33, 35. Another representative firm was the hardware manufacturer, Archibald Kenrick & Sons: Its restrictionist response to an increasingly difficult environment has been examined by Roy Church in *Essays in British Business History*, ed. Supple, 102-23.

97. Quoted in Leslie Hannah, *The Rise of the Corporate Economy: The British Experience* (London, 1976), 46; see also Alan Harding, *A Social History of English Law* (Harmondsworth, 1966), 412.

98. A. F. Lucas, *Industrial Reconstruction and the Control of Competition* (London, 1937), 352.

99. *The Managers*, 54. See also Blank, *Industry and Government in Britain*, on the concern for stability voiced repeatedly by the FBI.

100. See M. W. Kirby, "The Control of Competition in the British Coal-Mining Industry in the Thirties," *Economic History Review*, series 2, 26 (1973), esp. 283-4, and B. W. E. Alford, *Depression and Recovery? British Economic Growth, 1918-1939* (London, 1972), 52-3. In the steel industry of the thirties, its most recent historian has reminded us, "there was no great demand for rationalization. What the steelmasters wanted was rigid price agreements and a stiffer tariff"; they received both of these (John Vaizey, *The History of British Steel* [London, 1974], 65). For a somewhat more optimistic view of the value of reorganization and amalgamation, see Hannah, *The Rise of the Corporate Economy*, 141, 158-62, 182-3; but even Hannah is very cautious, ending in "restrained agnosticism" (192).

101. Quoted in Turner, *Business in Britain*, 65. See also Edwards and Townsend, *Business Enterprise*, 562-3.

102. See Channon, *Strategy and Structure of British Enterprise*, 215-16, 232, and passim.

103. See Hannah, *Rise of the Corporate Economy*, 177.

104. "The Coming Corporatism," *New Society 30* (10 October 1974), 72.

105. "The Entrepreneur and Social Order: Britain," *Business History 17* (1975), 186-7.

8. An overview and an assessment

1. See Frank Blackaby, ed., *De-Industrialization* (London, 1978); see also Peter Jenkins, "A Nation on the Skids," *Manchester Guardian Weekly*, 8 October 1978, and [Paul Barker], "Europe's Merseyside," *New Society 46* (14 December 1978), 623.

2. "Gentlemen and Players, " *Economic History Review*, series 2, 26 (1973), 115.

3. "What is the British Disease? " the *Times* (London), 29 April 1971.

4. *The Spirit of the People* (London, 1907), 151.

5. *Industrial Efficiency* (London, 1906), *II*, 459.

6. "Leaving the Village," *International Herald Tribune*, 2 August 1973. See also Lewis's comparison of English and American life, in which England comes out, for all its faults, the home of "human values" ("Notes on the New York Skyline . . .," *Atlantic*, June, 1971, 58-62).

7. Quoted in Krishan Kumar, "A Future in the Past? " *New Society 42* (24 November 1977), 418-19. See the reflections by Christopher Price, MP, provoked by Galbraith: "A Dunce as Prizewinner," *New Society 39* (3 March 1977), 452-3.

8. *Britain – A Future That Works* (Boston, Mass., 1978), 100.

9. *God is An Englishman*, (Sydney, Australia, 1969), 71.

10. Quoted by R. R. James, *Ambitions and Realities: British Politics, 1964-1970* (London, 1972), 293.

11. *The Two Cultures and the Scientific Revolution* (New York, 1959), 42.

12. "The Politics of the New Venice," *New Society 42* (17 November 1977), 352.

13. *Imperial Spain, 1469-1716* (London, 1963), 378. This was a failure, he stressed elsewhere, of a society, and not of a handful of leaders: "Behind this inert government . . . lay a whole social system and psychological attitude which themselves blocked the way to radical reform" ("The Decline of Spain" [1961], in *The Economic Decline of Empires*, ed. Carlo Cipolla [London, 1970], 185). "Spanish Main Gold," as Peter Jenkins recently remarked, "was to Castille what North Sea oil may prove for Britain – the agent of de-industrialization" ("Going Down with Great Britain," *Harper's*, December, 1979, 28).

14. See the *Guardian*, 26 November 1973.

15. See, for example, Wilfred Beckerman, *In Defense of Economic Growth* (London, 1974).

16. Review of James Alt, *The Politics of Economic Decline* (Cambridge, 1979), in *New Society 50* (8 November 1979), 332.

17. Preconference message to Conservative party workers, 28 September 1973, quoted in Sunday *Telegraph*, 30 September 1973.

18. Quoted in *Manchester Guardian Weekly*, 22 April 1979.

19. See, for a similar argument during the election compaign, Peregrine Worsthorne, "Do British Want to Lose Their Chains? " Sunday *Telegraph*, 8 April 1979, 16.

20. Tom Forester, "Do the British Sincerely Want to Be Rich? " *New Society 40* (28 April 1977), 158, 161.

21. *The Diaries of a Cabinet Minister* (New York, 1976), *I*, 351.

22. Glyn Jones and Michael Barnes, *Britain on Borrowed Time* (Harmondsworth, 1967), 268. Maude saw himself as keeper of the Tory conscience, and denounced preoccupation with economic growth as no part of the Conservative tradition. Echoing R. H. Tawney, he labeled it (in *The Consuming Society* [London, 1967]) a "fetish" producing "a sterile cycle of increasing production for increasing consumption of increasingly trivial things."

23. Anthony Lewis, "The Radical of 10 Downing Street," *New York Times Magazine*, 14 March 1971, 46.

24. See David Marquand, "Compromise Under Attack," *New Society 16*, (5 November 1970), 829, and Paul Johnson, "Ted Heath's Britain," *New Statesman 83* (18 February 1972), 196.

25. See David Butler and Dennis Kavanagh, *The British General Election of February 1974* (London, 1974), 125-6, 162-3; David Butler and Michael Pinto-Duschinsky, *The British General Election of 1970* (London, 1971), 169; and Robert Rhodes James, *Ambitions and Realities: British Politics,*

1964-1970 (London, 1972), 220, 239. See the suggestive analysis of the key words and phrases used by the candidates by Shelley Pinto-Duschinsky, "A Matter of Words," *New Society* 27 (7 March 1974), 570-1. Wilson continued this winning line in the October election: "What the people want," he affirmed, "what every family needs, is a bit of peace and quiet" (David Butler and Dennis Kavanagh, *The British General Election of October 1974* [London, 1975], 134).

26. Quoted in *People* (New York), March, 1977, 32.
27. "The Politics of Austerity," *New Statesman* 87 (3 May 1974), 607-8. The decade of the forties was harked back to as a model by a number of left-wing writers. It now seemed an age of elevating austerity and common purpose, before prosperity opened the floodgates of selfishness and the frantic pursuit of artificial wants. Mervyn Jones, novelist and regular contributor to the *New Statesman*, greeted the year 1975 ("A New Year Salute," *New Statesman* 89 [3 January 1975], 3-4) with a reassurance that prolonged zero growth was all for the best: "I never believed that human happiness can be measured in gross national product per capita." He and others, he recalled, had spent the fifties deploring the pursuit of affluence; they were right then, and should hardly be despondent now that "the affluence show is closed down," at least "for the time being." "There have been," he went on, "only two periods in my lifetime that justified a positive pride in being a citizen of this country: the war, and the early post-war years." In Attlee's Britain, for all the shortages, "the number of people who felt deprived, who got nothing of value out of life, was surely less than it is now." (The irony of such nostalgia is inescapable if one looks at a cartoon in the 4 October 1944 issue of *Punch*, in which a scene of a queue of shoppers draws the [humorous] observation from a bystander, "I suppose in about thirty years' time people will insist on describing this as the good old days." [Precisely on the nose!]).
28. "Labour After the Defeats," *New Statesman* 92 (12 November 1976), 659-60.
29. *Ramsay Macdonald* (London, 1977), 462.
30. Lincoln Allison, "The English Cultural Movement," *New Society* 43 (16 February 1978), 358-60. Allison offered a "culturist manifesto": "Join the organisations which oppose harmful modernization and development. Do it thoughtfully but with determination. Protect your communities. Learn ancient skills. Renovate old houses. Defend quality, whether of beer or of landscape; the substitutes rarely satisfy. In doing so you will reward not merely yourself, but your society."
31. "Farewell to Westminster," *New Statesman* 93 (7 January 1977), 2.
32. Anthony Hartley, *A State of England* (London, 1963), 129n.; see also Clive James, "Supplier of Poetry," *New Statesman* 88 (22 November 1974), 745: "The urge to preserve supplied him with his most important creative impulse."
33. *New Statesman* 85 (23 February 1973), 253.
34. Quoted in Allison, "English Cultural Movement," 360.
35. *The Edwardians* (London, 1970), 289; *The English* (London, 1973), 242.

Appendix: British retardation – The limits of economic explanation

1. *Economic Growth in France and Britain, 1851-1950* (Cambridge, Mass., 1964), 67-8.
2. Population growth, on the one side, and emigration and the expansion of service occupations, on the other, maintained a rough equilibrium in the labor market. Compared with the United States, Britain certainly

displayed a labor surplus, but explanations built on comparison with the unique American situation are apt to collapse when confronted with conditions in other nations. On the basis of a comparison between Britain and the United States, H. J. Habbakuk suggested (*American and British Technology in the 19th Century* [Cambridge, Mass., 1964], 196-9) that there was a lesser incentive in late-Victorian Britain to invest in labor-saving machinery because of lower wage rates. Such a suggestion has been repeated more recently by the social historian Paul Thompson (*The Edwardians: The Remaking of British Society* [London, 1975], 186-7). This argument would lead us to expect even less investment in such technical improvements in Germany and in all other industrializing nations, whose wage rates were all (in varying degrees) below Britain's. Such an expectation would be contradicted by the evidence. This argument is also weakened, perhaps fatally, by the fact that in the late nineteenth century, when a significant gap opened between the performance of the British economy and that of the United States and Germany in certain strategic industries, the level of wage costs was pressing harder than before upon British industrialists. Prices were falling, productivity increases were slowing down, yet money wage rates did not decline significantly. If wage rates exerted such influence upon technical investment, the late nineteenth century should have seen a striking upsurge in such investment in Britain, but it did not (see Peter Mathias, *The First Industrial Nation* [London, 1969], 426). R. A. Church ("Nineteenth Century Clock Technology in Britain, the United States and Switzerland," *Economic History Review*, series 2, *28* [1975], 616-30) found the Swiss, with similar craft traditions and probably lower (and certainly no higher) watchmakers' wage rates, leaving the British far behind in the second half of the nineteenth century in the adoption of labor-saving devices. Church concluded that "comparisons between British or European and American technology have stressed the importance of markets and relative factor prices, but our study suggests that social and institutional factors must also be counted among the crucial variables which explain the varied patterns of invention and innovation in the nineteenth century."

3. Although late Victorians worried about exhausting their coal reserves, for example, their fears were misplaced: During the succeeding century of use, proven reserves grew faster than production. Petroleum did not become an important resource until after the First World War, and even then Britain was in a better position, through its influence in the Middle East, than Germany, France, or Japan. The mere mention of Japan, a nation endowed with virtually none of the natural resources necessary for industrialization, should cast doubt on the significance of this factor. Rather than being checked by the depletion or absence of resources, British industry, as Kindleberger argued, "failed to adapt to the resources made valuable by technical change"(*Economic Growth in France and Britain*, 35).

4. See particularly L. H. Gann and Peter Duignan, *Burden of Empire* (New York, 1967), D. K. Fieldhouse, *Economics and Empire, 1830-1914* (Ithaca, N.Y., 1973), Ian Drummond, *Imperial Economic Policy, 1917-1939* (London, 1974), and, more generally, Bernard Porter, *The Lion's Share: A Short History of British Imperialism, 1850-1970* (London, 1975).

5. This line of inquiry was opened by the pioneers of entrepreneurial history. See David Landes, "Factor Costs and Demand: Determinants of

Economic Growth," *Business History* 7 (1965), 15-33, and *The Unbound Prometheus: Technological Change and Industrial Development in Western Europe from 1750 to the Present* (Cambridge, 1969), 331-58; D. H. Aldcroft, "The Entrepreneur and the British Economy, 1870-1914," *Economic History Review*, series 2, 17 (1964-5), 113-34; A. L. Levine, *Industrial Retardation in Britain, 1880-1914* (New York, 1967).

6. *Industry and Empire: An Economic History of Britain since 1750* (London, 1968), 157.
7. Ibid., 158.
8. *Essays on a Mature Economy: Britain since 1840* (London, 1971), ed. Donald McCloskey; see also McCloskey, *Economic Maturity and Entrepreneurial Decline: British Iron and Steel, 1870-1913* (Cambridge, Mass., 1973), and Roderick Floud, *The British Machine Tool Industry, 1850-1914* (Cambridge, 1976).
9. "Did Victorian Britain Fail?" *Economic History Review*, series 2, 23 (1970), 459. Charles K. Hyde (*Technological Change and the British Iron Industry, 1700-1870* [Princeton, N.J., 1977]) makes the persuasive argument – but only for the period before 1870 – that in all the major technological decisions, "the ironmasters were economically rational."
10. *Economic History Review*, series 2, 25 (1972), 590-2.
11. W. P. Kennedy, "Foreign Investment, Trade and Growth in the United Kingdom, 1870-1913," *Explorations in Economic History* (1973-74), 11, 416. Even a basically sympathetic economic historian, P. L. Payne (*British Entrepreneurship in the Nineteenth Century* [London, 1974], 50, conceded that "doubts remain." See Barry Supple's critical review of McCloskey's monograph in *Business History Review 48* (1974), 238-40, and S. B. Saul's of Floud's monograph in *Business History 20* (1978), 113-14. See also the general critique by the economist and historian Douglas North, "Discussion" (of Donald McCloskey's "Achievements of the Cliometric School"), *Journal of Economic History 38* (1978), 77-81. The method of McCloskey's original argument has been criticized in N. F. R. Crafts, "Victorian Britain Did Fail," *Economic History Review*, series 2, 32 (1979), 533-7.
12. Peter Marris, *Loss and Change* (New York, 1974), 117.
13. *The First Industrial Nation* (London, 1969), 426.
14. "Britain's Economic Growth and the 1870 Watershed," *Lloyds Bank Review 99* (January, 1971), 30. For a recent econometrical argument that the reasons for economic adaptability, crucial to growth, "appear to be cultural and institutional rather than purely economic," see Stanislaw Gomulka, "Britain's Slow Industrial Growth – Increasing Inefficiency vs. Low Rate of Technical Change," in *Slow Growth in Britain: Causes and Consequences*, ed. Wilfred Beckerman (Oxford, 1979), 166-93.
15. "The Development of British Industry and Foreign Competition 1875-1914," *Business History 12* (1970), 65.

Index